STRANGE BEDFELLOWS

NATO Marches East

GEORGE W. GRAYSON

University Press of America, Inc.
Lanham • New York • Oxford

Copyright © 1999 by
University Press of America,® Inc.
4720 Boston Way
Lanham, Maryland 20706

12 Hid's Copse Rd.
Cumnor Hill, Oxford OX2 9JJ

Library of Congress Cataloging-in-Publication Data

Grayson, George W.
Strange bedfellows : NATO marches east / George W. Grayson.
p.   cm.
Includes bibliographical references and index.
1. North Atlantic Treaty Organization—Membership. 2. North
Atlantic Treaty Organization—Europe, Eastern. 3. United States—
Foreign relations—1993- I. Title.
UA646.3.G73   1999 355'.031091821—dc21   99—12699 CIP

ISBN 0-7618-1359-4 (pbk: alk. ppr.)

⊖™ The paper used in this publication meets the minimum
requirements of American National Standard for Information
Sciences—Permanence of Paper for Printed Library Materials,
ANSI Z39.48—1984

DEDICATION

to

Jan and Jadwiga "Greta" Wolska Nowak

and

George F. Kennan

Although you disagreed over NATO expansion, the West is indebted
to you for your incomparable roles in winning the cold war.

•

Contents

Acknowledgments

I wish to thank more than one hundred current and past U.S. and European officials for enlightening me on the origins, history, structure, and mission of the North Atlantic Treaty Organization (NATO), as well as the pros and cons of enlarging the organization. In most cases, these individuals agreed to speak on the record, and their names appear in endnotes. On a few occasions, however, policymakers—often because of the sensitivity of their positions—asked to be interviewed on a background-only basis. Needless to say, I respected their wishes. At a time when it is all too fashionable to criticize bureaucrats, I wish to commend the public servants who assisted me for their intelligence, commitment, professionalism, and generosity of their time.

I also want to express my appreciation to the following individuals for comments on drafts of various chapters and sections of this manuscript. David C. Acheson, who as a young attorney attended the signing of the Washington Treaty that created NATO in 1949, and Gayden E. Thompson, executives of The Atlantic Council of the United States, provided particularly keen insights into the alliance. Only late in my research did I have the good luck to make contact with Peter Bird Swiers, a career foreign service officer for twenty-six years before accepting the post as vice president of The Atlantic Council and director of its Harriman Program for East-West studies. Not only did Mr. Swiers offer astute suggestions for strengthening the substance of Chapter 1, but he also helped to improve my roughly hewn prose. The Williamsburg area is indeed fortunate to have the Swiers as residents. Michael Mandelbaum, Christian A. Herter Professor of American Foreign Policy, the Nitze School of Advanced International Studies, the Johns Hopkins University, promptly and courteously returned phone calls and facsimiles even on weekends, to deepen my understanding of the most trenchant arguments against NATO's eastward expansion. Simon Serfaty, director of European Studies, the Center for Strategic & International Studies, furnished manifold assistance with respect to guiding my research, its organization, and content. He is truly a scholar's scholar.

Throughout the preparation of the manuscript, I benefitted greatly from the ideas, encouragement, and advice of several colleagues at the College of William & Mary: namely, Professors Brian Blouet, Clay Clemens, C. Lawrence Evans, John B. Gilmour, Ludwell H. Johnson, III, John J. McGlennon, Ronald Rappoport, and Alan J. Ward.

In addition, I am indebted to Tess Owens, Karen Hammer, and Nancy Currence for cheerfully and expertly typing portions of the manuscript; Anne Margaret Boyle, Sean Heuvel, and Greg Seare, William & Mary students, for performing yeoman's work in aiding with research and proofreading; and Ramzi Nemo of The American University, Anne Peregrine Shepherd, a Renaissance lady steeped in literature, mathematics, and military science, and Will Molineux, journalist par excellence with the *Daily Press*, for infusing grace, precision, and consistency into portions of the text.

It goes without saying that this book would never have seen the light of day without the extraordinary contributions of Peter Cooper, acquisitions editor of the University Press of America, Dorothy Albritton, President of Majestic Wordsmith, and professionals in the reference departments of Earl Gregg Swem Library, College of William & Mary, the Williamsburg Regional Library, and the State Library of Virginia. The latter displayed enormous imagination in ferreting out information that I believed could not have been found.

At every stage in this writing project, my legislative assistants Michael Abley and Ellen Moncure lent invaluable helping hands, as did Agnes Wasik and Svietlane Ilczuk, secretaries to the ambassador of the Republic of Poland in the United States. The Polish American Congress kindly supplied many of the photographs at the end of the text. Although I requested pictorial submissions from various organizations, only the PAC had access to suitable material.

In addition, David F. Morrill, managing editor of *Eighteenth-Century Life* and other scholarly publications, not only creatively and expertly copy-edited the manuscript, but he also demonstrated remarkable industriousness, imagination, and good humor in organizing and collecting

Acknowledgments

the material for publication. Thanks to David Morrill, Peter Cooper, and Dorothy Albritton the manuscript evolved from rough draft to an attractive volume within three months—a feat beyond the capability of most of the publishing industry.

Support from William & Mary's Class of 1938 and the College's Faculty Research Committee helped the author defray certain expenses incurred in researching and preparing the book.

Last but not least, Dr. Carmen Brissette Grayson, an ideal companion for thirty-six years, took time from her path-breaking study of the life and times of Civil War Quartermaster Montgomery Meigs to advance her husband's comparatively modest intellectual venture.

With so much help from so many people, the author must bear full responsibility for any errors of fact or interpretation that crept into these pages.

George W. Grayson
College of William & Mary
Williamsburg, Virginia

Map of Europe

Introduction

Shortly before 11 p.m. on April 30, 1998, a telephone rang in S-212 at the Capitol, breaking the silence of the Vice President's Office of Legislative Affairs, a chandeliered room just off the floor of the United States Senate. But the caller did not ask for Al Gore, then traveling in the Mideast.[1] Alone in the room, Mary Daly, a highly regarded foreign service officer, picked up the receiver, listened intently for several seconds, and then hurried to track down her boss. She found him in the hallway, exchanging congratulatory handshakes and hugs with senators, diplomats, and senior officials in the Clinton administration.

"Jeremy," she said assertively, "there's a call you have to take. Don't ask any questions!"

Once back in the office, Daly explained, "It's the White House. The president wants to talk to you."[2]

For the previous sixteen months, Jeremy Rosner, a forty-year-old special adviser to the president and secretary of state, had spent virtually every waking hour pursuing Bill Clinton's "top foreign-policy goal": the enlargement of the North Atlantic Treaty Organization (NATO).[3] A few minutes earlier, Rosner saw his efforts pay off spectacularly, as the Senate voted a bipartisan 80 to 19 to approve adding Poland, Hungary, and the Czech Republic to the sixteen-member security alliance. The fact that all the senators but one voted on the treaty indicated its historic importance. Indeed, Arizona's junior senator, John Kyl (R), had planned to cast a "yea" vote. After waiting as long he could for the roll call to begin, he had to rush to Dulles Airport to catch a flight to an international conference in Istanbul.[4]

As Rosner clutched the cream-colored phone waiting for Bill Clinton to come on the line, he observed the relative tranquility of his ornate surroundings, which for the past two weeks had resembled more a military command post than a vice-presidential enclave. There, Rosner and his colleagues from throughout the city, including his own staff in the State Department's NATO Enlargement Ratification Office—known by the acronym NERO—had encamped to prepare for the days of debate and dozens of possible amendments preceding the final vote. In early 1997, senior administration officials had decided to establish a small, single-purpose office headed by a dynamic expert in foreign policy-making. This decision revealed a determination by Secretary of State Madeleine Albright, Undersecretary of State Strobe Talbott, and other top departmental executives that efforts to expand the Atlantic alliance not bog down in the State Department's sprawling bureaucracy, sometimes referred to as the "Fudge Factory in Foggy Bottom."

Rosner had trained himself as a careful student of executive-legislative relations, graduating from Brandeis University *summa cum laude*, then earning a master's degree at Harvard's Kennedy School of Government. After holding several political and policy positions, he joined the National Security Council (NSC) in 1993, becoming the president's main international-affairs speechwriter.[5]

In this post, Rosner also received a crash course in Central Europe from Daniel Fried, an iconoclastic NSC staff member, who later became the council's senior director for European affairs before President Clinton named him ambassador to Poland in 1997. Fried—a history major at Cornell University who later received a master's degree in international affairs from Columbia University—impressed upon Rosner the foreign-policy establishment's myopia with respect to Central and Eastern Europe.

After the USSR's disintegration, Fried insisted, most scholars, military analysts, and U.S. bureaucrats gave top priority to productive financial, political, and diplomatic relations with Moscow in hopes of fostering a moderate, responsible postcommunist regime. They believed that once Washington had forged a condominium with the Kremlin, the United States could then focus on Central Europe. However, the United States' relationship with Poland, Hungary, Czechoslovakia, and other former eastern bloc members should not undermine Russian moderates, lest they incur the wrath of xenophobes, unreconstructed communists, and other extremists eager to recreate authoritarian rule.

In essence, Fried maintained, converting this "Russia-first" outlook into policy would accept the cold war division of Europe—with semireformed Central European states remaining subordinate to Russia.

As the State Department's Polish desk officer in the late 1980s, Fried had begun suggesting to colleagues that making Russia the pivot of U.S. Central European strategy constituted a recipe for instability: Moscow would reestablish some form of hegemony over its former satellites; ultranationalist, anti-Russian demagogues would command volatile followings in countries of the region; and an assortment of angry, bitter, quarreling states would dominate the landscape between the Oder-Neisse line and Russia's western border. Fried, along with others inside and outside the government, asserted that 1989 changed the world and afforded Washington the opportunity to avoid the parlous outcome he envisioned in the "Russia-first" viewpoint. Mikhail Gorbachev had not granted Warsaw Pact countries their independence in a fit of benevolence. Rather, Poland's Solidarity Movement and similar groups in the area had crashed through the corroded fences that once confined them. Fried declaimed the wisdom of reaching out to modern democrats in Warsaw, Prague, Budapest, and other Central European capitals, welcoming their return to the trans-Atlantic community whose values they shared. In short, he proposed neither accepting the European power structure dictated by Stalin in 1944 nor the quasi-authoritarian/quasi-democratic Central Europe of the 1930s. Instead, he advocated allowing the Poles, Czechs, Hungarians, and other peoples who so desired, to reintegrate into the West on principles enunciated by Prime Minister Winston Churchill and President Franklin D. Roosevelt in the 1941 Atlantic Charter.[6] As these countries benefitted from political openings, market economies, and a growing sense of military security, they could serve as nonthreatening sources of financial, technical, and entrepreneurial assistance to Russia. Such a win-win plan, Fried contended, would also depoliticize America's Russian policy at home where Democrats had traditionally shown greater sympathy for Moscow and Republicans for the "captive nations" of East and Central Europe.[7]

Rosner readily accepted Fried's logic. Starting in 1993, Rosner had helped Clinton and National Security Adviser W. Anthony Lake craft speeches that laid out an American strategy of consolidating and enlarging the community of free-market democracies in Central Europe and elsewhere. But Rosner faced a practical rather than a theoretical challenge in 1997. He knew that the Senate had approved most major treaties proposed by presidents in recent years. He also recalled how, almost seventy years earlier, Henry Cabot Lodge (R-MA)—the cantankerous, acutely partisan chairman of the Senate Foreign Relations Committee (SFRC)—despised Woodrow Wilson and thwarted the uncompromising Democratic president's attempt to guide the United States into the League of Nations. In 1998 as in 1920, an American president confronted a Senate controlled by his political opponents, not to mention an SFRC whose chairman, Jesse Helms (R-NC), reviled Clinton. Likewise, the chairman's colleagues reflected the public's overriding interest in domestic rather than foreign affairs after a period of intense international engagement. Thus, like Wilson after World War I, Clinton sought to embark upon new commitments after the cold war.

The painstaking work of Albright, Talbott, Lake and his successor, Samuel R. "Sandy" Berger, and others convinced most insiders that the NATO protocols would muster the required two-thirds majority to amend the Washington Treaty, which had created the Atlantic alliance in 1949. At the same time, they nevertheless worried that senators might somehow adopt amendments that would disturb, distort, delay, or denature the most significant revision of NATO since the collapse of the Berlin Wall. After all, "reservations" offered by Lodge and other "irreconcilables" had spelled defeat for U.S. ratification of the Versailles Treaty, not pure and simple opposition to America's joining an international pact to promote peace.

Above all, Rosner wanted a "good win." Among other things, this meant an outcome "showing broad, enthusiastic US support, both to make the . . . security guarantees [to incoming NATO allies] more meaningful, and to strengthen the US as it pursues other foreign goals."[8]

A self-identified "control freak," Rosner had spent the preceding months working with colleagues in the administration and on Capitol Hill to map out every possible change to the legislation that each senator's office might suggest.[9] On the eve of the vote, however, he had to activate his intelligence network—manned by friendly lawmakers and their lieutenants on Capitol Hill—to identify harmful amendments. As soon as any looming threats appeared on NERO's radar screen, Rosner and his cohorts immediately alerted friendly forces to neutralize them. At the same time, Rosner wanted to amass the biggest majority possible, which required expansion proponents to strike a delicate balance. On one hand, NERO and the SFRC's leadership had helped craft the proposals, using as much foresight and attention to detail as Stonewall Jackson had in preparing his 1862 Valley Campaign in Virginia.[10] On the other hand, bringing prospective supporters on board required that the enlargement side had to welcome "helpful" suggestions from all quarters, and give them serious consideration. NERO sought to avoid gratuitously alienating any lawmaker in hopes that even if he decided not to support the 1998 legislation, he might look favorably on the entry into the alliance of other Central European nations in future years.

For days, Rosner—whom everyone calls by his first name—listened affably as senators, their aides, committee staffers, and other assorted kibitzers rushed into S-212 with proposed changes. Often the NERO chief turned thumbs-down even on "friendly" amendments, always calmly explaining to their advocates the problems implied by the proffered language.

At other times, Rosner passed along proposals to Cameron Munter, another esteemed career diplomat who served as Rosner's deputy and who worked out of NERO's drab sixth-floor office at the State Department. Munter, a Johns Hopkins Ph.D. in German history who speaks five languages and taught at UCLA before entering the Foreign Service, had left the American embassy in Bonn to join Rosner in 1997. Tall, greying at the temples, well-spoken, and conservatively dressed, Munter epitomized Hollywood's version of a diplomat. But substance, not style, landed him the NERO job.

Munter had served in Poland during the 1980s, headed the State Department's Czech desk during the dramatic events of 1989, and exhibited an abiding interest in the politics, culture, and fate of Central Europe's new democracies. Munter believed fervently that expanding NATO would enhance U.S. and European security. Moreover, he liked the prospect of "seeing a project through from start to finish"—a rare experience for diplomats, who rotate from one post to another every two or three years.[11]

Upon receiving Rosner's inquiry, the swift-thinking, crisp-writing Munter "shotgunned" faxes to NERO's "virtual staff." This group embraced some two dozen policy and legal specialists in the departments of Defense and State, the National Security Council, the White House, and embassies abroad. Recipients of these communications often faced half-hour turnabout times to furnish unambiguous recommendations for each modification proposed. The difference in time zones enabled Fried, then ambassador to Poland, to read the *Washington Post*'s on-line edition six hours before official Washington began work. This advantage allowed the imaginative envoy to electronically mail suggestions—known by others in the virtual office as "Dan Fried's Daily Scream"—on how best to react to the latest inquiry or criticism arising in the expansion debate.[12]

Rosner and Munter boasted other secret weapons in this battle: Deputy Assistant Secretary of State for European and Canadian Affairs Ronald D. Asmus, a brilliant young scholar recruited by Talbott to manage the diplomacy of NATO enlargement, and his deputy, Robert Simmons. These two men, who knew the NATO issue backwards and forwards, frequently rushed to Capitol Hill as reinforcements for knock-down-drag-out sessions with Senate staff members. Rosner joked that he and NERO handled "sales" while Asmus, Simmons, and their colleagues took care of "engineering."

Before entering government, Asmus, along with two fellow RAND Corporation security specialists—Richard L. Kugler and F. Stephen Larrabee—had written a crucial *Foreign Affairs* article that set forth the intellectual rationale for NATO expansion.[13] A fruitful, symbiotic relationship developed between experts in the European bureau and NERO, and Asmus and Rosner often huddled late in the day to hammer out secret memorandums, letters, talking points, and opinion articles. To those on hand outside the Senate chamber on April 30, Asmus beamed as if he had just won the lottery.

Finally, NERO enjoyed one hundred percent backing from the president's national security team. Berger, who had recruited Rosner, was instrumental in establishing NERO and ensuring the president made speeches and calls on this issue at important junctures. Albright, although in Beijing on the day of the vote, burned up phone lines urging senators to oppose unacceptable amendments and support ratification. Secretary of Defense William S. Cohen played a key role in addressing the concerns of Senator Ted Stevens (R-AK), chairman of the appropriations committee, and other lawmakers who feared that the Pentagon would bear the financial brunt of NATO's move eastward. In addition, Talbott and other key officials made numerous contacts on behalf of the legislation.

Information supplied to Senator Joseph R. Biden (D-DE) and other sharpshooters brought down amendments offered by nine senators. For example, Senator John Warner (R-VA), the silver-maned former navy secretary, knew that his colleagues were about to vote for the three "Visegrad countries" to join NATO.[14] Still, he wanted a three-year ban on the admission of other nations. Although attracting the "ayes" of important lawmakers like Helms, the "freeze" amendment failed 41 to

59. Kay Bailey Hutchison (R-TX) saw her proposal to create within NATO a formal dispute-resolution mechanism lose 37 to 62. If adopted, such a device could have ended the alliance's culture of consensus decision-making, thus eliminating the U.S. veto. Daniel Patrick Moynihan (D-NY) fared even worse (17 to 83) with an initiative to delay NATO membership for the three countries until they had gained admission to the European Union (EU). John D. Ashcroft (R-MO), a dour Christian Coalition favorite then mulling a bid for the GOP presidential nomination in 2000, proposed that NATO's mission remain focused on the defense of members' territories. His craftily worded amendment discouraged the organization from undertaking missions outside of Western Europe, thus deterring new, Bosnia-style peacekeeping assignments. Asmus immediately perceived the threat to the alliance's future posed by Ashcroft's initiative and rallied Rosner and others in the administration to fight it hammer and tongs.

In this case, Trent Lott (R-MS) lent a strong helping hand to Biden, Asmus, and Rosner after Ashcroft's attempt at grandstanding irritated the majority leader. When late in the evening the Missourian demanded four hours of debate on his amendment, Lott suggested that Biden move to table the measure. Reluctant to anger a fellow member of the Senate "club," the Delaware lawmaker agreed to make the motion only if Lott would stand next to him to show bipartisanship. At first Lott demurred, but when Ashcroft proved intractable, the Mississippian came over to Biden and said, in effect, "make the motion," which Lott then seconded. The Senate tabled Ashcroft's item 82 to 18.

"It's a testimony to Jeremy's acumen that he adroitly killed the 'killer' amendments," said Tom Yazdgerdi, the State Department's desk officer for the Czech Republic and a NERO virtual office mainstay, who observed the prevote maneuvering.[15] Indeed, no one appealed Rosner's verdicts to his superiors: He enjoyed the full support of the White House and Albright; he possessed an encyclopedic knowledge of the legislation and its nuances; and he exuded a moral authority respected even by foes of the NATO initiative.[16]

But the vote had rendered enlargement "a done deal," in Washington parlance, and a smile washed over Rosner's boyish face as the president's voice interrupted his daydreaming. Although Rosner himself described the call as "confidential" and declines to divulge the contents, others in the room remember his telling the chief executive, "You were the driving force in the victory . . . . A lot of people helped get the job done," before thanking Clinton for the thoughtfulness of his call. Daly picked up Rosner's camera to snap photos of her exultant boss conversing with the leader of the free world.

High above Rosner's head, white-robed females—one representing the North, the other the South—floated toward each other on the frescoed ceiling of the vice-presidential office. The joy expressed by these peacemakers, symbolizing national reconciliation after the Civil War, could not have exceeded the contentment of the ratification team's key members, who savored their historic achievement. Munter also displayed satisfaction. He knew that the scores of speeches he had delivered, the hundreds of talking points he had jotted down, and the thousands of "blast-faxes" he had unleashed had helped seal the victory for expansion.

Another first-string player on the NERO team amply deserved his part in the after-vote celebration. President Clinton had appointed Nicholas A. Rey as ambassador to Poland in 1993. Rey, a Princeton graduate, humorously attributed his selection to the fact that his "sixteenth-century ancestor was the father of Polish literature, that country's Chaucer," and that he was "the only white-haired investment banker in captivity who spoke Polish."[17] It did not hurt his cause that he had backed Clinton's bid for the presidency and received the imprimatur of Democratic stalwarts Lane Kirkland and Zbigniew Brzezinski, both fellow board members of the Polish American Enterprise Fund conceived to stimulate investment in Poland.

After completing his four-year stint in Warsaw in November 1997, Rey convinced his friend Secretary Albright to assign him to the NATO expansion venture. Rosner and Munter—always having to beg, borrow, and steal staff—welcomed the new recruit with open arms. They liked his eagerness to roll up his sleeves and contribute to all phases of their work, whether speaking to a big-city world affairs council or collating pages for thick congressional briefing books. Thus, they promptly made him their top glad-hander and booked him on tours around the country. For the peripatetic Rey—whose family fled Poland at the same time Hitler's *Wehrmacht* stormed into the country—the April 30 outcome justified his grueling schedule of speeches, sessions with editorial boards, and other media appearances. "I even enjoyed flying through two snow storms and a thundersquall to reach Minot [North Dakota] in February," he remarked later.[18]

Rey remembers several "tension breakers" during the run-up to final Senate action. For example, two days before the vote, NERO's Capitol Hill office received a phone call from Fried, then American envoy in Warsaw. Fried, the embassy's political counselor from 1990 to 1993, had just revisited the Jasna Gora Monastery in Czestoschowa. No sooner had his black Lincoln Town Car pulled up to the Roman Catholic shrine when Father Szymon, whom Fried befriended during his previous tour in the country, extended warm greetings. After inquiring about several specific amendments that might water down the legislation, the monk said, "Mr. Ambassador, I understand you fellows are having a bit of trouble with the U.S. Senate. Perhaps we can offer some extra help." Even white-robed monks in Czestoschowa were keeping a sharp eye on the debate in Washington because of its significance to their nation. The fun-loving, irrepressible Fried immediately apprised Rosner's team of the prospect for divine intervention.[19]

Rey himself arrived late in the afternoon for the final Senate vote. He had spent part of the morning at the National Gallery of Art "seeking guidance" from *The Polish Nobleman*, a Rembrandt painting of Andrew Rey, a seventeenth-century ancestor, who served as Warsaw's ambassador to the Netherlands.[20]

The thirty-four-year-old Yazdgerdi called the NATO outcome "one of the most moving moments of my life." After all, he added, "my mother is Czech and I still have lots of relatives in Prague and Pilsen." In watching Biden and Rosner exchange ideas about strategy, he had a sense of watching "history being made."[21] Jon Liam Wasley, another virtual office hand who had rushed from his State Department office to the Capitol to witness the final vote, sensed that "I have completed a perfect stage of my life . . . that I was part of a historical process that has changed the world for eighty million Europeans . . . [and] changed the world for my children."[22]

No one displayed more emotion than Jan Nowak, who had devoted his adult life to freeing Poland first from Nazi occupation and then from communist oppression. From the Senate Visitors' Gallery, he walked proudly over to Poland's Ambassador Jerzy Kozminski, who had been seated in the Diplomatic Gallery. "I thank God for letting me live to see this day," said the eighty-five-year-old Nowak tearfully, as he threw his arms around the envoy.[23]

Born on the eve of World War I in a Warsaw under the thralldom of czarist Russia, Nowak had joined Czech President Václav Havel in preaching a powerful moral message to the senators. They proclaimed that expanding NATO would not only enhance trans-Atlantic security, but would reunite with Western Christendom countries grievously injured by international agreements at Munich in 1938, Tehran in 1943, and Yalta and Potsdam in 1945. Nowak, whose wartime service eclipsed the derring-do of John Le Carré characters, described the Senate action as "the pinnacle of my life."[24]

In contrast, one of America's most esteemed statesman—a gentleman possessed of even more international experience than Nowak—viewed the Senate outcome as the nadir of his life. Ninety-four-year-old diplomat/scholar George F. Kennan, the father of the post-World War II policy to "contain" the Soviets from projecting power beyond their borders, spoke for the Russia-first school when he mordantly condemned architects of the new NATO:

> Yes, tell your children, and your children's children, that you lived in the age of Bill Clinton and William Cohen, the age of Madeleine Albright and Sandy Berger, the age of Trent Lott and [Senator] Joe Lieberman, and you were present at the creation of the post-cold-war order, when these foreign policy Titans put their heads together and produced . . . a mouse.[25]

Foreign-policy expert Susan Eisenhower,[26] Johns Hopkins University scholar Michael Mandelbaum, *New York Times* columnist Thomas Friedman, former Senator Sam Nunn, ex-CIA director Stansfield Turner, Vice Admiral John J. Shanahan (ret.), and many other distinguished individuals and organizations shared Kennan's pessimism about adding the Visegrad states to the North Atlantic alliance. As will be discussed in Chapter 4, many considerations nurtured this apprehension. The foremost concern for Kennan revolved around the impact of NATO enlargement on Russia. He believed this initiative would undercut moderate democrats, impede reforms of the country's ramshackle economy, raise problems over the future of its huge arsenal of nuclear weapons, and chill its disposition to cooperate with the West during international crises. In agreeing with Kennan's points, Eisenhower inveighed against the betrayal of Russia. She pointed out that the

> Two Plus Four Settlement, which proved for the unification of Germany, had excluded the stationing of foreign troops and nuclear systems on the territory of the former German Democratic Republic, an assurance, in the Russian view, that NATO would not extend beyond the borders of Germany. After the Alliance declared its intention to expand eastward, the Russians felt further humiliated by the unilateral nature of the decision.[27]

As examined later, strong NATO proponents like Senator Nunn also feared that expanding the alliance could dissipate its effectiveness and involve the United States in conflicts for which it had no national interest. Although agreeing with Nunn, most Pentagon officials recoiled at the idea of America's armed forces assuming new responsibilities in the face of sharp budget cuts, with countries whose armies would dilute rather than enhance NATO's military strength. On the other side of the political spectrum, the Cato Institute and other libertarian organizations decried future—and many current—U.S. commitments abroad.

Candidate Clinton

NATO may have become a hot topic by the spring of 1998, but it had not always occupied center stage. If a latter-day Rip Van Winkle, asleep for six years, had awakened to observe rejoicing over NATO expansion, he would have rubbed his eyes in disbelief.

After all, during the 1992 campaign, candidate Clinton emphasized domestic over international affairs in his presidential race against George Bush, while the Republicans paid little attention to the Atlantic alliance as they sought to fend off attacks on their handling of the economy. The NATO issue simply did not appear on America's national radar screen. The Arkansan presented himself as a centrist "New Democrat," determined to avoid the gauzy, ideologically charged stands of Michael Dukakis and other party standard-bearers. Clinton had lasered-in on the pocketbook complaints of blue-collar and middle-class voters: "People are working harder than ever, spending less time with their children,

Pros and Cons of NATO Expansion

Issues	Proponents	Opponents
Institutional	* Keeps the United States engaged in Europe. * Allows the organization to engage in new missions, thus preventing its stagnation.	* Weakens the organization by adding new states with militaries inferior to those of existing members. * Paves the way for even less qualified countries to seek admission. * Puts the cart before the horse because Central European nations should enter the EU and other economic/political organizations before pursuing membership in NATO.
Political	* Fortifies nascent democracies in Central Europe. * Provides West with means to promote human rights within new members. * Returns deserving nations to the bosom of the West, redressing wrongs they suffered at the Munich and Yalta conferences. * Enjoys support in public opinion polls. * Helps to overcome the partisan conflict over U.S. policy toward Russia.	* Provides an issue for extremists to use against moderates in Russia, thereby imperiling the country's transition to democracy. * Finds the United States breaking its promise at time of Two-Plus-Four agreement not to move NATO eastward. * Benefits the military-industrial complex in the West. * Constitutes a rush to judgment, which deprived the American public of a national debate on the issue.

(cont'd.)

Pros and Cons of NATO Expansion (Cont'd.)

Issues	Proponents	Opponents
Economic	* Encourages market-oriented economies. * Expands the marketplace for American goods and services.	* Diverts scarce resources from social to military spending.
Security	* Fills the security vacuum between Russia and Germany. * Militates against Germany's attempting to manage the security zone to its east. * Obviates the likelihood that Poland or other Central European states will acquire nuclear weapons. * Provides the United States with additional well-prepared allies to call upon in the case of international crises. * Reduces potential threats to Russia by fostering democracy, development, and a sense of security in Central Europe.	* Gratuitously antagonizes nationalists, xenophobes, militarists and others in former USSR, which poses no treat to its neighbors. * Discourages Duma's approving the START II Treaty and other arms control agreements. * Risks requiring U.S. troops to settle simmering border disputes between Central European states like Hungary and Romania.

working nights and weekends on the job instead of going to PTA and Little League or Scouts," he thundered in his acceptance speech at the Democratic Convention, "[a]nd their incomes are still going down, their taxes are going up, and the costs of housing, health care and education are going through the roof. Meanwhile, more and more of our best people are falling into poverty, even though they work 40 hours a week."[28]

In speech after speech, he castigated George Bush for neglecting people's pressing economic problems because of a fixation on the past. "The Cold War is over. Soviet Communism has collapsed," Clinton told four thousand cheering delegates assembled in New York City for the Democratic National Convention that July. "And our values— freedom, democracy, individual rights and free enterprise—they have triumphed all around the world. And yet just as we have won the Cold War abroad, we are losing the battles for economic opportunity here at home."[29] The Democratic National Committee embellished this theme by distributing T-shirts that proclaimed "George Bush: THE ANYWHERE BUT AMERICA TOUR," a barbed reference to the incumbent's frequent forays abroad during a sustained recession.[30]

Although Bush's public approval ratings had soared to ninety-one percent in the wake of the dramatic Gulf War victory in early 1991, Clinton was one of the few Democratic notables who perceived that average Americans would shift their attention from the successful conclusion of hostilities more quickly than most establishment politicians. He believed that the "forgotten middle class" would opt for a future-oriented advocate of creating jobs, improving their kids' schools, and broadening access to affordable health care, shunning an incumbent who reminded them of a past that became less relevant to their daily lives with each new round of layoffs. Appearing together on *60 Minutes*, Governor Clinton and his wife Hillary largely laid to rest the "character issue" at the time of the New Hampshire primary, so that by Election Day voters praised the Democratic nominee for "caring about people like us." This perception benefitted Clinton even at the time of his mid-August 1998 televised mea culpa concerning "inappropriate [sexual] behavior" with former White House intern Monica S. Lewinsky and during the ensuing impeachment by the House of Representatives on December 19, 1998.[31]

While promising to keep the United States engaged in world affairs, Clinton devoted less than ten percent of his campaign pronouncements to global matters. At first, the Republicans ridiculed the five-term Southern governor's provincialism. Bush joked, for example, that his opponent had gained his overseas experience at the International House of Pancakes, where he liked to indulge his hearty appetite.[32] As the campaign progressed, however, Clinton astutely seized upon foreign policy to neutralize Republican attacks on him and even score points against his GOP competitor.

First, Clinton parried Republican charges that his avoidance of service in Vietnam would make him a weak commander in chief. Although he temporarily wavered over congressional authorization of force in the Persian Gulf, the Democrat backed U.S. intervention against Iraq in January 1991. Three months later, he said that the nation's leader must be prepared "to act with force . . . [and] I will not shrink from using military force responsibly. And I will see that we maintain the forces we need to win, and win decisively, should that necessity arise."[33]

With respect to the ethnic conflict in the former Yugoslavia, Clinton upbraided the Republican standard-bearer for indecision and vacillation. "When I argued that the United States, in cooperation with international community efforts, should be prepared to use military force to help the UN relief effort in Bosnia, Mr. Bush's spokesman quickly denounced me as reckless," the Democratic nominee told the Institute of World Affairs in Milwaukee. "Yet a few days later, the administration adopted the very same position."[34]

This assertiveness and Clinton's domestic agenda drew ringing endorsements from Admiral William J. Crowe, chairman of the Joint Chiefs of Staff under Reagan and Bush, Lieutenant General Calvin Waller, deputy commander of U.S. forces in the Persian Gulf, General William Odom, the *New York Times*, the *Washington Post*, and other pillars of the foreign affairs establishment. Clinton's enunciation of a credible defense policy also allowed him to avoid the image of weakness and aversion to force projected by the Democrats in 1988, when Governor Dukakis, suffering free-fall in public-opinion polls, invited scorn by appearing in a television commercial wearing a helmet and riding in a tank.

Second, Clinton jumped on the mishandling of U.S. relations with a major trading partner to highlight Bush's domestic failures. In a speech to the Los Angeles World Affairs Council, he lamented that

> Mr. Bush's economic neglect has invited foreign pity—literally. You remember the Japanese trip, which ended with the Japanese prime minister saying he felt sympathy for the United States. . . . He felt sympathy for us because he thought we had refused to address our problems here at home, we had gone into a period of economic decline, and our best days might be behind us. It is time for economic leadership that inspires foreign respect.[35]

Third, the challenger from Arkansas excoriated the Republican administration's generous assistance to Saddam Hussein up to Iraq's invasion of Kuwait and after an Iraqi attack on the USS *Stark* in May 1989. In so doing, he raised doubts whether Americans could really have confidence in Bush, who had claimed that the campaign centered on "trust"—a euphemism for Clinton's alleged draft dodging and womanizing.[36]

In the same vein, Clinton blasted the incumbent's readiness to "coddle [Beijing's] aging rulers with undisguised contempt for democracy, for human rights, and for the need to control the spread of dangerous technologies. Such forbearance . . . might have been justified during the Cold War . . . when China was a counterweight to the Soviet Union. But it makes no sense to play that China card now, when our opponents have thrown in their hand."[37] The Clinton White House would, he promised, "link China's trading privileges to its human rights record and its conduct . . . [with respect to] weapon sales."[38]

Fourth, the Democratic aspirant took Bush to task for his inattention to Moscow, warning that an absence of solid support for Boris Yeltsin's elected government could lead to its replacement by communists or ultranationalists. Former President Richard M. Nixon's scathing March 1992 critique of Bush's "pathetically inadequate response" to post-communist Russia obviated the possibility of tagging Clinton as "soft" on the Russians.[39]

Finally, Clinton adopted a stand in favor of a modified version of the North American Free Trade Agreement (NAFTA), reaffirming his credentials as a New Democrat. His party's traditional pillar, organized labor, had lambasted the trilateral commercial accord among the United

States, Mexico, and Canada. Nevertheless, Clinton not only pledged to back a slightly altered agreement, but also used the debate to underline Bush's hapless inability to articulate a sense of purpose and mission for the country—what the incumbent called the "vision thing."

One month before the election, Clinton told an audience in Raleigh, North Carolina, that he would not renegotiate NAFTA, but would improve it through supplemental agreements. Calling omissions to the text "serious," he declared that he could not sign the pact as it stood. His reservations centered on a belief that NAFTA should dovetail with plans to better prepare the American economy and workforce for the challenges of the twenty-first century. "The issue," he declared, "is not whether we should support free trade or open markets. Of course we should. The real question is whether or not we will have a national economic strategy to make sure we reap its benefits."[40]

NATO Expansion

Although the Democratic Platform called for "reducing the size of . . . [U.S.] forces in Europe while meeting our obligations to NATO," at no point did expanding the alliance surface as a campaign issue in 1992.[41] NATO's future had precipitated discussions on both sides of the Atlantic; however, such deliberations occurred largely among a handful of U.S. officials at the State Department and National Security Council, at NATO headquarters in Brussels, at defense and foreign ministries in Central Europe, in the councils of the German government, and at think tanks like the RAND Corporation in Santa Monica, California, renowned for its research on military and security matters for the U.S. Department of Defense and other governmental agencies.[42]

In 1992, several considerations weighed against Clinton's devoting scarce time and resources to this issue, much less throwing his weight behind augmenting NATO's size and role. First, Hillary Clinton, George Stephanopoulos, Ira Magaziner, Robert Reich, and other prominent liberals in Clinton's entourage regarded military-related issues as a throwback to the old days of power politics, virulent anticommunism, huge Pentagon budgets, and the insidious greed of defense contractors. Along with labor allies in the American Federation of Labor and Congress of Industrial Organizations (AFL-CIO), they looked forward to devoting the "peace dividend" to repairing and fortifying a frayed social safety net, not refurbishing and revitalizing the nation's military machine. In-house liberals shared Vice President Gore's view that the United States confronted a profoundly different array of international topics in the post-cold war era. In his 1992 book, *Earth in the Balance: Ecology and the Human Spirit*,[43] Gore had stressed the need to address problems that Bush and his business-oriented advisers had mishandled, ignored, or dismissed, including global pollution, depletion of the ozone layer, the spread of dangerous chemicals, proliferation of nuclear weapons, and threats to democracy and human rights. Gore and Clinton contended that, rather than using traditional means, Washington should pursue solutions to such challenges multilaterally, preferably through international organizations.

Second, the president's chief political consultants—"Ragin' Cajun" James Carville and Paul Begala—held scant regard for foreign policy, which they viewed with all the enthusiasm of town drunks at a temperance meeting. They determined to keep their client's attention riveted on the domestic message, and continually reminded his foreign-policy advisers that "kitchen-table" concerns—not arcane global matters—enabled Bill Clinton to pile up 370 of 538 electoral votes en route to 1600 Pennsylvania Avenue. Moreover, every poll showed the public rejecting isolationism, but resonating to domestic over international matters. Whether a cause or effect of public apathy, in recent years major networks have halved their coverage of international affairs during their evening news broadcasts.[44]

Third, many lawmakers appeared unreceptive to foreign entanglements now that the Berlin Wall had tumbled, the Soviet Union had dissolved, and captive nations had achieved independence. For them, involvement abroad conjured bloated images of the United Nations, the World Bank, the International Monetary Fund, and other contemptible sinkholes for the hard-earned dollars of American taxpayers. With the cold war's termination, many dyed-in-the-wool conservatives moved from bashing atheistic communists abroad to boosting the Christian Coalition at home. In addition, lawmakers from the hard right disdained Clinton not just for capturing the presidency, but because of his draft avoidance, equivocation on marijuana use, highly publicized philandering, outreach to gays, and marriage to an extremely intelligent, outspoken feminist. Worst of all, this veritable anti-Christ boasted consistently high approval ratings with average, working families.

Fourth, Pentagon analysts expressed concern that NATO enlargement could overextend U.S. armed forces. As noted above, to the degree that they even considered the issue, civilian and uniformed executives in the Defense Department shied from assuming new responsibilities at a time of declining budgets and existing security commitments on five continents.

Fifth, alliance members had witnessed profound geostrategic changes recently in the Euro-Atlantic region. The Polish American Congress (PAC), the Hungarian American Coalition (HAC), and a dozen or more ethnic organizations had already begun echoing pleas from Warsaw, Budapest, and other East European capitals that NATO open its doors to new members. But few if any reasons compelled attention to their entreaties.

At the same time, Russia of the early 1990s bore little resemblance to the "evil empire" against which President Ronald Reagan had unleashed both his ire and billions of dollars of national-security spending. Indeed, the former USSR had suffered serious military, economic, and social reversals. For the first time in history, life expectancy began declining in a European nation, and Moscow posed no imminent threat to either its erstwhile satellites or its former foes. The last thing Yeltsin wanted or needed was a foreign conflict that would consume more lives and scarce resources.

Along the lines of Kennan's criticism, the few early academic critics of NATO expansion argued that enlargement would pose a gratuitous threat to Russia, and potentially help the prospects of nationalist hardliners or communists. To broaden the alliance, they insisted, would ignore the post-World War II wisdom of Harry Truman, George C. Marshall, Dean Acheson, and a host of European statesmen. Early academic critics held that these men understood the imperative to welcome the West's former enemy—in their time, Germany—into the bosom of the Euro-Atlantic community rather than treating it as an outsider, if not an outright pariah. Nonetheless, in fewer than six years, NATO expansion moved from a nonissue on the American political scene to the apex of Clinton's foreign-affairs agenda.

What accounted for this change of priorities? I argue that the *Foreign Affairs* essay by Asmus, Kugler, and Larrabee—who became known as the "RAND troika," the "RAND boys," or the "gang of three"—gave impulse to the pro-expansion effort, much as Kennan's remarkable "X" article nearly a half-century earlier laid the foundation of America's containment strategy toward the Soviet Union.[45] The Asmus et al. article resonated in Congress, especially with Senator Richard G. Lugar (R-IN); with both Admiral Ulrich Weisser, head of policy planning for the German Defense Ministry, and Defense Minister Volker Rühe; and with Daniel Fried and core players in the National Security Council, who became known as the "NSC troika." Until 1994, however, pro-enlargement advocates found themselves in a distinct minority in Washington's international affairs bureaucracy, which often displayed outright hostility to their quest. Only after President Clinton fully endorsed NATO's growth in speeches in Central Europe did the foreign-policy Fudge Factory begin to respond positively.

Put briefly, NATO's expansion (1) sprang from the RAND troika's deft articulation of Trumanesque ideas about U.S. vital interests and European security; (2) picked up momentum as a result of backing from moderate internationalist senators, the German Defense Ministry, and the Polish government and key Polish American intellectuals; (3) became official U.S. policy through statements of a "New Democratic" president reinforced in an action plan developed by National Security Adviser Lake and several NSC colleagues, and endorsed by Secretary of State Warren Christopher and Talbott; (4) gained a critical mass of bureaucratic backing thanks to herculean efforts by Lake and Assistant Secretary of State for European and Canadian Affairs Richard C. Holbrooke; (5) reached fruition under the strong leadership of Christopher's successor, Albright, who pursued a diplomatic strategy crafted by Talbott, initially an opponent of enlargement; and (6) won overwhelming Senate approval because of early, indefatigable efforts by bright, highly motivated activists in NERO, on Capitol Hill, in the business community, in think tanks, in Central European embassies, and among ethnic-American organizations. Foes of expansion suffered from the lack of: a single leader, an ideologically similar alliance, a walk-through-fire senator who would champion their cause, and sufficient resources—at least until Ben Cohen, president of Ben & Jerry's Ice Cream, joined the fray at the eleventh hour.

Introduction

To place the historic April 1998 Senate vote in perspective, Chapter 1 summarizes NATO's origin, evolution, and post-cold war options. Chapter 2 examines the latter-day "X" article and its impact on decisionmakers on both sides of the Atlantic. Chapter 3 describes how, in the face of fierce bureaucratic opposition, Lake, the NSC troika, and top State Department officials framed and advanced the pro-enlargement effort within the executive branch with the formidable assistance of "enforcer" Holbrooke and others. Chapter 4 discusses the creation and activities of NERO and its activism in the clash between pro- and anti-expansionists. Chapter 5 outlines the role in achieving ratification played by NATO members, their ethnic and political confreres in the United States, and distinguished intellectuals. And Chapter 6 explores changes in the U.S. Senate with respect to international affairs, the actual vote on NATO expansion, and lessons in policy-making and coalition-building derived from the ratification episode.

Notes

1. Although Article 1, Section 3, of the *Constitution* designates the vice president as "President of the Senate," he rarely discharges this role except on ceremonial occasions or when he might be called upon to break a deadlock. With Republicans holding a 55- to 45-seat advantage over the Democrats, Gore had neither cast a tiebreaking vote nor presided over the Senate in 1998. In fact, he had voted only four times since taking office five years earlier.
2. Mary Daly, Foreign Service officer, interview by author, Washington, D.C., September 28, 1998.
3. The author could not find a presidential statement to the effect that NATO enlargement stood at the top of the president's agenda; however, for two successive years, alliance expansion headed the foreign-policy section of the State of the Union Address, a traditional predictor of presidential priorities.
4. Even though twenty-five miles from the Capitol when his colleagues voted, Kyl had offered a friendly amendment, adopted 90 to 9, expressing the sense of the Senate that NATO retain its strategic priorities.
5. Warren Christopher, *In the Stream of History: Shaping Foreign Policy for a New Era* (Stanford: Stanford University Press, 1998), p. 19, fn. 4.
6. This "charter," issued as a news release following a Churchill-Roosevelt meeting off the Newfoundland coast in August 1941, blended elements of Wilson's Fourteen Points (self-determination, democracy, free trade, freedom of the seas, abandonment of force) and Roosevelt's New Deal (improved labor standards, economic advancement, social security, and freedom from want and fear); see Thomas A. Bailey, *A Diplomatic History of the American People*, 7th ed. (New York: Appleton-Century-Crofts, 1964), pp. 728-29.
7. Ambassador Daniel Fried, interview by author, Washington, D.C., December 28, 1998.
8. Jeremy Rosner and Cameron Munter, "Mission Statement: NATO Enlargement Ratification Office (NERO)," photocopy, March 5, 1998.
9. Jeremy Rosner, interview by author, Washington, D.C., August 5, 1998.
10. Senator Jesse Helms (R-NC) chairs the panel, while Senator Joseph R. Biden, Jr. (D-DE) serves as ranking minority member. As will become evident, Biden became the driving force for ratification in the Senate, acting as de facto floor manager of the legislation.
11. Cameron Munter, interview by author, Washington, D.C., July 21, 1998.
12. Alexander "Sandy" Vershbow, U.S. ambassador to NATO, also contributed to the work of the virtual office (Fried, interview, December 28, 1998).
13. Ronald D. Asmus, Richard L. Kugler, and F. Stephen Larrabee, "Building

a New NATO," *Foreign Affairs* 72, no. 4 (September/October 1993): 28-40. See note 42 below for more on the RAND Corporation.

14. The allusion to Visegrad arose from a mid-February 1991 summit in Visegrad, Hungary, attended by leaders of Poland, Hungary, and Czechoslovakia (which separated into the Czech Republic and Slovakia on January 1, 1993). At this session, the representatives of those nations pledged to harmonize their cooperation with European institutions, to consult on security matters, to promote economic collaboration, and to improve ties in areas like ecology, transportation, and information. See, F. Stephen Larrabee, *East European Security After the Cold War* (Santa Monica: RAND Corporation, 1993), p. 101.

15. Tom Yazdgerdi, desk officer for the Czech Republic, U.S. Department of State, interview by author, Washington, D.C., August 18, 1998.

16. Cameron Munter, telephone interview by author, September 1, 1998.

17. Ambassador Nicholas Rey, interview by author, Washington, D.C., August 5, 1998.

18. Rey, interview, August 5, 1998.

19. Daniel Fried, electronic mail to author, December 15, 1998.

20. Rosner, telephone interview by author, October 12, 1998; Rey, facsimile to author, October 30, 1998.

21. Yazdgerdi, interview, August 18, 1998.

22. Jon Liam Wasley, desk officer for Hungary, U.S. Department of State, interview by author, Washington, D.C., August 31, 1998.

23. Ambassador Jerzy Kozminski, interview by author, Washington, D.C., October 19, 1998; Jan Nowak, national director, Polish American Congress, telephone interview, November 16, 1998.

24. Nowak, telephone interview by author, November 16, 1998.

25. Quoted by Thomas Friedman, "Now a Word from X," *New York Times*, May 2, 1998, p. 15.

26. Former President Dwight David Eisenhower's granddaughter serves as chairman of the Center for Political and Strategic Studies, in Washington, D.C.

27. Susan Eisenhower, "Russian Perspectives on the Expansion of NATO," in *NATO and the Quest for Post-Cold War Security*, ed. Clay Clemens (New York: St. Martin's Press, 1997), p. 141. Two Plus Four refers to the four World War II allies—France, the Soviet Union, the United Kingdom, and the United States—recognizing the sovereignty of a reunified Germany.

28. "Nominee Clinton Describes Vision of 'New Covenant,'" *1992 CQ Almanac*, vol. 48 (Washington, D.C.: Congressional Quarterly, 1993), p. 55-A.

29. "Nominee Clinton Describes Vision of 'New Covenant,'" p. 54-A.

30. Thomas Omestad, "Why Bush Lost," *Foreign Policy*, no. 89 (winter 1992-93): 73.
31. Victor Fingerhut, associate professor of political science and public-opinion expert, Mary Washington College, telephone interview by author, August 5, 1998.
32. Republican presidential aspirant Patrick Buchanan used the IHOP remark during the primaries; Bush picked it up during the fall campaign. See *Newsday*, November 29, 1992, p. 31.
33. Quoted from Bill Clinton, Speech to the Foreign Policy Association, "Major Foreign Policy Speech," LEXIS-NEXIS, Academic Universe, April 1, 1992, p. 2.
34. Quoted in Bill Clinton, "Stump Speech: Clinton at University of Wisconsin," broadcast on National Public Radio, Academic Universe, LEXIS-NEXIS, October 13, 1992, p. 2.
35. Quoted in Bill Clinton, Speech to the World Affairs Council of Los Angeles, August 13, 1992.
36. Omestad, "Why Bush Lost," p. 77.
37. Quoted from speech delivered to the Foreign Policy Association, New York, April 1, 1992, p. 2.
38. Quoted from speech delivered to the World Affairs Council of Los Angeles, August 13, 1992.
39. For a discussion of Nixon's widely leaked "How to Lose the Cold War" onslaught against Bush's policy toward Yeltsin, see Marvin Kalb, *The Nixon Memo: Political Respectability, Russia, and the Press* (Chicago: University of Chicago Press, 1994); the book's appendix carries the document, pp. 217-23.
40. Stuart Auerbach, "Bush, Clinton Differ on Government's Role," *Washington Post*, October 8, 1992, p. A-30.
41. "Democratic Platform," *1992 CQ Almanac*, p. 63-A.
42. Founded in 1948 by the U.S. Air Force as the RAND Research and Development Corporation, the organization developed strategic policies for the Air Force—including plans for the Strategic Air Command—that contributed to this service's dominance in nuclear strategy. Although technically independent of the government, the RAND Corporation still receives the lion's share of its contracts from the Pentagon. See, "Rand Corporation," in Thomas S. Arms, *Encyclopedia of the Cold War* (New York: Facts on File, 1994), p. 476.
43. (Boston/New York: Houghton Mifflin Company, 1992).
44. Richard N. Haass, "Fatal Distraction: Bill Clinton's Foreign Policy," *Foreign Policy*, no. 108 (fall 1997): 114.
45. For Kennan's famous article, see "The Sources of Soviet Conduct," *Foreign Affairs* 25, no. 4 (July 1947): 566-82.

Chapter 1

ॐ

NATO's Origins, Evolution, and Post-Cold War Prospects

The Post-World War I Backdrop

T he evolution of modern Euro-Atlantic security did not begin at the cold war's passing, and the story of NATO reaches back at least as far as the other side of the twentieth century. Following World War I, the victorious Allies treated their vanquished enemy, Imperial Germany, like a heinous criminal. In particular, leaders in Paris vowed to avenge not only the 1,397,000 French lives lost to the kaiser's military between 1914 and 1918,[1] but also the humiliation suffered when Otto von Bismarck defeated Napoleon III in the 1870 Franco-Prussian War. Although less vengeful than the French, officials from Belgium—scene of many of the bloodiest battles—joined the British government, whose empire had lost nearly one million men and women,[2] in agreeing to a draconian peace.

The Allies infused the Versailles Treaty of 1919 with their animus toward the so-called "Huns." President Woodrow Wilson did soften the peace settlement by insisting, whenever convenient, on the "self-determination" of peoples. Still, the hefty two-hundred-page peace treaty specified that Germany must return the border region of Alsace and Lorraine, seized during the Franco-Prussian War, to France, which would also administer the coal-endowed Saar Valley for fifteen years. In addition, Berlin vowed to cede colonies in Africa, Asia, and the Pacific, which would become "mandates" under the general supervision of the newly created League of Nations until deemed ready for independence. The treaty also required Germany to forfeit its status as Europe's most powerful military regime by giving up most of its navy, renouncing the creation of an air force, and converting its army into a small peacekeeping force. Germany's rulers further agreed not to station forces in the Rhineland on the French frontier and granted Poland access to the Baltic port of Danzig (Gdansk) through what came to be known as the "Polish corridor."

Above all, the German government accepted "guilt" for the war in the infamous Article 231 and pledged to pay $33 billion in reparations to the victors. At the same time, the Allied leaders concluded the Security Treaty of 1919, which called for a united front should Germany launch an unprovoked attack against France.

German militarists—dominated by east-Prussian land barons—demanded that liberal civilians attend the humiliating signing ceremony held in Louis XIV's great Hall of Mirrors. In this same magnificent room forty-eight years earlier, Bismarck had established the Second Reich, following his victory in the Franco-Prussian war. As a result, the democratic Weimar Republic that emerged to govern Germany carried with it the stigma of "betraying" the fatherland and "stabbing in the back" millions of brave German soldiers who had perished in a war filled with unprecedented horrors. Chief of Staff General Erich Ludendorff lay the seeds for the opprobrium that would befall civilian parties when he told the section chiefs of the High Command in October 1918:

> I have asked His Majesty to bring those people into the government who are largely responsible for things having turned out as they have. We shall, therefore, see these gentlemen enter the ministries, and they must now make the peace which has to be made. They must now eat the soup which they have served us![3]

Ludendorff's bombast mirrored the hostility that political groupings from across the political spectrum evinced toward the Versailles Treaty in general and the "war guilt" clause in particular.

As mentioned in the Introduction, the U.S. Senate rejected proposals that the United States join the League of Nations. Isolationists and rabid Republicans blocked ratification of the Versailles pact, while Wilson believed it would replace the Hobbesian world of power politics with a means to resolve differences through reasoned debate rather than mindless bloodshed. Equally important was the United States' failure to remain in the European security equation as a guarantor of the Franco-German border accord in 1919. After the war, American bankers and businessmen did pursue financial and commercial opportunities in Europe, but joining the league or vouchsafing the Franco-German frontier would have encouraged official Washington's continued involvement in Europe's high politics. However, defeat of the league and Wilson's death preceded the U.S. government's retreat from international obligations and preference for domestic matters. In the words of English writer H.G. Wells, "Every time Europe looks across the Atlantic to see the American eagle, it observes only the rear end of an ostrich."[4]

In the 1920 presidential contest, the American electorate overwhelmingly sent to the White House Warren G. Harding, a popular, seductively handsome Ohioan, who wooed the country with promises of "normalcy not nostrums." For political reasons, the Republican nominee hedged his position on the league during the campaign. After his inauguration, though, he made his stance plain. "My administration," he proclaimed, "doesn't propose to enter [the league] now by the side door, back door, or cellar door."[5]

Twenty-four countries founded the League of Nations. But France, and to a lesser degree England, failed in both nurturing Germany's Weimar Republic and standing firm against emerging tyrants until it was too late. Germany's open parliamentary system sharply contrasted with the rigid traditionalism that pervaded industry, agriculture, the judiciary, the civil service, the police, and other key institutions of German society. Instead of recognizing the ubiquity and extremism of the fragile Weimar Republic's enemies, Paris demanded prompt payment of the war debt. When Berlin fell in arrears, President Alexandre Millerande's government dispatched the French army to reoccupy the Rhineland in January 1923. This incident sparked a runaway inflation that diminished the regime's legitimacy in the eyes of its most important constituency, the middle class, who watched their savings evaporate as the exchange rate plummeted from eighteen thousand marks to the dollar at the beginning of the year to 4.2 trillion marks to the dollar in November 1923. Fortunately for Germany, American loans helped its economy rebound to the point that 1926 living standards surpassed those of the prewar era. After a few years of apparent stability, Weimar fell like a house of cards when swept by the winds of the Great Depression. The crisis opened the door to

Adolph Hitler, National Socialism, the German-Austrian Anschluss, the 1938 Munich Conference, the invasion of Poland, and World War II. The isolationism pervading the United States until Pearl Harbor raised doubts whether Washington, even if a league member, would have proven more resolute against the totalitarian menace.

The Post-World War II Challenge

Despite George Washington's injunctions against entangling alliances, a second world war erupting in Europe convinced many policymakers on both sides of the Atlantic that European stability depended upon sustained trans-Atlantic coordination of security matters. But even after 256,275 American deaths suffered during four years of combat,[6] some Washington decisionmakers stood ready to repeat Harding's policy and disengage from Europe. They claimed that by its nature European politics incubated power rivalries, Machiavellian duplicity, national jealousies, and thus inevitable conflicts. Following the conclusion of hostilities in 1945, the United States rapidly demobilized its military, slashing its forces from twelve million men and women in mid-1945 to 1.5 million by the end of 1946.[7] Former British Prime Minister Winston Churchill's ominous warning—voiced in a March 1946 speech in Fulton, Missouri—that the Russians would ring down an "Iron Curtain" over Central Europe disquieted many Americans, who remembered "Uncle Joe" Stalin as a war ally. Student protesters at Harvard lofted a banner that proclaimed: "Winnie, Winnie, go away, G.I. Joe is home to stay."[8]

Truman, who had acceded to the presidency after Franklin Roosevelt's death in April 1945, grew up in the midwest where isolationist sentiment flourished. Regional preferences aside, though, the plain-speaking Missourian admired Woodrow Wilson for pursuing international harmony. For decades, Truman, a World War I veteran, had carried in his billfold the lines from Tennyson's *Locksley Hall*, which ran

> Till the war-drum throbb'd no longer,
> And the battle flags were furled
> In the Parliament of man,
> The Federation of the world.[9]

In keeping with this sentiment, Truman welcomed delegates from fifty countries to San Francisco to create the United Nations. They completed their work in just two months, concluding the organization's charter on June 25, 1945. By crafting the charter before the formal conclusion of hostilities, its framers avoided the post-World War I snare of simultaneously striving to forge a peace and create an international organization.

Overwhelming grassroots support for the UN propelled the charter through the U.S. Senate. In mid-1945, for instance, four out of five Americans favored UN membership, according to public-opinion polls. Nevertheless, at public hearings, a few witnesses excoriated the UN Charter as a "communist plot," and a "godless and unconstitutional document" drafted by wicked foreigners. One critic even denounced the initiative as a "British-Israel World Federation movement" to establish "a world state with the Duke of Windsor as King"! Senators Henrik Shipstead (R-MN), William Langer (R-ND), and other less flamboyant isolationists insisted that the UN represented a superstate and that U.S. membership would violate the constitution.[10]

In contrast to 1919, however, presidential efforts toward multilateralism after World War II found a willing collaborator in the Foreign Relations Committee's chair. Unlike Lodge and the Versailles Treaty, Senator Tom Connally (D-TX) enthusiastically endorsed the United Nations. Recalling the rejection of the League of Nations Covenant, he shouted: "Can you not still see the blood on the floor?"[11] On July 28, 1945, the Senate approved the legislation by a vote of 89 to 2. Truman and Connally enjoyed the backing of powerful Michigan Republican Arthur H. Vandenberg, Jr., ranking member of the SFRC, whose profound isolationism had given way to internationalism once Japan bombed Pearl Harbor on December 7, 1941.

Scholars commonly attribute the difference between the ratification votes to the significant distinction between the league's and the UN's decision structures: In the UN, decisions on key issues would come from a Security Council, comprised of delegates from fifteen states. While ten members would rotate regularly, each of the five major World War II Allies would have permanent membership and a veto over all decisions.[12] Nevertheless, Senator Hiram W. Johnson (R-CA)—an irreconcilable who had stubbornly opposed the league twenty-six years before—sent word from his deathbed that, if in the chamber, he would have voted "no" to the United Nations.[13] Soon, U.S. officials realized that the USSR could paralyze the UN with its Security Council veto. Thus, the world body would not prevent Stalin from threatening Central and Western Europe directly or through proxies.

Shortly after V-E Day, an ungrateful British electorate—tired of wartime stress and deprivation—ousted from power Winston Churchill's Conservatives in favor of Clement Attlee's Labor Party. Soon after taking office, Attlee and Foreign Secretary Ernest Bevin attended the Allies' mid-1945 conference in the Berlin suburb of Potsdam. Among other issues, this "Big Three" summit addressed Germany's postwar status, the punishment of Nazi war criminals, and tentative new boundaries for Germany and Poland. Truman sought to establish a rapport with Stalin, and on one occasion entertained the ruthless Soviet chief with a piano rendition of Paderewski's *Minuet in G.*

Bevin felt less sanguine about preserving the West's wartime alliance with Moscow. After all, the Soviet leader had shown no interest in implementing the decisions of the February 1945 Yalta Conference. At that time, Roosevelt, Churchill, and Stalin issued a "Declaration on Liberated Europe," solemnly pledging that the Soviet-backed Lublin government in Poland would reorganize on "a broader democratic basis" that included representatives of other, noncommunist political groups. This restructuring would pave the way for "free and unfettered elections" in Poland, as other Central European states also selected leaders "responsive to the will of the people." Rather than keep his word, Stalin crassly manipulated puppet regimes in Bulgaria, Czechoslovakia, Hungary, Poland, and Romania. The Crimean charter ratified Russia's demand, first asserted at the late 1943 Teheran Conference, that the Curzon Line running from Grodno through Brest-Litovsk to the Bug River form the Polish-Russian border. Even though Poland was compensated with German territories east of the Oder-Neisse,[14] the country lost approximately one-third of its pre-1939 eastern territory, arousing bitter denunciations by Polish and Roman Catholic groups. The American public may have approved of this outcome, but Polish American congressmen Alvin E. O'Konski (D-WI) and John Lesinski, Jr. (D-MI) assailed the "crime of Crimea" as a "stab in the back" for Poland and as a "second Munich."[15]

Such diatribes overlooked the reasons why the Allies yielded to Stalin at Yalta. The Red Army occupied Central Europe and neither the British nor the American public favored a war of liberation against Russia. Roosevelt and Churchill, too, mistakenly believed they would need the Soviet Union to help them defeat Japan in the Pacific and Manchuria.

Just as Stalin's reneging on his "free-election" pledge proved an eye-opener for many observers, Moscow's machinations at Potsdam alerted the new British government to the perfidy of the USSR's leader. Upon the foreign secretary's return from the conference, a colleague in the House of Commons asked, "Ernie, what are those Soviets like?" Bevin replied that "[t]hey're just like the bloody Communists," in a disparaging reference to left-wing extremists in Britain's Transport and General Workers Union.[16]

Truman Doctrine

Although Truman had already thwarted Stalin's efforts to retain control of northern Iran in 1946, the first major postwar demand for U.S. re-engagement arose in southern Europe. In early 1947, the British embassy in Washington unexpectedly delivered an *aide-mémoire* to the State Department. This "blue piece of paper," in diplomatic parlance, explained that "His Majesty's Government, in view of their own [dire financial] situation, find it impossible to grant further financial assistance to Greece." The document's second part advised that: "In their existing financial situation, His Majesty's Government could not, as the United States will readily appreciate, contemplate themselves making any further credits available to Turkey."[17] The withdrawal of British aid from the Eastern Mediterranean enhanced the possibility that communist insurgents, aided and abetted by Yugoslavia's Marxist regime, would seize power in Greece. The conditions in Turkey posed just as much of a dilemma as Stalin followed the tradition of the czars in striving to gain control of the strategically vital Black Sea Straits.

On February 26, 1947, the secretaries of state, war, and the navy advised President Truman to take "immediate steps" to extend all possible aid to Greece and, on a lesser scale, to Turkey. Truman concurred with this advice, but Senator Vandenberg advised that "if that's what you want [an aid program for the pro-Western governments in Athens and Ankara] there's only one way to get it. This is to make a personal appearance before Congress and scare hell out of the country."[18] During a surprise visit to the Capitol building on March 12, 1947, Truman did just that, telling the lawmakers:

> One of the primary objectives of the foreign policy of the United States is the creation of conditions in which we and other nations will be able to work out a way of life free from coercion . . . . We shall not realize our objectives, however, unless we are willing to help free

peoples to maintain their free institutions and their national integrity against aggressive movements that seek to impose upon them totalitarian regimes. This is no more than a frank recognition that totalitarian regimes imposed on free peoples, by direct or indirect aggression, undermine the foundations of international peace and hence the security of the United States.[19]

Within two months, Congress had appropriated $400 million for Greece and Turkey with overwhelming votes in the House of Representatives (287 to 107) and Senate (67 to 23). This sum pales in comparison with subsequent aid donations, but the political message embodied in the "Truman Doctrine" reverberated beyond Capitol Hill. For the first time, Washington had reversed the nonintervention principle of the original Monroe Doctrine, making a major international commitment outside the Americas during peacetime.[20] "The Truman Doctrine marked a watershed," notes Henry Kissinger, "because, once America had thrown down the moral gauntlet, the kind of *realpolitik* Stalin understood best would be forever at an end, and bargaining over reciprocal concessions would be out of the question."[21]

Containment

The Truman Doctrine launched in a spectacular fashion the policy of "containment." First articulated by diplomat George Kennan in an eight-thousand-word "Long Telegram" dispatched from the U.S. embassy in Moscow and reiterated in *Foreign Affairs* in mid-1947, this policy rested on several premises: (1) ideological incompatibility characterizes American capitalism and Soviet communism; (2) Russia's dictatorship arose because the "Communists represented only a tiny minority of the Russian people"; (3) Moscow's hostility to the outside world sprang from the "necessity" of justifying authoritarianism at home; (4) its sense of "infallibility" propels the Communist Party to impose an "iron discipline" on its society; (5) conviction of its monopoly over truth means that Moscow's leaders feel no "ideological compulsion" to achieve their goals in a hurry; (6) the "United States has it in its power to increase enormously the strains under which Soviet policy must operate, to force upon the Kremlin a far greater degree of moderation" that will accelerate the "break-up or the gradual mellowing of Soviet power"; and (7) it is likely that repeated failures at home and abroad, exacerbated by containment, would force Moscow's autocrats to curb their ambitions and restructure their system.

Rather than decry the Kremlin's hostility toward American society, the thoughtful observer will

> experience a certain gratitude to a Providence which, by providing the American people with this implacable challenge, has made their entire security as a nation dependent on their pulling themselves together and accepting the responsibilities of moral and political leadership that history plainly intended them to bear.[22]

Kennan felt strongly that the USSR had nothing to gain by starting a war. Rather, he believed that the main danger from Russia lay in political subversion. Thus, he emphasized the economic component of containment, lest extremists—preying on acute shortages of jobs, housing, and hope—gain sway in war-ravaged countries.

Not only did U.S. assistance to Greece and Turkey comfort beleaguered Aegean regimes, but this bilateral program also prepared the American people for the $13.3 billion multilateral Marshall Plan, named after Secretary of State George C. Marshall and shaped by the New Deal assumption that instability springs from the gap between "haves" and "have nots."

Launched in 1948 with its second biggest contribution directed to a vanquished Germany, the Marshall Plan prevented widespread starvation, which would have increased chances for communist subversion. In the final analysis, this collaborative plan sparked unity and recovery of Western Europe's war-torn economies, diminished the attraction of Soviet-style communism, helped forestall the emergence of a Fourth Reich, and attracted expatriated capital back to the Continent. In fact, West Germany, formally known as the Federal Republic of Germany, rapidly became the core of an ever-more united and democratic Western Europe. The prospect of a revitalized Europe—purchasing substantial amounts of "Made in USA" goods and services—added a healthy dose of pragmatism to the security concerns and altruism implied in this unprecedented venture. After World War I, the European Allies sought retribution over reconstruction; after World War II, Washington's leadership of the victorious Alliance ensured the primacy of reconstruction and reconciliation over a security commitment. Thus, the Truman administration promoted the Marshall Plan and even the idea of a united Europe before seeking to establish a collective-defense organization.[23]

Move Toward NATO

Animated by his own distrust of Moscow, Ernest Bevin proposed that the United Kingdom depart from its tradition of aloofness from Europe. Specifically, Bevin promoted the Anglo-French Dunkirk Treaty of 1947, which constituted an automatic alliance aimed at Germany. Although not requiring the deployment of British troops on the Continent, this agreement was the very type that London had refused to make before World War I. Bevin then also urged the formation of a mutual-defense accord through which England and France would ally with Belgium, the Netherlands, and Luxembourg— known as the Benelux countries.

This so-called "vital step" to enhance security in the North Atlantic community became a reality in March 1948 with the signing of the Brussels Pact. Bevin's proposal won approval of middle-level officials in Washington. Theodore C. Achilles, the State Department's director for Western European Affairs, remembers telling his boss at a New Year's Eve party:

> I don't care whether entangling alliances have been considered worse than original sin since George Washington's time. We've got to negotiate a military alliance with Western Europe in peacetime and we've got to do it quickly."[24]

A half-century after the fact, David C. Acheson, president of The Atlantic Council of the United States and son of the former secretary of state, affirmed that "Bevin deserves more credit for NATO than anyone else" because of his determined leadership in security matters.[25]

After initially balking at a formal American guarantee of the initiative, Truman asked the U.S. Congress to restore completely the Selective Service, declaring that the Brussels Pact deserved full backing of the United States "by appropriate means."[26] This document reflected the U.S. influence in widening Europe's security concerns, emphasizing the need for reconciliation with the former enemy in Central Europe (Germany) by pointing to the growing threat of a new adversary farther east (Russia).[27]

North Atlantic Treaty

In 1948, the takeover of Czechoslovakia by Moscow-aligned forces, the USSR's enveloping Finland in a distasteful alliance, and the Soviet blockade of Berlin increased support on both sides of the Atlantic for an anti-Soviet strategic pact to complement the Marshall Plan. The Senate paved the way for such trans-Atlantic collaboration by adopting Senate Resolution 239 on June 11. Prepared by Senator Vandenberg, then chairing the Foreign Relations Committee, the "Vandenberg Resolution" urged the United States to pursue several objectives in the context of the UN Charter, including "association of the U.S. by constitutional processes, with such regional and other collective arrangements as are based on continuous and effective self-help and mutual aid and as affect its national security." The nonbinding resolution expressed the sense of the Senate that the United States safeguard world peace "by making clear its determination to exercise the right of individual or collective self-defense under Article 51 [of the UN Charter] should an armed attack occur affecting its national security."[28]

Kennan, however, cautioned that a military alliance would impede European unification, aggravate Soviet suspicions, fuel a dangerous arms race, and extend the time required for his containment policy to succeed. This opposition aside, Truman emphasized the importance of the North Atlantic Treaty in his inaugural address on January 20, 1949. He highlighted NATO as an extension of a foreign policy that also embraced the UN, the Marshall Plan, and the "Point Four" program of aid to Latin America, Asia, and Africa. On April 4, 1949, the Truman administration joined eleven allies in concluding NATO's founding act in Washington, D.C. (By the mid-1980s, NATO would expand to sixteen members with the affiliation of Greece and Turkey in 1951, West Germany in 1955, and Spain in 1982.)

At the signing ceremony, Truman told the assembled dignitaries that the pact constituted "a shield against aggression" everywhere in the world. Had NATO existed in 1914 and in 1939, he said, the alliance would have prevented two world wars, adding that "[f]or us, war is not inevitable." The chief executive further asserted:

> We do not believe that there are blind tides of history which sweep men one way or the other. In our own time we have seen brave men overcome obstacles that seemed insurmountable and forces that seemed overwhelming. Men with courage and vision can still determine their own destiny. They can choose slavery or freedom—war or peace. . . .
> I have no doubt which they will choose. The treaty we are signing here today is evidence of the path they will follow.[29]

The president's speech highlighted festivities in the same blue-domed auditorium where eight-and-a-half years before, officials had drawn numbers from a goldfish bowl, opening America's first peacetime draft. Then, millions of young men kept their ears glued to radios and their eyes fixed on registration cards to learn the order in which they would leave their communities for boot camp. In 1949, listeners around the world tuned into the historic proceedings, hoping that NATO would protect future generations from the demands of war. In forty-three languages, short-wave radios beamed out the message that the West would maintain a solid front against all threats.[30]

Ironic and informal touches enlivened the one-hour-and-fifty-two-minute program. For example, at least two speakers quoted the famous "peace is indivisible" phrase of Maxim Litvinov, the onetime Soviet foreign minister who had fallen out of favor in Moscow. On a lighter note, as the audience gathered, the Marine Corps Band Orchestra surprised some guests by playing "It Ain't Necessarily So" and "I Got Plenty of Nothin." For Dean Acheson, who had succeeded Marshall as secretary of state, these tunes added an "unexpected realism" to the program. With First Lady Bess Truman seated in the front row, the musicians also rendered another Gershwin classic: "Bess, You Is My Woman Now."[31]

While the music and activities may have delighted Mrs. Truman, displeasure ran high on Capitol Hill, because the State Department's original guest list omitted a majority of senators. SFRC chairman Connally charged the department with "poor taste and bad finesse." Majority Leader Scott W. Lucas, an Illinois Democrat, expressed similar pique: "The State Department has been very lax," he said. "Certainly this has been something of a blunder. After all, they have got to depend on the United States Senate for ratification of the pact. They might better have looked out after the Senate than someone else." Red-faced State Department officials scurried to find seats for all lawmakers who wished to attend.[32]

The senators quickly forgot this faux pas as they settled down for hearings on the legislation. Acheson and other administration witnesses contended that the North Atlantic Treaty differed from previous military alliances. While necessitated by Soviet belligerence, Acheson observed, "the North Atlantic Treaty is far more than a defensive arrangement. It is an affirmation of the moral and spiritual values which we hold in common." These included "democracy, individual liberty and the rule of law."[33]

Washington Treaty

In framing the treaty, Acheson noted that the State Department relied on flexible guidelines, rather than specific strictures for achieving these lofty goals. Except for the North Atlantic Council and the defense committee specified in Article 9, the document remained silent on military strategy, defense structures, and bureaucratic entities. The pact's open-endedness reinforced Acheson's avowal that it would not prove "a static one," but a document capable of allowing changes dictated by future circumstances.

In their testimony, Acheson and other drafters paid attention to many senators' hopes that the UN would ensure world order through peaceful means. For example, the treaty's preamble reaffirmed the parties' "faith and the purposes and principles of the Charter of the United Nations and their desire to live in peace with all peoples and all Governments"; Article 1 disavowed the "use of force in any manner inconsistent with the purposes of the United Nations"; and Article 7 stressed that the treaty neither affected members' rights and duties under the UN Charter nor diminished "the prime responsibility of the Security Council for the maintenance of international peace and security."[34]

Championed by Canada, Article 2 set forth sociopolitical objectives. This provision committed NATO members to further international harmony "by strengthening their free institutions, by bringing about a better understanding of the principles upon which these institutions are founded, and by promoting conditions of stability and well-being." The objectives of this section would figure prominently in future debates on expansion. Article 4, which also attracted attention during the 1997-98 debate over altering NATO's membership and mission, specified that the "Parties will consult together whenever, in the opinion of any of them, the territorial integrity, political independence or security of any of the Parties is threatened."

Article 5 enshrined the heart of the treaty and even today is the foremost reason why new democracies in Central Europe, with their residual fear of Russia, seek to be NATO members rather than "partners" of the organization. This provision stipulated that signatories should regard armed aggression against any member as an attack against all members. This language made clear that NATO constituted a mutual-defense alliance to safeguard members from "outside" threats in contrast to the League of Nations and other collective-security organizations, which promoted peaceful relations among its members by maintaining a balance of power and interests. However, at Washington's insistence, Article 5 responses would not occur automatically, but were subject to each member's sovereign decision-making.

Article 6 defined areas in which an armed attack on one member constituted an attack on all signatories. Such areas were: the parties' territory in Europe or North America; Algeria, when it was a department of France; the occupational forces of any member in Europe, on the islands under the jurisdiction of any party in the North Atlantic area north of the Tropic of Cancer or any signatory's vessels and aircraft in this region. Although a matter of major concern to the United States at the time of its adoption, this article today impedes obtaining alliance consensus for out-of-area operations.

Article 10 empowered the twelve original signatories to extend membership by unanimous agreement to "any other European State in a position to further the principles of this Treaty and to contribute to the security of the North Atlantic area . . . ." United States senators made clear, however, that the executive branch should treat any enlargement of NATO as a treaty commitment, which the president would submit for the requisite Senate approval.

Before the ratification vote took place, robust majorities turned back several efforts to hobble the accord. Ohio's Robert A. Taft—widely known as "Mr. Republican"—believed that the United States could best protect its interests in Europe by extending the Monroe Doctrine. Thus, he wanted the Senate to disavow any commitment, "morally or legally," to provide NATO allies with military assistance, "including atomic bombs and information relating thereto." This reservation, defeated 74 to 21, targeted Article 3 of the covenant, by which "the Parties, separately and jointly, by means of continuous and effective self-help and mutual aid, will maintain and develop their individual and collective capacity to resist armed attack." Thrown back in their first thrust, treaty opponents next proposed language, offered by Senator Arthur V. Watkins (R-UT), to require Congress to approve any U.S. military action to rescue an invaded partner. After losing a second time (84 to 11), the isolationist forces took aim at the so-called "heart" of the pact—namely, Article 5, which avows that an attack on one ally constitutes aggression against all NATO members. This measure garnered only eight "ayes" while 87 senators voted "nay."[35]

Ironically, repairs to the Capitol forced the final roll call to take place in the Old Senate Chamber, a small semicircular room where Daniel

Webster, Henry Clay, and John C. Calhoun had held memorable debates in the nineteenth century and where, in 1821, lawmakers had approved the Monroe Doctrine with its pugnacious admonition against European meddling in the Western Hemisphere. Mindful of this historic milieu, legislators on both sides of the aisle declaimed the legislation's merits before casting the decisive vote. Connally summed up the views of many of his colleagues when he said:

> We cannot afford to deny to the Europeans our cooperation and assistance—and if need be, our arms—and if they are attacked we must go to their rescue and preserve their lives. This is a world-wide contest between tyranny and freedom—between slavery and democracy. Where shall we stand?[36]

In early July 1949, the Senate voted to ratify the treaty 82 to 13, action that accurately reflected public opinion. Earlier in the year, sixty-seven percent of respondents to a Gallup Poll concurred that the United States and Western European nations should "come to each other's defense immediately if any of them is attacked." Only sixteen percent of those interviewed opposed creating a mutual-defense pact, while seventeen percent of the sample expressed no opinion.[37] Most newspaper editorial writers applauded NATO; however, naysayers fulminated. The *New York Daily News* (March 18) warned that "Uncle Sap" was "scrapping Pres. George Washington's solemn warning for this country to keep out of foreign entanglements." Not to be outdone, the *New York Mirror* (March 19) opined that Congress's exclusive right to declare war would "cease to be."[38]

A few hours after signing the treaty legislation on July 25, 1949, Truman requested Congress to authorize $1.4 billion for military assistance to show America's commitment to its new obligations. At this point, the once cooperative Vandenberg accused the president of seeking dictatorial powers. In a letter to his wife, the Michigan senator lamented:

> It's almost unbelievable in its grant of unlimited power to the Chief Executive. It would permit the President to sell, lease or give away anything we've got at any time to any country. . . . It would virtually make him the number one war lord of the earth. . . . The old bipartisan business is certainly "out the window" on this one. . . . So it's a pretty tight "poker game" between Acheson and me.[39]

In reaction to this sentiment, Acheson brought Secretary of Defense Louis Johnson, Ambassador Averell Harriman, General Omar Bradley, and General Marshall to the Hill to testify on the need for the legislation. After these meetings and a period of harrumphing, Vandenberg placed his imprimatur on a "new bill [in which] the State Department . . . surrendered on eighty per cent of my criticisms"—even though it contained only ninety dollars less in authorizations that the original measure.[40]

NSC-68

Although strongly endorsed by a dozen Western nations, the alliance remained essentially a paper pact for its first two years. A working group struggled to define its organization and mission. Meanwhile, Moscow's explosion of an atomic bomb and Mao Zedong's victory in the Chinese civil war convinced Truman of the need to develop a global policy to arrest the spread of communism. In response, Paul H. Nitze and his colleagues on the State Department's Policy Planning Staff drafted National Security Council Memorandum 68 (NSC-68). This document reiterated Kennan's dark view of the Soviet Union as a totalitarian state incapable of enduring diversity, finding that the "existence and persistence of the idea of freedom is a permanent and continuous threat to the foundation of the slave society; and it therefore regards as intolerable the long continued existence of freedom in the world." NSC-68 endorsed a worldwide system of anticommunist alliances, construction of the hydrogen bomb, and a massive buildup of conventional forces.[41]

Even though Kennan suggested a geographically limited version of containment, the strategy evolved under NSC-68 to constitute a U.S. commitment to counter Soviet pressures for the indefinite future around a "vast periphery" that embraced recognizably differing conditions in Asia, the Mideast, and Europe. The Kremlin was, moreover

> free to select its point of attack, presumably only where it calculated it would have the greatest advantage. Throughout subsequent crises, the American political objective was deemed to be the preservation of the status quo, with the overall effort producing communism's final collapse only after a protracted series of ostensibly inconclusive conflicts.[42]

Although submitted in April 1950, the treaty's prescriptions were only adopted by Truman after North Korea invaded South Korea on June

23. The increased focus on defense led the president to raise the ceiling on military expenditures from $13.5 billion to $48.2 billion for fiscal year 1951 and prompted discussions of re-arming West Germany.

Disquieting events in the Soviet Union and on the Korean peninsula forced Washington to view NATO in a new light. Truman's bold response to North Korea's mid-1950 invasion reassured Europeans that the United States would stand firm against communist onslaughts. Still, they worried that the conflict in Asia might divert American attention from the Atlantic community: U.S. leaders believed that Moscow sought to test Washington's and the West's resolve by dispatching North Korean minions across the 38th Parallel. If this ploy proved successful, the Kremlin might try to repeat their victory in the divided Germanies in "a European analogue to the divided Koreas."[43] In Bonn, Chancellor Konrad Adenauer averred that "Stalin was planning the same procedure for Western Germany as had been used in Korea."[44] This image of Stalin as chief puppeteer, though overstated, convinced the Truman administration that it must endow NATO with military muscle to discourage the Red Army's lunging into Western Europe.

NATO's Evolution

To sell this policy at home and in Europe, Truman proposed that General Dwight D. Eisenhower reprise his World War II role as supreme allied commander in Europe. In addition, the president ordered the Pentagon to send four divisions to Europe, supplementing the forces already in place. This proposal sparked virulent criticism from former ambassador to the United Kingdom Joseph Kennedy, ex-President Herbert Hoover, and Senators Robert Taft (R-OH) and William Knowland (R-CA). These views differed sharply from those on Main Street, where seventy-two percent of Americans backed a European army under Eisenhower's command. The Senate's approval of the presidential request sounded in many ways "the last hurrah of isolationism."[45]

By early 1952, the allies had fleshed out NATO's organization. The North Atlantic Council, formed in 1949 and composed of the member countries' heads of state or their representatives, constituted the top policy-making body. All council decisions required unanimity. The defense ministers of participating states would constitute the Defense Planning Committee, which was to meet semiannually and receive reports from a Military Committee of top-ranking generals and admirals from all signatory nations. A secretary-general, selected on the basis of merit, would chair the North Atlantic Council, preside over its most important committees, and supervise a sprawling NATO bureaucracy. The first secretary-general—Britain's Sandhurst-educated Lord Ismay—left an indelible imprint on the organization's structure. Moreover, he coined one of the alliance's best-known aphorisms, suggesting that NATO should strive to "keep the Americans in, the Russians out, and the Germans down." He made this saying in the context of simultaneously complementing U.S. deployment of troops in Europe with re-arming the Germans. Bonn's forces would be subordinated, first, to the European Defense Community (EDC), and next, when the EDC failed in 1954, to NATO's own integrated command.

The Military Committee would possess the highest military authority in the alliance, as this body collected member states' chiefs of staff or permanent military representatives. The new organizational chart placed NATO's forces under three major commands: the Supreme Allied Commander, Europe (SACEUR), located at the Supreme Headquarters Allied Powers Europe (SHAPE); the Supreme Allied Commander, Atlantic (SACLANT), headquartered in Norfolk, Virginia; and the Allied Commander in Chief for the Channel (ACCHAN).[46] There would also be a Canada-U.S. Regional Planning Group. In 1967, SHAPE moved from Paris to Casteau, outside Brussels, Belgium.

Frictions that Beset the Alliance

Frictions have beset the alliance almost from the day of its foundation. Such challenges fall under four categories: *Who leads? Whose forces? Who cares?* and *Who pays?*

Who leads?

Early on, disagreements erupted over the allocation of key assignments. While agreeing that an American general should assume the SACEUR post, the United Kingdom sought the SACLANT slot for one of its admirals. Despite the fact that World War I marked the end of British primacy at sea, pride for its maritime tradition animated London's intense, but unsuccessful, lobbying for the top naval position. Subsequent disputes centered on the selection of general and flag officers for the four commands that fall under SHAPE: Allied Forces Northern Europe, Central Europe, Southern Europe, and the Mediterranean.

Beginning with President Charles DeGaulle in 1958, the French have complained vigorously of "Anglo-Saxon hegemony" over France and Europe. DeGaulle recommended ending this primacy by replacing NATO with a tripartite Atlantic Directorate, which would enable the United States, Great Britain, and France to collaborate as equal partners on all "political and strategic questions of world importance." In particular, DeGaulle doubted the credibility of America's guarantee to use nuclear weapons in case of an attack on Western Europe. When Washington and London rejected DeGaulle's overture, the French president withdrew the French Mediterranean fleet from NATO control, and moved to develop a French nuclear capability or *"Force de Frappe."* DeGaulle grew increasingly bitter toward the "special relationship" between the Americans and the British, by which he believed the United Kingdom acquiesced too readily to U.S. foreign policy interests. This resentment culminated in DeGaulle's early 1967 announcement that France would withdraw from the alliance's integrated military structure—while remaining in NATO's political bodies—and give the organization a year to move its headquarters from France.

Whose Forces?

Proposals to re-arm West Germany precipitated shrill opposition in France in the late 1940s, in light of the historic enmity between the neighbors. Nevertheless, the increased defense burden of the Korean War convinced Eisenhower, now U.S. president, of the wisdom of welcoming West Germany into NATO, albeit on a limited basis. Such participation would prove all the more necessary because the Federal Republic's eastern border formed the line of defense against a potential Soviet invasion of Western Europe. After four years of quadrangular haggling involving Paris, London, Washington, and Bonn—and failure to devise an integrated European defense structure, the EDC—the French government agreed to the Federal Republic's admission under a scheme that British Foreign Secretary Anthony Eden hatched while lounging in his bathtub.

In September 1954, the London Conference adopted Eden's compromise to address fears of a remilitarized Germany. Britain strengthened its commitment to the Continent by joining a fifty-year defense alliance, called the Western European Union (WEU) and agreeing to maintain four divisions on the Continent; the United States implicitly provided a guarantee against German revanchism by informally sponsoring Bonn's

NATO membership and pledging to keep troops in Europe for fifty years; and Chancellor Adenauer placed West German troops under NATO control, at the same time renouncing manufacture of atomic, biological, or chemical weapons. Nine days after West Germany's formal admission to the Atlantic alliance in May 1955, the Soviets reacted by forming the Warsaw Pact to counter NATO. The new pact's provisos mirrored NATO with respect to responses to external aggression, mutual aid, the establishment of a political council, and the twenty-year initial duration. In the words of security analyst Andrej Korbonski, "one might venture to guess that those responsible for the final version of the Warsaw Treaty had a copy of the NATO text at their elbows."[47]

Europeans continually worried about the strength of Washington's resolve to defend them should the Red Army surge across the Fulda Gap. Before the autumn of 1957, Russia lacked long-range ballistic missiles with which to attack the continental United States. Nonetheless, the Europeans expressed skepticism over Washington's reiterated pledge to engage in "massive [nuclear] retaliation" should the Soviets invade Western Europe. The USSR's October 1957 launch of the Sputnik satellite showed that the Kremlin had the missile technology needed to menace U.S. cities. In view of newly revealed Soviet might, would the United States risk the destruction of Boston, New York, and Washington to defend Paris, Rome, and Hamburg? Once the Europeans got used to the more comforting idea that the United States and Russia might wage war "over Europe's head," Washington shifted its doctrine from "massive retaliation" to a step-by-step "flexible" response to Russian aggression. This change, impelled by Secretary of Defense Robert McNamara, sharpened the Europeans' anxiety over the possibility of a ground war on their Continent.

Who Cares?

Neocolonialism and other "out-of-area" challenges have generated intense frictions between the Europeans and the Americans. The *Quai d'Orsay*, for instance, expressed outrage at Washington's failure to back Premier Pierre Mendes-France when French forces in Indochina suffered an ignominious defeat at Dien Bien Phu in 1954. Two years later, the British and French decried the Eisenhower administration's stern rebuke of their attempt, in league with Israeli commandos, to retake the Suez Canal, after its nationalization by Egyptian President Gamal Abdel Nasser.

Payback time came in the 1960s and early 1970s, when most European nations expressed misgivings about the United States' major commitment to a war in Vietnam. Then in 1973 several European governments refused landing rights to U.S. military aircraft bound for the Mideast during the Yom Kippur War between Israel and its Arab neighbors.

In more recent times, the very definition of security has pitted Washington against its European allies. President Ronald Reagan's reaction to the Urengoy Pipeline reveals such a conflict. Eager to diminish their reliance on Persian Gulf energy sources, seven European governments struck a deal in 1982 to finance a $1 billion natural gas pipeline from the Soviet Union to the West. Following the imposition of martial law in Poland the previous December, Washington forbade the use of U.S.-made equipment for the artery. Shortly thereafter, the United States extended this ban to American subsidiaries and licensees abroad, a provision that would have tied the hands of many European companies involved in the multi-billion-dollar arrangement. The contretemps was said to have "reflected badly on NATO" because the White House had not used the alliance as a forum for consultation. The parties ultimately resolved their differences through diplomatic channels. Nevertheless, the dispute exemplified the chasm between the views of the early Reagan administration and many West European governments on dealing with the Soviet Union.[48]

Intra-European conflicts also endanger western security. The European Union has balked at admitting Turkey to the organization, in large measure because of Greece's truculence toward the Ankara government. An even greater threat to the trans-Atlantic alliance would erupt should the member-states accede to Athens' demand and admit only the Greek portion of Cyprus to the EU rather than requiring the Cypriots to resolve their conflict as a condition of affiliation. Welcoming only a segment of Cyprus to the organization would embalm in amber the Greece-Turkey antipathy.

Who Pays?

Sharing defense burdens has proven the most nagging and persistent irritant among NATO allies. Many U.S. legislators have accused Europeans of failing to contribute enough to defense, leaving U.S. taxpayers to carry a disproportionately heavy load. In the 1950s, officials from Norway to Italy argued that rebuilding their war-torn economies would best enhance their stability and, thereby, ward off communist threats. As economic recovery accelerated, Senator Mike Mansfield (D-MT) raised the prospect of substantial cuts in American forces stationed on the Continent if Europeans failed to make "military contributions commensurate with their newfound economic strength."[49]　As early as the 1960s, many Europeans contended that Americans exaggerated the Soviet danger—an assertion made ever more stridently up to the fall of the Berlin Wall in 1989.

The Alliance's Post-Cold War Status?

Once the Berlin Wall tumbled and the Soviet Union imploded, NATO faced an uncertain future; after all, few alliances survive victory. For example, after uniting to defeat Napoleon, the Quadruple Alliance disintegrated in the 1820s and 1830s; and the Allies went their separate ways after winning World War I. Thus, in the early 1990s, NATO's sixteen member-states confronted at least six options, several of which— 5 and 6, for example—were not mutually exclusive: (1) dismantle the pact; (2) maintain the status quo; (3) "de-Americanize" the European security system; (4) convert NATO from a military alliance to one focused on social and economic issues; (5) expand the organization's mission to include security threats arising in the Balkans, North Africa, and other regions outside Western Europe; or (6) offer membership to former Soviet satellites, beginning with those in Central Europe.

Dismantle

Except for a handful of journalists and scholars, few observers recommended dismantling NATO, even after *glasnost* and *perestroika* had swept Russia, and the Warsaw Pact had disbanded. In fact, one senior official noted a sharp rise in the number of meetings held at NATO headquarters. "Every wife in the harem wants to have her night of pleasure, and the alliance faces a problem in being overwhelmed by pressing demands from so many countries," he said. "On the other hand," he added, "the absence of a common denominator makes it easier to define certain issues on a regional basis, such as the Balkans or the Caucasus, that will provide a clear division of labor."[50]

Rather than scrap NATO, the North Atlantic Council met in Rome in December 1991 to reevaluate the alliance. The council adopted a "New Strategic Concept," which (1) diminished reliance on nuclear weapons, including an eighty percent reduction in sub-strategic forces; (2) stressed the need for rapid reaction forces "to assist in crisis management or to respond to aggression"; (3) pruned its military structure, eliminating the Allied Commander in Chief Channel or CINCHAN; (4) reorganized its Major Subordinate Commands in Europe; and (5) recommended creation of the North Atlantic Cooperation Council or NACC. Twenty-five countries would make up the NACC,[51] including NATO signatories, nations affiliated with the defunct Warsaw Pact, and successor republics of the Soviet Union. A High Level Working Group attached to the NACC coordinated a 1990 East-West accord to reduce conventional forces in Europe (CFE), with verification accomplished from the Atlantic to the Urals through a 1992 Open Skies Agreement.

While ensuring NATO's continuation, the Rome summit did not resolve the thorny issues of new functions and additional members. In establishing the NACC and addressing Continent-wide issues, however, the meeting did raise hopes in Warsaw and other Central European capitals that their countries might eventually join NATO.

Status Quo

Senators Nunn and Warner—longtime colleagues on the Armed Services Committee until the former retired in 1996—have enunciated the view: "If it ain't broke, don't fix it." They insist that NATO's strength lies in pursuing a specific mission (preventing Soviet aggression) in a definite area (Western Europe) with a limited number of signatories (sixteen). Accepting new responsibilities, new theaters of operation, and new members, Nunn and Warner contend, would thrust unreasonable burdens on history's most successful military alliance, particularly at a time when NATO states have pared defense budgets, the Warsaw Pact has vanished, and Russia poses no threat to Europe. Until mid-1994, officials in the State Department's European Bureau also decried the "gratuitous" baiting of the Russian bear implicit in enlargement. At the same time, military and civilian personnel in the Defense Department have reiterated the Nunn-Warner admonition that any change in the alliance would likely require the Pentagon to do more with less, a concern shared by members of the NATO secretariat.

De-Americanize

Gaullist frustration at what was seen as American hegemony in Europe has survived the cold war, albeit in a more moderate form. Indeed, in the early 1990s, French leaders led calls for a European Security and Defense Identity (ESDI) through the European Union, while fortifying the European pillar of the Atlantic alliance through the Western European Union.[52]   French officials reasoned that an integrating Europe should control its strategic destiny, particularly since Washington's disengagement from the Continent seemed probable in light of the Soviet Union's collapse, America's obligations in other parts of the world, and a mounting cry in the United States for politicians to address domestic problems.   Paris dismissed as a "facade" of Europeanization the all-European Rapid Reaction Corps, spawned by NATO's 1990-91 military reorganization. Greater European cohesion vis-à-vis Washington manifested itself in an October 1991 initiative to create a Franco-German Eurocorps and the December 1991 signing of the Maastricht Treaty, foreshadowing the EU's adopting a single currency in 1999.

But real support for diminishing Washington's role in Europe's security system ended at the Paris city limits.   While most continental leaders sought greater equality with the United States on decisions concerning defense matters, none cried "Yankee Go Home!"—at least in public.   Which other country, for example, could serve to balance the power of a unified Germany?

By early 1993, French aloofness gave way to a degree of rapprochement with the alliance.   Robert P. Grant, an expert on French defense policy, provides four reasons to explain this turnabout.   First, even before winning the presidency in 1995, former Prime Minister Jacques Chirac realized that working through NATO, rather than crossing swords with the United States, marked the better course for ultimately reconfiguring relations within the Atlantic alliance.   In Chirac's view, endowing the WEU with a bigger role would proceed more smoothly with American help than without it.

Second, the EU nations' lack of resolve in managing the Balkan crisis alerted the French to the dangers of U.S. disengagement at a time of shrinking defense budgets.   Apparently, the Foreign Ministry came reluctantly to appreciate Belgian Foreign Minister Mark Eysken's remark during the Gulf Crisis that the European Union had proven itself an economic giant, but still a political dwarf, and a military worm.[53]

Third, the Clinton administration—eager to reduce Pentagon spending—applauded greater European defense cooperation, including the European Security and Defense Identity.

Finally, the election of a conservative-center majority in the National Assembly in early 1993 laid the groundwork for greater cooperation between France and NATO. In the words of then-Prime Minister Alain Juppé, "the time has passed for an attitude of haughty reserve towards [NATO]." In December 1995, the French defense minister announced that his country would again participate fully in NATO's Military Committee, but French policy remains in limbo.

Update Mission

Among others, Senator Lugar—who chaired the Senate Foreign Relations Committee in the mid-1980s—recalled Acheson's characterization of the alliance as a dynamic rather than a static or hidebound arrangement. In times of crisis, Lugar observed, the United States has looked to NATO members for support, even when the organization did not activate its military structure. It stood to reason, therefore, that adding reliable members to the organization would expand the number of potential allies upon which Washington could call when facing a nontraditional challenge. Defense expert Stanley R. Sloan accentuated the point:

> NATO remains an organization of sovereign nation states, and no member can be compelled to participate in a military operation that it does not support. Defense cooperation . . . cannot guarantee that the Allies will respond to any given political or military challenge. But NATO can be used to build political consensus and create military options to back up or implement political goals. U.S. and allied policymakers would have fewer credible coalition military options if their military leaders and forces were not working together on a day-to-day basis, developing interoperability of those forces, planning for contingency operations, and exercising their military capabilities. This day-to-day work develops habits of cooperation, at the political and military level, which underpin the ability to work together when required to do so under pressure or, more importantly, under fire.[54]

Out of Area

As will be discussed in Chapter 2, Asmus and his RAND colleagues insisted that the Cold War extinguished any strategic distinction between

Europe's center and periphery. As a result, new challenges now lie along two "arcs of crisis": In the view of Asmus and his fellow scholars, the eastern arc connotes a zone of instability running from Northern Europe through Germany and Russia into Turkey, the Caucasus and Central Asia. The southern arc courses through North Africa and the Mediterranean into the Mideast and Southwest Asia. Conflicts in both of these areas erupt continually from authoritarian ideologies hostile to those of Western Europe and the nascent democracies of the former Soviet bloc. Such conflicts promise only difficult and partial management, involve major powers' interests, and risk reactivating old fault lines and dormant historical rivalries, namely, "geopolitical competition between Germany and Russia along the eastern arc, or a conflict between the West and Islam in the south." If NATO fails to address the security challenges confronting Europe from the two arcs, Asmus and his colleagues find it will become increasingly irrelevant, concluding that "NATO must go out of area or it will go out of business."[55]

Enlargement to Central Europe

The Poles, followed by leaders of other Visegrad countries, first raised the prospect of their inclusion in NATO. Cameron Munter—who served as desk officer for Czechoslovakia in the early 1990s along with other State Department officials with responsibility for Central Europe—discussed the region's future among themselves and with Washington-area scholars, including Czech-born Madeleine Albright during her tenure at Georgetown University. Although then-Professor Albright cautioned against impulsive acts, she and most of the diplomats and scholars concluded that extending NATO eastward would stabilize a precarious zone around the old Soviet Union, where ethnic, religious, and boundary disputes flourish. Just as admitting the Bonn government to the alliance contributed to West Germany's development as a stable democracy, they argued, opening membership to Central European states would promote their progress along democratic, market-oriented lines, free from concerns about a Russian military renaissance. In addition, courageous anticommunists like Walesa and Havel had fixed as their highest priority reintegrating their countries into the trans-Atlantic community. Once securely in the Western camp, they contended, Poland, the Czech Republic, and other countries could act as important links to Russia.

Although the integration of Poland, Hungary, the Czech Republic, and other nations into the West could occur through the European Union, a number of factors make EU accession for Central European states a long-term process: West Europe's protectionism; current members' concern about refugee flows from the east; the reticence of the union to dispense the same huge volume of aid to newcomers that has flowed to Spain, Portugal, and Ireland; and the difficulty of integrating economies at such distinctly different stages of development.

Conclusion

NATO's advocates disagreed about the organization's future, but they took heart from the alliance's having promoted the security and prosperity of the trans-Atlantic community—arguably even better than did the two world wars that preceded the cold war. Indeed, NATO's achievements have far overshadowed its problems. First, the alliance powerfully deterred the USSR from invading Western Europe. Second, as Truman contemplated, the pact erected a shield behind which societies decimated by World War II could rebuild, prosper, and become integrated through creation of the EU and other European institutions of cooperation that were able to emerge under the U.S. umbrella. Third, NATO reinforced a nascent German democracy, and helped bring the country back into the Western fold, after its unification in 1990. Fourth, through Article 2, the alliance promoted civilian control of militaries within member states. Fifth, the organization has served to strengthen democratic institutions within participating countries like Spain, Portugal, Greece, and Turkey. Sixth, while Greece and Turkey continue to spar over Cyprus, and the United Kingdom and Spain to squabble over Gibraltar, NATO has encouraged allies to resolve problems peacefully as a condition of membership. Seventh, the organization has produced an influential Euro-Atlantic constituency, composed of military, diplomatic, and intelligence personnel who have worked in the alliance. In addition, scores of academics, professionals, lawmakers, and business leaders identify with this constituency, many of whom belong to the Atlantic Council of the United States and its counterparts abroad. Finally, NATO has kept the United States engaged in what diplomats and scholars refer to as "the trans-Atlantic bargain." Retired foreign service officer Peter Bird Swiers has defined the concept as follows:

In exchange for the United States' treaty commitment to defend, or—as since evidenced by one of the longest periods of peace in Europe's history—to deter aggression against its European NATO partners, Europeans acknowledged the right and role of the United States in the affairs of a Continent responsible for two castastrophic world wars in this century alone.[56]

In some important senses, the story of final passage of the 1998 legislation begins quite late in the annals of NATO expansion. Legislative and executive staffs do not cobble bills together, and congressional leaders do not shepherd them through their chambers, without strong motives, whether principled or expedient. As many ideas vied for the scarce attention and time of policymakers, which proponents of enlargement attracted attention? From where did these ideas originate, and whom did they first impress? Chapter 2 explains how the *Foreign Affairs* article written by Asmus, Kugler, and Larrabee promoted a spirited debate on both sides of the Atlantic that, pursuant to an NSC-crafted action plan fully backed by the State Department's top echelon, ultimately expanded NATO's mission and membership, beginning with the addition of three Central European states.

Notes

1. R. Ernest Dupuy and Trevor Dupuy, *Encyclopedia of Military History from 3500 B.C. to the Present* (New York: Harper & Row, 1986), p. 990.
2. Dupuy and Dupuy, *Encyclopedia*, p. 990.
3. Quoted in V.R. Berghahn, *Modern Germany: Society, Economy and Politics in the Twentieth Century* (Cambridge: Cambridge University Press, 1982), p. 59.
4. Quoted in "The Cold War," a Cable News Network (CNN) documentary broadcast in October 1998.
5. Quoted in Denna F. Fleming, *The United States and the League of Nations, 1918-1920* (New York: Putnam, 1932), p. 1.
6. Dupuy and Dupuy, *Encyclopedia*, p. 990.
7. Joseph Smith, ed., *The Origins of NATO* (Exeter: BPCC Wheatons Ltd., 1990), p. 68.
8. Quoted in the *New York Times*, March 27, 1946, p. 28.
9. Quoted in Clark M. Clifford, "A Landmark of the Truman Presidency," in André de Staercke et al., *NATO's Anxious Birth: The Prophetic Vision of the 1940s* (New York: St. Martin's Press, 1985), p. 2.
10. Bailey, *Diplomatic History*, pp. 771-72; U.S. Senate, *The Charter of the United Nations*, Hearing before the Senate Committee on Foreign Relations, 79 Cong. 1 sess. (1945), p. 405; and Ruth B. Russell, *A History of the United Nations Charter* (Washington, D.C.: Brookings Institution, 1958), p. 942.
11. Quoted in C.P. Trussell, "Senator for Speed," *New York Times*, July 29, 1945, p. 1.
12. The five "permanent" Security Council members were the United States, the Soviet Union, the United Kingdom, France, and the Republic of China (later replaced by the People's Republic of China).
13. Bailey, *Diplomatic History*, p. 772.
14. With the exception of Königsberg (Kaliningrad).
15. A Gallup Poll (March 10, 1945) found sixty-one percent favorable, nine percent unfavorable, and thirty percent undecided (*Public Opinion Quarterly*, IX, p. 95); cited in Bailey, *Diplomatic History*, p. 764.
16. Quoted in a floor speech by Sen. Daniel Patrick Moynihan in a debate on "Protocols to the North Atlantic Treaty of 1949 on Accession of Poland, Hungary, and the Czech Republic," April 27, 1998, *Congressional Record*, Internet edition.
17. Clifford, "Landmark," pp. 4-5.
18. Jules David, *America and the World of Our Time: United States Diplomacy in the Twentieth Century* (New York: Random House, 1964), p. 403.
19. Quoted in *New York Times*, March 13, 1947, p. 1.

20. Monroe had promised to stay out of Greece; Truman championed America's going into Greece (Bailey, *Diplomatic History*, p. 799).

21. Henry Kissinger, "Reflections on Containment," *Foreign Affairs* 73, no. 3 (May/June 1994): 118.

22. Kennan, "The Sources of Soviet Conduct"; and John Lewis Gaddis, *The United States and the End of the Cold War: Implications, Reconsiderations, Provocations* (New York: Oxford University Press, 1992), p. 27.

23. For this insight, I am obliged to Professor Simon Serfaty, director of European Studies, the Center for Strategic & International Studies, Washington, D.C., letter to author, October 5, 1998.

24. Oral History Interview, Theodore C. Achilles, Harry S. Truman Library, Independence, MO; cited in Lawrence S. Kaplan, *NATO and the United States: The Enduring Alliance* (Boston: Twayne Publishers, 1988), p. 19.

25. David C. Acheson, telephone interview by author, January 6, 1999.

26. Clifford, "Landmark," p. 7.

27. Serfaty, letter to author, October 5, 1998.

28. "Vandenberg Resolution," in *Encyclopedia of the Cold War*, pp. 564-65.

29. Quoted in the *New York Times*, April 5, 1949, p. 1.

30. "12 Nations Sign Atlantic Treaty; Stress Aim to Uphold the U.N.; Truman Sees Aggression 'Shield,'" *New York Times*, April 5, 1949, pp. 1, 3.

31. Dean Acheson, *Present at the Creation: My Years in the State Department* (New York: W.W. Norton & Co., 1969), p. 284; and W. H. Lawrence, "12 Nations Sign Atlantic Treaty," *New York Times*, April 5, 1949, p. 3.

32. "Congress Solemn on Signing; Invitation Mix-Up Irks Senate," *New York Times*, April 5, 1949, pp. 1, 2.

33. Acheson discusses his arguments for the Washington Treaty in *Present at the Creation*, pp. 276-313. On p. 281, the urbane policymaker confided that Senator Forrest C. Donnell (R-MO) was not "my favorite senator." The "irresponsible" Missouri lawmaker based his opposition to NATO on the gossip of an "irresponsible" reporter. In Acheson's view, Donnell "combined the courtliness of Mr. Pickwick and the suavity of an experienced waiter with the manner of a prosecuting attorney in the movies—the gimlet eye, the piercing question. In administering the *coup de grâce* he would do it with a napkin over his arm and his ears sticking out perpendicularly like an alert elephant's."

34. The text of the North Atlantic Treaty appears on the official NATO website, as well as in any major book on the organization, including Kaplan, *NATO and the United States*, pp. 219-21.

35. William S. White, "Pledge to Europe: Three Efforts to Soften Text by Restrictions Decisively Beaten," *New York Times*, July 22, 1949, p. 1.

36. Quoted in C.L. Sultzberger, "Senate, 82 to 13, Votes Atlantic Pact Binding 12 Nations to Resist Attack; Truman to Move Soon for Arms Aid," *New York Times*, July 22, 1949, p. 2.

37. The Gallup Poll, Interviewing date 1/22-1/27/1949, p. 792.
38. *Facts on File*, March 13-19, 1949, p. 91.
39. Arthur H. Vandenberg, ed., *The Private Papers of Senator Vandenberg* (Boston: Houghton Mifflin Company, 1951), pp. 503-4.
40. Acheson, *Present at the Creation*, p. 310.
41. For a concise description and analysis of the document, see "National Security Council Memorandum-68," in *The Cold War 1945-91*, vol. 3, ed. Benjamin Frankel (Detroit/Washington: Gale Research Inc., 1992), pp. 213-14.
42. Kissinger, "Reflections on Containment," p. 121.
43. Kaplan, *NATO and the United States*, p. 44.
44. Konrad Adenauer, *Memoirs, 1945-64* (Chicago: Henry Regnery Co., 1965), p. 273.
45. Kaplan, *NATO and the United States*, p. 48.
46. A 1994 reorganization eliminated ACCHAN, folding this command's duties into those of SACEUR.
47. Andrej Korbonski, "The Warsaw Pact," *International Conciliation,* no. 573 (May 1969): 13.
48. Clive Archer, *Organizing Europe: The Institutions of Integration*, 2d ed. (London: Edward Arnold, 1994), pp. 215-16.
49. Quoted in Archer, *Organizing Europe*, p. 214.
50. William Drozdiak, "NATO Ponders Future, Effectiveness," *Washington Post*, May 30, 1998, p. A-16.
51. This number had risen to forty by 1999.
52. This discussion of French policy relies heavily on Robert P. Grant, "France's New Relationship with NATO," in Philip. H. Gordon, ed., *NATO's Transformation: The Changing Shape of the Atlantic Alliance* (Lanham: Rowman & Littlefield Publishers, 1997), pp. 53-76.
53. Quoted in Asmus et al., "Building a New NATO," p. 31.
54. Stanley R. Sloan, with assistance of J. Michelle Forrest, *NATO's Evolving Role and Missions*, CRS Report for Congress, Congressional Research Service, The Library of Congress, 97-708F (Updated March 13, 1998), Washington, D.C.
55. Asmus et al., "Building a New NATO," p. 31.
56. Swiers, facsimile to author, January 15, 1999. In addition to a distinguished diplomatic career, Swiers served as vice president and director of the Harriman Chair for East-West Studies, The Atlantic Council of the United States.

Chapter 2

❧

The "RAND BOYS" Article and Capitol Hill Initiatives

Introduction

Three RAND Corporation senior analysts—Asmus, Kugler, and Larrabee[1]—impelled the idea of enlarging NATO's mission and membership in what turned out to be one of the most important essays on trans-Atlantic security since Kennan's "X" article seized policymakers' attention in 1947. This essay formed a key element in a mutually reinforcing dynamic which involved, in addition to American officials, German Defense Minister Rühe, Czech President Havel, Polish President Walesa, Polish American intellectuals, and a host of pro-expansionist organizations.[2] The RAND experts' thesis contributed to the work of three U.S. foreign-policy experts—christened the "NSC troika" by National Security Adviser Lake—who devised the action plan that spelled out the steps, procedures, and timing of NATO enlargement.

During the 1992 campaign, Asmus, who holds a doctorate in European Studies from the Johns Hopkins University's Nitze School of Advanced International Studies, occasionally participated in a small group that prepared issue briefs, policy analyses, and background papers for candidate Bill Clinton. Headed by Washington attorney John D. Holum, later to head the Arms Control and Disarmament Agency (ACDA) before becoming undersecretary of state for Arms Control and International Security Affairs, the group also included Kugler and Jenonne R. Walker, an international-affairs expert, former State Department official, and Democratic activist. Walker, who subsequently acted as the Clinton transition team's liaison to the State Department's European Bureau, became the NSC's senior director for European Affairs.

In an argument that previewed the differences within the Clinton administration, Asmus and Kugler pressed strongly for an assertive policy toward Europe that centered on NATO reform, including the addition of Central European states to the organization. Walker, on the other hand, opposed expansion and insisted that U.S. policy should focus on strengthening the Organization for Security and Cooperation in Europe (OSCE), while avoiding antagonizing Russia.[3] Such intramural skirmishes took place completely out of the limelight; they involved relatively few security strategists whose views gained scant recognition in a campaign dominated by domestic "It's the economy stupid!" issues. As Asmus summed it up later: "I don't think anyone ever read our work."[4] The impassioned in-house debate prefigured future clashes over policy.

Asmus saw no one on the new administration's defense and foreign-policy team, especially officials with responsibility for Europe, likely to champion changes in the size and mission of the Atlantic alliance.[5] Thus, he set to work to shape U.S. security policy from outside the beltway in a manner that would garner bipartisan support. As described in the Introduction, he led an effort, joined by Kugler and Larrabee, to prepare a manuscript on NATO for submission to *Foreign Affairs*. The three scholars hoped to generate a broad discussion of the alliance's future and spur the Clinton administration to vigorously promote NATO reform.

While many Republicans would subsequently claim NATO enlargement as a "GOP idea," Asmus, Kugler, and Larrabee considered themselves centrist Democrats who had supported Governor Clinton in his 1992 quest for the presidency. Asmus in particular had studied the career of the then-Arkansas governor and identified with his domestic goals. He also sensed that Clinton harbored a positive predisposition toward Europe. Not only had Clinton studied and traveled in Europe as a Rhodes Scholar at Oxford University, but he clearly drew upon the European experience of activist government to craft his "New Democrat" agenda and give momentum to what has become known as the "third way."[6]   This approach emphasizes a less-taxing, leaner government's cooperation with the private sector to improve efficiency in the global marketplace, while upgrading the quality of education, health-care, and other social programs.   Moreover, Asmus hoped that Clinton, as the first post-cold war president, might show a willingness to rethink the American-European partnership. According to the RAND Boys, NATO's growth would, in the tradition of Harry Truman and former Senator Henry "Scoop" Jackson (D-WA), weave a synthesis of liberalism and conservatism in his foreign policy.[7]

RAND Boys

The authors brought three different types of expertise to their task. Asmus, a fluent German speaker, has studied both European and Soviet/ East European affairs, eventually concentrating on Germany, Central Europe, and broader East-West issues.   He had followed closely the debate on German reunification, the topic of his doctoral thesis. Asmus observed the foreign-policy establishment's consensus that "unification shouldn't happen; therefore, it couldn't happen," a view that flew in the face of his own analytical instincts. In retrospect, he regretted being "a bit too timid," adding that "I figured that all of those smart and distinguished people in the community whom I admired so much couldn't be wrong. But they were! Afterwards I vowed to stick to the courage of my convictions even if it brought me into conflict with mainstream thinking."[8]

Larrabee, a Columbia University Ph.D. who speaks French, German, Greek, and Russian, concentrated on Russia, Ukraine, and Eastern Europe. Like Asmus, he had worked at Radio Free Europe and Radio Liberty for several years, an experience that exposed both men to the German point of view—specifically, "that Central Europe forms part of Europe; that instability in that region imperils the entire Continent; [and] that Germany and the United States must take the lead in spurring European integration."[9] Asmus and Larrabee enjoyed extensive high-level contacts in Western and Central Europe, including good relations with many anticommunist dissidents. The scholars had followed closely the early thinking about NATO enlargement among the area's intellectuals, many of whom had moved from dissenters to ministers in Warsaw, Prague, and Budapest. The men had also spent long evenings in coffeehouses and beer halls talking about NATO's prospects with these senior officials who were themselves struggling to define their own priorities vis-à-vis the West. For Larrabee, NATO's opening its doors to the Central Europeans would ensure that America would play a pivotal role in promoting European security.[10]

Kugler, who earned a doctorate at the Massachusetts Institute of Technology and whose "foreign language is systems analysis and formal mathematical modeling,"[11] had long studied geopolitics, defense analysis, military strategy, and NATO. He brought to the mix something that Asmus and Larrabee lacked: a detailed understanding of the Atlantic alliance's history and military structure. His firm grasp of the organization's inner workings and the evolution of its strategic doctrine proved crucial to the team. In addition, unlike his RAND colleagues, Kugler had served in the armed forces as an Air Force officer in Vietnam. Later, he worked in the Office of the Secretary of Defense and at the National Defense University before joining RAND in 1989.

The gang of three had collaborated at RAND on many key projects, which precipitated debate among themselves about Europe's future. They had reached consensus on several major points, the first of which maintained that the collapse of communism and the Soviet Union constituted the "twin revolutions" overturning the systems created at Versailles and Yalta. Second, post-cold war Europe needed a new security architecture, lest the Continent slip back to a period reminiscent of the inter-war era highlighted by America's withdrawal and a new round of geopolitical jockeying. Third, the primary challenge lay in filling the security vacuum in East and Central Europe. Fourth, enlarging NATO represented the best means to address this security challenge. Fifth, the United States had to remain engaged in Europe to preserve stability. Finally, enlargement involved moral as well as strategic imperatives: the West waged the cold war in part, at least, to advance moral values; and the preservation of those values required devising a satisfactory relationship among Germany, Poland, and Russia.[12]

Pursuit of a Foreign Affairs Article

In December 1992, Asmus sought to introduce these ideas into the first draft of the article at the RAND Corporation's beach-side headquarters in Santa Monica, California, where he and Larrabee worked in nearby offices. Asmus focused his energy on defining and stressing the risks emanating from the "twin arcs of crisis" so important to trans-Atlantic security. Among other things, Larrabee contributed the sections on the need for NATO security partnerships with Russia and Ukraine. He also infused the text with a clarion call to action. Kugler, at RAND's Washington office, had written a paper entitled "Necessity to Act," which, in his words, addressed post-cold war military issues from a "dry and analytical" perspective. He zeroed in on the need for the alliance to engage in out-of-area missions. The initial draft ran forty-three typed pages, too long for a publication such as *Foreign Affairs*. As a result, the authors began the excruciating task of paring their prose. Kugler's five-plus pages of estimates of the fighting units needed for out-of-area operations required major condensation, as did Asmus's allusions to the nationalistic philosophies of German J. G. Herder and Italian idealist Giuseppe Mazzini. The authors submitted their manuscript to *Foreign Affairs* in March 1993; the journal's managing editor Fareed Zakaria notified them of its acceptance within two months, and asked that they provide a final version in June. Upon receipt of this text, the editors boiled the material down to twelve-and-a-half printed pages, again excising mostly nuts-and-bolts material on defense matters.

Editor James F. Hoge's and Zakaria's enthusiasm for the article sprang from their belief that, in Zakaria's words, "what happens to NATO—with lots of members and a sizable budget—constituted one of the most important foreign policy issues in the post-cold war period."[13] Yet he bemoaned the surprising lack of debate about the alliance's future among international-relations experts, much less among average citizens. Consequently, Hoge and Zakaria elected to publish the RAND scholars' pro-enlargement article along with a blistering critique of expansion written by Owen Harries, editor of the *National Interest*.[14]

This to-ing and fro-ing obviated any chance of the journal's publishing the article in its summer issue. In the meantime, word spread of the RAND troika's thesis, precipitating scores of phone calls to their offices. The most bizarre request for a copy of the manuscript came from the foreign affairs adviser to seventy-four-year-old Giulio Andreotti, forced out of Italy's premiership because of alleged Mafia-related corruption.[15]

Sensing the importance of the NATO-expansion issue, Zakaria alerted Katherine J. "Katie" Roberts, opinion-page editor of the *New York Times*, to his journal's upcoming pieces. She agreed that the subject was relevant, and ran back-to-back condensed versions of the two articles on the *Times'* influential op-ed page.[16]

Meanwhile, the savvy Hoge informed members of the Council on Foreign Relations, publisher of *Foreign Affairs*, of the catalytic impact the September/October number could have on the debate on U.S.-European defense questions. Hence, the council sponsored a luncheon to release the issue and provide a venue for the RAND Boys and Harries to cross intellectual swords. Although creating only "rumbles" at first, the Asmus-Kugler-Larrabee article caught fire after about six months, and enjoyed a "long shelf life." In terms of reprint requests, Zakaria ranked it "probably among the top ten articles in recent years."[17]

The authors began their article with an apocalyptic warning designed to grab the lapels of Washington policymakers:

> Three years after the fall of the Berlin Wall, Europe is headed toward crisis. Memories of democracy's triumph have faded. The immense problems facing the new democracies in the East are increasingly compounded by political gridlock, economic recession and resurgent nationalism.[18]

In the second paragraph, they issued a challenge to President Clinton and other Western leaders. "Nationalism and ethnic conflict have already led to two world wars in Europe," they wrote. "Whether Europe unravels for a third time this century depends on if the West summons the political will and strategic vision to address the causes of potential instability and conflict before it is too late."[19]

The scholars concurred on three central propositions: First, they asserted that Europe's post-cold war strategic challenges lay almost exclusively along two "arcs of crisis" (see Chapter 1 and below). Second, they argued that nationalism and ethnic conflicts posed the greatest danger to Central Europe's fledgling democracies. Finally, they believed that NATO, led by a fully engaged United States, provided the most appropriate mechanism for addressing security threats in these regions. The inability of EU members to halt the "ethnic cleansing" in Bosnia reinforced their conclusion that Washington should continue to play an active role in Europe, managing conflict and serving as a counterweight to Germany and Russia.

The RAND troika insisted that the end of the cold war had permanently erased any strategic line between Europe's center and periphery. As a result, new challenges now lay along two arcs: one traversing North Europe through Germany and Russia into Turkey, the Caucasus and Central Asia; the other cutting through Northern Africa and the

Mediterranean, into the Mideast and Southwest Asia. The Soviet Union's collapse left in its wake several states characterized by politically dominant militaries, uneven weapons stockpiles, and virulent nationalism. "East-Central Europe is littered with potential mini-Weimar Republics, each capable of inflicting immense violence on the others," the authors wrote, adding that these countries lacked the ability to fend off powerful aggressors, harbored fears of a resurgent Russia, and desperately sought means to protect themselves. In the RAND analysts' view, trends would aggravate geopolitical competition, arms proliferation, and strategic uncertainty, giving rise to the possibility that individual states might unilaterally seek to gain real or perceived security. They noted that as in the preludes to the world wars, "[i]deological mobilization alongside a security vacuum is once again proving to be Europe's classic recipe for instability and conflict."[20]

From some perspectives, turmoil along either arc might appear remote to safeguarding the Franco-German region, Europe's traditional core. Nevertheless, conflicts in both of these areas had sprung periodically from aggression by dictators contemptuous of democratic values. More likely than not, these confrontations would permit only partial and difficult management; they could involve major powers' interests, and risk reactivating old political fault lines and dormant historical rivalries. Asmus, Kugler, and Larrabee specifically cited "geopolitical competition between Germany and Russia along the eastern arc, or a conflict between the West and Islam in the south." If the Atlantic alliance failed to address the security challenges confronting Europe along these two axes, the RAND team concluded, the organization would become increasingly irrelevant. In short, "NATO must go out of area [i.e., defend Western Europe] or it will go out of business."[21]

As a framework to allow NATO to adapt to these new realities, the authors called for a seven-step program to develop a new "U.S.-European strategic bargain," namely:

1. Conversion of NATO from a collective-defense organization against a specific threat to "an alliance committed to projecting democracy, stability and crisis management in a broader strategic sense."

2. United States' acceptance of a stronger European identity in security matters conditioned on Europe's willingness to bear its share of defense costs and commitments.

3. Germany's readiness to assume new security roles not envisioned in its postwar constitution, including combat assignments outside its borders.

4. Integration of the Visegrad countries into the EU and NATO— a move that would "strengthen the Atlanticist orientation of the alliance and provide greater internal [NATO] support for U.S. views on key security issues."

5. Development of a "security partnership" with democratic forces in Moscow, emphasizing the connection between stability in East-Central Europe and Russian national interests.

6. Incorporation of Ukraine into pan-European and regional groupings as a guarantee against its being drawn into any new Russian empire that might emerge.

7. Creation of new NATO structures—a Committee for Preventative Diplomacy and Crisis Management and a Force Projection Command—to improve the alliance's ability to manage crises and conduct operations beyond its traditional geographic bounds.[22]

Throughout the text, the authors keyed on "Central" or "East-Central" rather than "Eastern" Europe. They realized that detractors of expansion stressed Eastern Europe's marginality to U.S. interests compared with the risk of alienating Russia. No such assertion could be made about Central Europe, which embraces Germany, figured prominently in two world wars, formed the cold war's main battleground, and clearly holds great salience for America's well-being.

In a subsequent interview, Kugler expressed his personal concern— one rejected by his co-authors—that failure to reconfigure NATO to fill the power vacuum around the old Soviet Union raised the specter of an "imperial German army rushing across a nuclear-armed Poland to defend itself against a revanchist Russia."[23] In essence, *Mittellage*—being trapped in the middle—posed Germany's traditional strategic predicament. Failure to resolve this challenge had cost Europe, including Germany, dearly. A unified Germany again confronted this dilemma, with its biggest national security issue revolving around how to stabilize its Eastern border. Its membership in the EU and NATO might hold the answer, but the inability to address Bonn's top security concerns through an institutional approach could lead Germany to undertake unilateral action to fill the security void east of the Oder River. For Germany, NATO enlargement obviated any need to resurrect old geopolitical rivalries and strategies. The key to building a political coalition for expansion lay along the American-German-Polish axis.

"RAND BOYS" Article Compared to "X" Article

As early as mid-1993, a German-defense expert compared the Asmus-Kugler-Larrabee essay to Kennan's famous "X" article on containment. Yet journalist Fred Kempe, who publicized the analogy, averred that the "odds are long that NATO will follow the authors' blunt call for the alliance to redefine the threat, to expand membership eastward and accept as its natural calling the pursuit of security challenges occurring on its periphery."[24]

As described later, NATO members have adopted most of the several proposals advanced by the RAND troika. But acceptance of the precepts in "Building a New NATO" should not blind us to the article's differences with Kennan's masterpiece.

First, while Asmus and his colleagues—like Kennan—concentrated on Europe, the RAND boys sought to revitalize NATO as a means to a larger end: stabilizing all of Europe, anchoring Germany, and equipping the West to handle emerging threats. In other words, theirs was "a strategy for reshaping European security on a pan-European basis."[25] In contrast, the author of the "Long Telegram" set forth a blueprint for preserving, on a world-wide basis, the peace achieved in World War II.

Second, the gang of three focused on Europe and, to a lesser extent, North Africa and Central Asia. The more ambitious gambit of the late 1940s had global ramifications, especially when Truman, Marshall, Acheson, Nitze and others added a powerful military component to what Kennan contemplated as essentially an economic, political, and philosophical strategy. Although their emphasis on power projection and out-of-area challenges implied a broadening of NATO's scope, the RAND troika's article envisioned keeping the alliance Euro-centered. To counter the USSR's post-World War II expansionism, however, the United States had dispatched troops to Grenada as well as to Germany, to Korea as well as to the United Kingdom, to Saigon as well as to Spain—all in the name of containment.

Third, compared with Kennan's fixation on Russia, Asmus et al. lavished attention on several dozen countries that could engender strife in Europe either because of deeply rooted ethnic and religious animosities on their soil or because their striving for security might lead them into a crazy-quilt of military alliances and other ad hoc pacts. While each such accord might involve only a handful of nations, such agreements could prove so threatening to neighboring states as to actuate the signing of new *ententes* or the launching of preemptive strikes, particularly if nuclear arms complicated the picture.[26]

Finally, the RAND team had no interest in spawning a neo-containment strategy. To the contrary, they focused on the security vacuum that imperiled peace in Central Europe. They contended that NATO expansion would promote democracy, economic growth, and a sense of security, a sine qua non for reconciliation between the countries of that region and Russia. "We believed . . . that enlargement was not inherently anti-Russian and that, indeed, the last thing Russia should want was insecure and unstable countries on its Western border."[27]

Administration Reaction

Many administration officials took a jaundiced view of the RAND boys' thesis, considered radical in mainstream Atlantic community circles. For example, three-star General Barry McCaffrey, hero of Desert Storm-Desert Shield, reflected the views of many senior officers when he told Asmus in the fall of 1993: "My daughter will be chairman of the Joint Chiefs of Staff before these countries get into NATO—and that won't happen anytime soon."[28] Jenonne Walker, the National Security Council's senior director for European Affairs who believed that enlargement would weaken NATO, told Asmus and Larrabee that "[e]veryone in Washington thinks you're mad, except two people [the president and his national security adviser]." Larrabee started to differ with her when Asmus said, "Steve, let's go." Upon reflection, they both agreed that having Clinton and Lake in their corner augured well for achieving their goal.[29] Other high-level officials and statesmen told the scholars they were "crazy" and their reputations would be "damaged" by advocating enlargement.[30] In contrast, in his memoirs, ex-Secretary of State Warren Christopher identified "'Building a New NATO' as a useful article that influenced my thinking [about NATO's future]."[31]

From his own conversations, Asmus believed that the article also shaped the views of Daniel Fried; Lynn E. Davis, undersecretary of state for International Security;[32] James Steinberg, who read a draft of the *Foreign Affairs* essay at RAND before becoming head of the State Department's Policy Planning Staff, a position he left to assume the post of deputy national security adviser; Alexander "Sandy" Vershbow, a State Department professional who succeeded Walker at the NSC in mid-1994 and whom Clinton later named ambassador to NATO; and Strobe Talbott and Richard C. Holbrooke, to whom we will return.

With respect to the article, Fried said that he had come to support NATO enlargement by the spring of 1993, when he was completing three years as political counselor in Warsaw. "But I was still sorting out the strategic pieces when I read his piece. I was struck with the parallel between Ron's thinking and the thinking of the most serious Polish foreign policy specialists," he stated. The RAND scholars and Fried's Polish contacts were trying to overcome the traditional view of NATO as an anti-Soviet alliance by emphasizing the organization's potential for integrating Europe. The *Foreign Affairs* manifesto countered the conventional wisdom that U.S. policy toward the alliance amounted to a zero-sum game—with Russia's winning at the expense of the Central European states or vice versa. "The RAND analysts demonstrated that Washington didn't have to choose between the two parties, but could reincorporate Central Europe into the West, while ensuring the Russians a place in a new security architecture," Fried added.[33] As pro- and anti-enlargement forces within the administration prepared for a bruising internal battle over NATO's future, a key senator warmly embraced the RAND troika and their thesis.

Lugar Circulates the Article

Before submitting their provocative manuscript for publication, the analysts circulated it among security experts in the Washington area. Asmus said that his quest for a "sanity check" prompted him to forward the essay to Ken Myers, a longtime friend and top aide to Senator Richard G. Lugar.[34] The article so impressed Myers that he passed it along to Lugar, a Rhodes Scholar and former Naval Intelligence Officer, who soon emerged as Capitol Hill's prime mover on expansion. Since his election in 1976, Lugar had honed his knowledge of international affairs as a member of the Senate Foreign Relations Committee, which he chaired in 1985-86. He had worked for ratification of the Intermediate-Range Nuclear Forces in Europe Treaty (INF) in 1988, the Strategic Arms Reduction Treaty (START I) in 1992, START II in 1996, and the Chemical Weapons Convention (CWC) in 1997.[35] In 1991, Lugar joined with fellow moderate and good friend Sam Nunn to enact the Cooperative

Threat Reduction Program (CTR), commonly known as the Nunn-Lugar bill. CTR earmarked hundreds of millions of dollars to convert nuclear arms plants to nonmilitary production and to destroy nuclear, chemical, and biological weapons and infrastructure in Russia, Ukraine, Belarus, and Kazakhstan. This initiative sought to reduce the risk that nuclear weapons technology or fissile materials might fall into the hands of rogue states or terrorists.

When Thomas Huxley first read Charles Darwin's *On the Origin of Species*, he reportedly said, "It's so simple, why didn't I think of that?" The *Foreign Affairs* article did not represent such an epiphany to Lugar, who had been pondering security issues for a generation, but he was nevertheless deeply impressed. As a result, his staff—regarded as one of the leanest and best on Capitol Hill—invited Asmus, Kugler, and Larrabee to come over to discuss their ideas. Although the analysts expected to talk briefly with Lugar and his aides, they were surprised that the lawmaker so enthusiastically treated their views and asked if he might draw on them for a speech. They were also delighted that he spent an hour of give-and-take of substantive ideas with them. Having marked and underlined the draft, the senator not only concurred with the scholars' thesis, but also observed that in times of crisis the United States turns for support to NATO allies, even if U.S. policies do not elicit consensus among all members of the Pact. In addition, Lugar expressed the hope that granting the alliance more relevant missions would shore up its domestic support. Furthermore, Lugar and his guests agreed that the Visegrad states exhibited staunch Atlanticist tendencies—that is, their leaders' views on defense matters often coincided with those expressed by the United States, the United Kingdom, Portugal, and the Netherlands. In the senator's view, then, admitting new states to the alliance would increase the number of potential partners from which Washington could seek assistance at critical moments.[36] In mid-1993, the senator delivered a major speech on European security in which, with the authors' hearty approval, he employed "out of area or out of business," "two arcs of crisis," "a new strategic bargain requires that the West develop a constructive policy toward Ukraine," and other phrases from the *Foreign Affairs* article.[37]

Just as Kennan's "X" article shaped opinions of policymakers on both sides of the Atlantic in 1947, nearly a half-century later, the Asmus-Kugler-Larrabee analysis helped unleash a chain reaction.[38] The reception accorded their research surpassed the authors' most optimistic outlook. Kugler said that he and his colleagues "had no realistic expectation that the article would trigger a strategic revolution in U.S. policy . . . [toward] Europe. Being sobered by lots of previous experience at this enterprise, we expected to have a marginal impact. The clamor [following the article] caught us by surprise."[39]

Lugar found their thesis so compelling that he took it upon himself to carry the message to the ever-widening circles of decisionmakers who frequently solicited his advice. "We always called him the E.F. Hutton of the Senate," a former press secretary said, noting that "[h]e isn't a headline grabber. But when he says something, people listen."[40] Lugar began his proselytizing with legislative colleagues who exert the greatest influence over foreign affairs. Although the Indianan has never disclosed names of the fellow lawmakers with whom he discussed NATO expansion, likely candidates included Senators Biden, Warner, Dole, Nunn, John Kerry (D-MA), Carl Levin (D-MI), Joseph I. Lieberman (D-CT), John McCain (R-AZ), and Stevens.[41] He moved next to talks with Christopher, Perry, Berger, and other administration notables. Subsequently, he and Senator Nunn cohosted informal dinners at Capitol Hill's popular Monocle Restaurant to discuss NATO's future.[42]

Sponsored by the Carnegie Corporation and held under the auspices of the RAND Corporation, these gatherings brought together not only the RAND trio, but also pro-expansionists (Holbrooke, Steiner), anti-expansionists (Senator Warner, Lieutenant General Wesley K. Clark, Professor Mandelbaum, former ambassador to the Soviet Union Jack Matlock, former Assistant Secretary of Defense Joseph S. Nye, Jr.), and key members of the Bush administration like former National Security Adviser Brent Scowcroft, former Undersecretary of State Robert B. Zoellick, and Ambassador Robert Blackwill. In addition, Lugar discussed the Asmus-Kugler-Larrabee article and NATO's future with European foreign and defense ministers, starting with Germany's Rühe. The talks yielded the desired results: both men endorsed an outward-looking NATO in speeches to the Overseas Press Club early in the summer of 1993.

The German Connection

The views of the RAND troika dovetailed with those of Admiral Ulrich Weisser, head of policy planning at the German Defense Ministry, who had written Chancellor Helmut Schmidt's 1979 "Alistair Buchan Memorial Lecture" on Intermediate-Range Nuclear Forces in Europe, a speech delivered to the illustrious International Institute of Strategic Studies

(IISS) in London. Ironically, the gang of three's article reached Weisser just as he was laboring over the Alistair Buchan address that Defense Minister Rühe had agreed to present at the IISS in March 1993. Weisser, who had known Asmus for ten years, shared ideas about NATO enlargement with his longtime friend as the former was drafting Rühe's presentation on the same subject. Rühe had already fully embraced expansion; thus, the Asmus-Weisser exchange provided additional rationale for adding new countries, as well as arguments with which to disarm critics. Rühe's lecture emphasized that the alliance should not become a "closed shop" and questioned whether EU affiliation should necessarily precede NATO membership. He told the IISS audience that "[w]ithout our neighbors in central and eastern Europe, the strategic unity of Europe would remain a torso and an illusion."[43] By this time Rühe, who epitomized the self-confident, pro-Atlanticist German politician, established himself as West Europe's foremost champion of expansion. In the words of Asmus, "[a]bsent Rühe and Lugar, we might've remained just a bunch of think-tankers with some interesting ideas."[44]

The RAND experts' work so pleased Rühe that he asked them to flesh out their thinking in a project for his ministry. Before agreeing, Asmus phoned RAND's chief executive officer James A. Thompson in Santa Monica, who checked with the Pentagon and other corporate clients before giving Asmus and the Germans the go-ahead. This contract represented the first time that RAND had actually carried out national security research for a non-American client.[45] Although the Department of Defense registered no objection to RAND's European debut, some officers looked askance at the German Defense Ministry's funding the think tank's pro-enlargement research. The troika's findings flew in the face of the Pentagon's support for looser East-West cooperation through what would become the "Partnership for Peace" (PFP) rather than the admission of Central European states to the alliance. At least one assistant secretary of defense informed the RAND boys that it would not be helpful to the department if they publicized their views before the January 1994 NATO summit in Brussels. By deciding to hire RAND, Rühe provided resources and cover for the gang of three. He permitted them to make the analytic case that enlargement served the best interests of the United States and Europe at a time of serious divisions over the issue among policymakers in Washington and, to a lesser extent, in Bonn. The dissemination of their views—particularly in *Survival*[46] and in a second *Foreign Affairs* contribution[47] —helped advance the intellectual arguments with respect to the costs and sequencing of expansion while Lugar, Rühe, and their allies waged the political battle.

Although Lugar could trade ideas with Rühe, the Clinton administration had to treat the German defense minister with kid gloves. He was much more bullish on NATO expansion than Foreign Minister Klaus Kinkel, whom Rühe—a political rival—accused of dissuading Chancellor Helmut Kohl from endorsing the addition of Central European nations to the pact.[48]

Asmus, Kugler, and Larrabee also kept U.S. ambassador to Germany Holbrooke abreast of their ideas, to which the envoy proved extremely receptive. Asmus first met Holbrooke, the son of European refugees, in Washington at an informational seminar organized for him as ambassador-designate in 1993. The RAND scholar spoke on Germany's prospects and his reasons for believing that NATO growth would benefit the Bonn government. At this point, James Dobbins, principal deputy assistant secretary of state in the European Bureau, launched a frontal assault on Asmus and enlargement. After the criticism, Holbrooke turned to Asmus and asked: "Ron, why don't you defend yourself and your colleagues?" Following a lively exchange with Dobbins and the audience, Holbrooke said to Dobbins, "Jim, I think Ron has the better arguments."[49]

Holbrooke, who had served as assistant secretary of state for Far Eastern Affairs, arrived in Bonn without the anti-expansion mind-set that pervaded the State Department's European Bureau. After thinking about NATO's future and discussing the alternatives with Rühe, the two men came to complete each other's sentences. Holbrooke's brief tenure in Germany made him a true believer in enlargement. As Admiral Weisser once joked: "It was the combination of RAND and Rühe that turned Dick into one of the strongest supporters of enlargement and a key figure in bringing it about." The failure of EU members to manage the Bosnian crisis also contributed to Holbrooke's belief that an active American presence was crucial to European stability. "With a bond dealer's instinct for spotting a trend, and leveraging it, Holbrooke came to share the German's view that Washington and Bonn must co-manage the volatile area between Germany and Russia."[50]

Yeltsin's About-Face on Poland's Entering NATO

Meanwhile, Lugar traveled to Warsaw in August 1993, where he broached the subject of NATO's growth with President Walesa, who was about to meet alone with his Russian counterpart, Boris Yeltsin, another visitor to Poland's ancient capital. Encouraged by Lugar—who counseled the Polish president regarding tactics—Walesa raised the possibility of Poland's joining NATO with his Russian guest during a long dinner accompanied by a "river of vodka."[51] Before returning to Moscow, Yeltsin and Walesa issued a joint statement reiterating Poland's wish to enter the Atlantic alliance and noting Yeltsin's "understanding" of that desire. In other goodwill gestures, the Russian leader laid a wreath at a monument commemorating the murder in 1940 of some four thousand Polish military officers at the hands of Stalin's secret police. In addition, he advanced by three months, to October 1, 1993, the withdrawal of the remaining one thousand Russian troops stationed in Poland.[52]

Yeltsin's apparent acquiescence in their nation's joining NATO sent the Poles scurrying to contact U.S. officials in Warsaw and Washington: they believed an important breakthrough had just taken place. Fried received the news at the NSC and immediately contacted the State Department's NATO office to gauge its reaction. He found to his "horror" that neither the department nor the U.S. government was prepared intellectually or with policy options for an expanded alliance. In fact, the State Department's "press guidance" consisted of a reminder that "NATO enlargement is not on the agenda." "I was appalled and depressed," Fried said later. "No NSC demand or push from me could change this [situation] fast. There would be a long, hard road ahead," he concluded.[53]

Under fierce pressure from apparatchiks at home, Yeltsin soon did a volte-face on Poland's entry into NATO. On September 15, Russia's ambassador in Warsaw claimed that the media had oversimplified and misunderstood Yeltsin's statements and that Poland's membership in the alliance should be viewed as an event that could occur only in the distant future as part of the larger process of European integration. Using even stronger language, Russian Foreign Minister Andrei Kozyrev contended that it "would be unfortunate if the former Warsaw Pact states joined NATO in the near future, because this step would relegate Russia to a much more isolated position." In late September, Yeltsin reportedly wrote the leaders of the United States, France, Germany, and the United Kingdom, invoking the Two Plus Four agreement on German unification, signed on September 12, 1990, as evidence that the West had pledged to consider Russia's interests in European military alliance arrangements.[54]

Additional Senators Join In

Lugar worked quietly behind the scenes in Washington, while delivering more than thirty speeches on NATO expansion throughout the United States and Europe. When the drive toward enlargement appeared to stall in December 1993, Lugar kept up the momentum with another ringing speech on the subject in which he underlined America's importance to European security. He said, in part

> Either the U.S. takes the lead in constructing a new NATO to deal with the new dangers and instabilities emerging in Europe, east and west, and thereby anchors itself in Europe, or NATO's relevance crisis could prove terminal with respect to robust American participation and presence, as both the executive and legislative branches of government adjust U.S. national interests downward to fit the numbers of a "bottom-up" defense review.[55]

Meanwhile, other senators sympathetic to NATO growth joined the dialogue, as Lugar's public involvement receded.[56] As early as 1993, Biden and Senator William V. Roth, Jr. (R-DE) had sponsored a study of the implications of expanding the alliance. Senator Barbara A. Mikulski (D-MD) energetically backed enlargement. Also prominent was Senator Hank Brown (R-CO), who developed his sensitivity to the plight of Central Europeans while a student at the University of Colorado. There he heard poignant lectures about the savage abridgement of freedom in the region from Polish-born professor Edward J. Rozek, who suffered severe injuries and earned four Purple Hearts as a World War II tank commander.[57] Brown strongly supported the "NATO Participation Act of 1994," designed to specify eligibility criteria for states to enter the alliance. The bill encouraged NATO admission for PFP participants that had made substantial progress toward establishing democratic political systems, free-market economies, civilian control of their armed forces, human-rights guarantees for their citizens, and peaceful relations with neighboring nations. To assist the expansion process, the proposal authorized military and economic aid for countries evincing strong potential for membership. The legislation required the president to report to Congress on the issue, particularly with respect to the qualifications of four such states: Poland, Hungary, the Czech Republic, and Slovakia.

Opposition from the administration forced Brown to convince the Senate to pass the Expansion Act three times before David Obey (D-WI), who chaired the House Appropriations Committee, would accept the provisions in the final version of the legislation. The Senate-House conference committee twice deleted the NATO language because critics convinced Obey, himself no advocate of enlargement, that the Poles were selling arms to terrorists and thus did not merit entry into the alliance.[58] As discussed later, GOP Minority Leader Newt Gingrich included an endorsement of NATO's growth in the ten-point "Contract With America" issued in 1994.

In 1995, Brown would sponsor amendments to the 1994 legislation in order to add the Baltic nations and Ukraine to the possible membership list. The Colorado lawmaker paid no heed to White House reservations: the president's national security team opposed both measures, citing their arbitrariness, provocation of Russia, and usurpation of executive prerogatives in foreign affairs. Brown's zeal for NATO enlargement even led him to append his proposals to vital appropriations bills to force colleagues to vote for them. The fearless senator adopted this tactic knowing he would complicate his relations with powerful Appropriations Committee chairman Ted Stevens, a titan whose legislation typically sails through the chamber unscathed.

When asked later about this perceived incautiousness, Brown said, "I wasn't excited about playing a traditional role in the Senate; I wanted to change foreign policy, which was viewed as largely the preserve of the executive branch." Brown developed good ties with most of the Senate leadership, especially Lott whom he had nominated for minority leader when the two men served in the House. Brown also backed the conservative Mississippian for the same post in the Senate.[59]

Although applauding Brown's intelligence, thoughtfulness, and zeal, some fellow senators regarded him as the proverbial bull in the china shop because of his unremitting efforts to name specific countries for NATO membership. His colleagues warned that, while heartening to the designated states, identifying Poland, Hungary, and the Czech Republic for affiliation could discourage Slovakia, Slovenia, Romania, and other initially excluded aspirants from promoting the difficult reforms required to join the alliance. More to the point, only the sixteen signatories to the Washington Treaty—not the United States Senate—could admit new members to NATO.

Nevertheless, in 1996 Brown successfully attached the "NATO Enlargement Facilitation Act" (NEFA) to the House Foreign Operations Appropriations bill. Although slightly different from the 1995 measure by the removal of Slovakia, the initiative praised Poland, Hungary, the

Czech Republic, and Slovenia for their commitment to political and economic pluralism. Brown's language also authorized $60 million worth of grants and loans to assist these countries in integrating their militaries with NATO structures and doctrines.

In an effort to highlight his differences with the president over foreign affairs, Dole had introduced the original version of the NATO facilitation act in the Senate on June 4. He unveiled the legislation while flanked by Walesa and a group of his GOP legislative colleagues.[60]

Operatives in the National Security Council tried to persuade senators on the other side of the aisle from Brown and Dole to submit their own version of the NEFA, but pro-expansion Democrats had cooperated so closely with their GOP counterparts that none wanted to inject partisan politics into an issue that had taken on the hallmark of a moral crusade. Besides, the administration could only answer "no" when asked if it had genuine alternatives to propose.[61]

The House of Representatives approved its own facilitation act sponsored by International Relations Committee Chairman Benjamin Gilman (R-NY), 353 to 65, on July 23. Two days later, Dole's Senate bill, supported by Senators Biden, Roth, Stevens, Lugar, Lieberman, and other heavyweights, won approval 81 to 16.

Yet Senator Nunn's action on that day gave rise to one of the "what ifs" of the NATO expansion drama. Unhappy with the prospect of enlarging the alliance, the highly respected Georgian had initially objected to the facilitation act and even threatened to speak for several hours against the measure. This prospect engendered a flurry of activity. Brown, Dole, and Lieberman immediately instructed their aides to work with Richard DeBobes, Nunn's staff designee, to modify the language of the 1996 initiative. The Georgian feared that the original wording came too close to a declaration that the four favored countries should be admitted to the alliance. Proponents revised the measure to state that the enlargement process "should not be limited to consideration of" admitting the four states. Brown also accepted Senator Simon's proposal that some members did not accept nuclear arms on their territory—an effort to calm Moscow's fears that NATO-controlled nuclear weapons might be placed on Polish or Hungarian soil.[62]

Although never committing himself to support even an attenuated NEFA, Nunn arrived early during the roll call and cast an "aye" vote. At that point, he sat stonefaced in his seat while his colleagues made their preferences known. Senator Kay Bailey Hutchison engaged Nunn

Table 1: Legislation Related to NATO

Legislation	Purpose	Action by Senate	Date	Action by House	Date
Protocols of Accession to NATO	Approve entry of Poland, Hungary, and the Czech Republic into NATO	Approved 80 to 19	April 30, 1998	None required	
Roth-Lieberman concurrent resolution (S. CON RES.5)	Reiterate congressional support for NATO expansion		February 1997		February 1997
NATO Enlargement Facilitation Act (S1830; HR 3540)	Authorizes $60 million for transitional assistance for Central European countries to join NATO; and names Poland, Hungary, Slovekia, and the Czec Republic as participants eligible for Alliance membership	Adopted 81 to 16	July 25, 1996	Approved 353 to 65	July 23, 1996
NATO Participation Act Amendments	Speeds up incorporation into NATO of emerging democracies in Central and Eastern Europe; strengthens certain provisions of the NATO Participation Act of 1994 by establishing joint planning, training and military exercises with NATO forces, encouraging greater interoperability of military equipment, air defense systems and command, communications and control systems; and permitting greater conformity of military doctrine.		Approved 241 to 81		
NATO Participation Act of 1994 (Brown amendments to HR 4426)	Makes Poland, Hungary, and the Czech Republic eligible for certain NATO benefits, including the transfer of military materiél	Adopted 76 to 22	July 14, 1994		November 1994
State Department Authorization/NATO Expansion (S1281)	Expresses sense of the Senate that the U.S. should urge immediate admission to NATO for European nations that support collective-defense requirements, free and fair elections, civilian control of the military, territorial integrity, individual liberties and other established democratic practices.	Adopted 94 to 3	January 17, 1944	None required	

in animated conversation at his desk, expressing her doubts about the legislation. Just before the clerk closed the roll, Nunn switched his vote to "nay." Had he originally voted in the negative, a score or more of senators might have followed his lead. Nunn himself immodestly estimates that an original "no" vote could have swayed four or five colleagues, while his attacking the bill could have changed the position of ten or twelve senators. Even if Nunn's position had influenced fewer legislators, Senate-watchers would have interpreted his stance as evidence of continued Pentagon reservations over alliance enlargement. After all, Nunn held the reputation as the Senate's premier defense expert, enjoyed an excellent rapport with top Department of Defense officials, and had chaired the Senate Armed Services Committee for six years until the Republicans regained the majority in 1995. While thirty or thirty-five "nays" would not have defeated the NEFA, a robust number of votes against the measure could have prompted more senators to ponder the consequences of adding additional countries to the pact. Some colleagues who accepted Nunn's recommendations believed that he had reneged on an implied agreement to back the amended version; others expressed consternation that he had changed his vote.[63]

In any case, passage of the bill constituted the last NATO-related action before the national political conventions, and substantial Senate opposition to adding more countries to the alliance could have tempered the pro-enlargement planks of the party platforms.

What accounted for Nunn's reversal? At the outset, he had prepared to fight the measure tooth and nail if the administration backed him. In the absence of White House support, he believed the initiative would sail through. Still, he continued to feel uneasy with the measure, even though his amendments had "taken away its punch." In the course of the vote, eight to ten Democratic colleagues—in addition to Hutchison—approached him with their own qualms about the bill. Their concerns made Nunn, one of the most skilled nose-counters on Capitol Hill, realize that he had underestimated the opposition's strength. Nevertheless, proponents had accepted his changes, and Nunn—a member of the Senate Club that considers a colleague's word his bond—sought out Brown before changing his stance. "Hank, am I committed to vote yes?" he asked the Coloradan. When Brown reassured him that he had never agreed to support the measure, Nunn reversed his vote.[64]

As Nunn suspected, the administration had shifted from opposition to quiet support for the act. Unable to produce its own version, the

White House finally acquiesced with congressional leaders on the Brown and Gilman initiatives, which flew through Congress just as the president prepared to launch his reelection bid. Although disputed by Democrats, Senator Brown remained convinced that electoral politics motivated the stance of Clinton, who seldom drew a line between governing and campaigning.[65]

A further sign of consensus on NATO's future appeared in both major-party platforms. The Democrats applauded "the Clinton-Gore Administration's efforts to foster a peaceful, democratic and undivided Europe—including expanded support for reform in former communist states; dramatically increased assistance to Ukraine; the Partnership for Peace . . . with Europe's new democracies; [and] its steady, determined work to add new Central European members to NATO in the near future."[66]

> In their platform, the GOP faithful affirmed the same spirit . . . [in which] Ronald Reagan called for the integration of Spain into the NATO alliance, we call for the immediate expansion of the framework for peace to include those countries of Central Europe which demonstrate the strongest commitment to the democratic ideals NATO was created to protect.

Pointedly, the Republican platform also "strongly endorse[d] Bob Dole's call for Poland, the Czech Republic, and Hungary to enter NATO by 1998."[67]

Conclusion

In summary, while media accounts have underscored executive branch initiatives to expand NATO, an abundance of evidence suggests that ideas hatched in a private think tank and embraced by a powerful U.S. senator provided the main impetus for acceptance of NATO expansion, even as key bureaucratic players clashed over the administration's position. The RAND troika's blueprint on alliance enlargement had an interactive effect with ideas emanating from Western and Central Europe. In their first *Foreign Affairs* article and in subsequent publications, they anticipated—and, in most cases, addressed—such nettlesome questions as: Why expand? How can NATO accomplish enlargement? What will the addition of Central European countries cost? Moreover, through scores, possibly hundreds, of talks, Asmus, Kugler, and Larrabee erected the framework of the European security debate, while helping to build a consensus for a new trans-Atlantic arrangement designed to prevent the kinds of outcomes that followed the end of two world wars. The men found intellectual soulmates in Lugar, Rühe, Lake, Albright, Holbrooke, Havel and Walesa, as well as Fried, Lynn Davis, and Steve Flanagan. As one journalist lyrically explained the convergence of ideas,

> . . . the most important geopolitical shift of the late 20th century was not a foregone conclusion. NATO could have disintegrated, the US could have abandoned European defense, Europe could have dissolved into quarreling fiefdoms, and Russia could have been pushed to the brink. Instead, history turned favourably on a chance meeting of minds and a couple of unlikely personal relationships. Personal chemistry made international policy.[68]

"Personal chemistry" aside, Asmus, Kugler, and Larrabee had provided the intellectual blueprint that three diplomats—NSC counterparts to the RAND troika—turned into a policy instrument for NATO expansion. An intra-administration donnybrook preceded the Clinton White House's adoption of this action program, which entailed an unambiguous commitment to alliance membership for the Visegrad states. Chapter 3 examines the factors that compelled Foggy Bottom's redoubtable Fudge Factory and other citadels of resistance to execute a 180-degree turn on NATO.

Notes

1. Their places and dates of birth are: Asmus (Milwaukee, June 29, 1957); Kugler (Minneapolis, May 24, 1945); and Larrabee (Boston, November 24, 1944).
2. For this insight, I am indebted to Clay Clemens, associate professor of Government at the College of William & Mary, and editor of *NATO and the Quest for Post-Cold War Security* (New York: St. Martin's Press, 1997).
3. The OSCE, successor to the Conference on Security and Cooperation in Europe (CSCE), emerged to advance the tenets enunciated in the Helsinki Final Act, signed by the leaders of the United States, Europe, and Canada in August 1975. The Helsinki principles include the signatories' respect for sovereign equality, territorial integrity, free elections, inviolable frontiers, peaceful settlement of disputes, cooperation among states, equal rights and self-determination of peoples, human rights, and international law.
4. Ronald D. Asmus, deputy assistant secretary of state for European and Canadian Affairs, interview by author, Washington, D.C., October 1, 1998.
5. Asmus and his colleagues adamantly refused to mention members of the new foreign-affairs team unsympathetic to adding additional countries to NATO. Nonetheless, careful observers of this issue have cited the opposition and misgivings of: Ambassador-at-Large and Special Adviser to the Secretary of State on New Independent States Strobe Talbott; Assistant Secretary of State for European and Canadian Affairs Steve Oxman; Oxman's deputy John Kornblum; and the NSC's top Europe hand, Jenonne Walker; see James M. Goldgeier, "NATO Expansion: The Anatomy of a Decision," *Washington Quarterly* 21, no. 4 (winter 1998): 85-102; and Nowak, interview by author, October 16, 1998, and Charles Gati, former adviser to the Policy Planning Staff, interview by author, Washington, D.C., November 6, 1998.
6. For a sketch of the "third way" as related to Clinton, British Prime Minister Tony Blair, German Chancellor Gerhard Schroder, and French Premier Lionel Jospin, see Ian Hargreaves, "The Commanding Heights: A European View," *IntellectualCapital.com*, July 16, 1998, Internet.
7. Asmus, interview, October 1, 1998; and Asmus, electronic mail to author, October 23, 1998.
8. Asmus, electronic mail to author, October 23, 1998.
9. F. Stephen Larrabee, senior analyst, RAND Corporation, interview by author, Washington, D.C., September 25, 1998.
10. Larrabee, interview, September 25, 1998.
11. Richard L. Kugler, telephone interview by author, October 10, 1998.
12. Asmus, electronic mail to author, October 23, 1998.

13. Fareed Zakaria, telephone interview by author, November 2, 1998; facsimile to author, November 18, 1998.

14. Zakaria, telephone interview, November 2, 1998; Harries' article was titled "The Collapse of the West," *Foreign Affairs* 72, no. 4 (September/ October 1993): 41-53.

15. Asmus, interview, October 1, 1998.

16. The journal's editors welcomed the *New York Times* publishing the essay, "Strategic Alliance," August 27, 1993, p. A-29; Harries' op-ed, "'The West' is only a Flag of Convenience," appeared on August 28, 1993, p. 19. Two weeks earlier, Asmus acquaintance Frederick Kempe wrote, "NATO: Out of Area or Out of Business," *Wall Street Journal Europe*, August 11, 1993, p. A-8.

17. Zakaria, telephone interview, November 2, 1998.

18. Asmus et al., "Building a New NATO," p. 28.

19. Asmus et al., "Building a New NATO," p. 28.

20. Asmus et al., "Building a New NATO," p. 29.

21. Asmus et al., "Building a New NATO," p. 32.

22. Asmus et al., "Building a New NATO," pp. 32-39.

23. Richard L. Kugler, National Defense University, Washington, D.C., interview by author, August 18, 1998.

24. Kempe, "NATO: Out of Area or Out of Business," p. 6.

25. Alexander Vershbow, U.S. ambassador to NATO, electronic mail to author, December 10, 1998.

26. Although never a policy of Poland's government, some Polish officers brainstormed about the possibility of acquiring nuclear weapons if the West prevented their country's admission to NATO.

27. Asmus, electronic mail, October 23, 1998.

28. Asmus, interview, October 1, 1998.

29. In our August 24, 1998 interview, Lake claims never to have come across the "Building a New NATO" article; I have used the version of the quotation found in Bruce Clark, "How the East Was Won," *Financial Times*, July 5 and 6, 1997, Internet edition.

30. Asmus, electronic mail to author, October 23, 1998.

31. Christopher, *In the Stream of History*, p. 129, fn 2.

32. When a vice president at RAND and director of the think tank's Arroyo Center, Davis claims to have been "instrumental" in getting the RAND troika's analysis underway. She agrees the *Foreign Affairs* article "played a role in the debate within the government in 1993 that led to the Administration's decision to go forward with NATO expansion." She does not, however, accord the essay the "central role" suggested in this chapter (Lynn E. Davis, electronic mail to author, November 30, 1998).

33. Fried, electronic mail to author, December 15, 1998, p. 2; interview, December 28, 1998.

34. Asmus, interview, October 1, 1998.

35. The Strategic Arms Reduction Treaty (START I), which limited the United States and Russia to a total of 1,600 long-range land- and sea-based heavy bombers and ballistic missiles, won approval of the U.S. Senate and the Russian Duma. The treaty between the United States of America and the Russian Federation on Further Reduction and Limitation of Strategic Offensive Arms (START II) not only stipulated that both sides' nuclear stockpiles must fall to 3,000 to 3,500 warheads over a decade, but also eliminated multiple warheads on all ballistic missiles. The U.S. Senate ratified START II 87 to 4 on January 26, 1996, but the Duma has yet to act on this initiative. The Chemical Weapons Convention (CWC), which bans the use, storage, and transfer of chemical weapons, got caught up in the 1996 campaign when Senator Dole withdrew his support for the measure. However, on April 24, 1997, the Senate ratified CWC by a vote of 74 to 26.

36. Larrabee makes this point in *East European Security after the Cold War*, p. 176.

37. Excerpts from Lugar's July 14, 1993 speech appear in "Viewpoint," *Aviation Week & Space Technology*, August 30, 1993, p. 66.

38. The editors of *Foreign Affairs* believed the article so important that they leaked its contents to the *New York Times* before the issue hit the newsstand. The *Wall Street Journal* (European edition) and the *Washington Post* also reported the basic analysis.

39. Richard Kugler, facsimile to author on "NATO Expansion," September 11, 1998.

40. Quoted in George Lardner, Jr., "Lugar Can Cross Allies, Charm Foes and Outdo Roger Staubach," *Washington Post*, April 27, 1982, p. A-2.

41. Of course, Nunn did not seek reelection in 1996. Observers point to several GOP 'rising stars' in foreign affairs, among them Gordon H. Smith (R-OR) and Chuck Hagel (R-NE).

42. Opened in 1961 by the father of current owner John Valanos, the Monocle gained attention when Vice President Lyndon B. Johnson brought a party of friends to the restaurant without having first made a reservation. The maitre d' asked if any of the diners would relinquish his table to the veep. When no one volunteered, Johnson stormed out in a snit.

43. Rühe, "Shaping Euro-Atlantic Policies: A Grand Strategy for a New Era," *Survival* 35, no. 2 (summer 1993): 135.

44. Asmus, electronic mail to author, October 23, 1998.

45. Quoted in Clark, "How the East Was Won,"; Rühe presented his London talk in March 1993 (Larrabee, interview, Washington, D.C., September 25, 1998).

46. Asmus, Kugler, and Larrabee, "NATO Expansion: The Next Steps," *Survival* 37, no. 1 (spring 1995): 7-33; and "What Will NATO Enlargement Cost?" *Survival* 38, no. 3 (autumn 1996): 5-26.

47. Asmus and Larrabee, "NATO and the Have-Nots: Reassurance after Enlargement," *Foreign Affairs* 75, no. 6 (November/December 1996): 13-20.
48. Clemens, memorandum to author, November 5, 1998.
49. Asmus, electronic mail, October 23, 1998.
50. Clark, "How the East Was Won."
51. Nowak, interview, October 16, 1998. Although not at the dinner, Nowak has talked to Walesa about the evening.
52. *Facts on File*, August 25, 1993, p. 636.
53. Fried, electronic mail to author, December 15, 1998.
54. Cited in Suzanne Crow, "Russian Stand on Poland's NATO Membership Biased," *RFE/RL Research Report*, 2, no. 41 (October 15, 1993): 21-22. See also F. Stephen Larrabee, "East Central Europe: Problems, Prospects and Policy Dilemmas," in *NATO and the Quest for Post-Cold War Security*, p. 98.
55. Richard G. Lugar, "NATO's 'Near Abroad': New Membership, New Missions," Speech to The Atlantic Council of the United States, December 9, 1993.
56. Lugar increasingly found himself at odds with Senator Helms, who had exercised his prerogative, based on seniority, to supplant the Indiana senator as "ranking member" on the Senate Foreign Relations Committee; when the GOP gained the majority in 1996, Helms assumed the committee's chair. In addition, Lugar's backing Thad Cochran (R-MS) for senate majority leader did little to endear him to the victorious Trent Lott. Finally, Lugar's brief pursuit of his party's presidential nomination in 1996 excited tensions between him and Senator Dole, the eventual Republican nominee.
57. Rozek, the author of *Allied War Diplomacy* (New York: Wiley & Sons, 1958), remembers Brown as an apt student in courses on East European Governments and Soviet Foreign Policy. Rozek, the only member of his department to vote GOP, also befriended Brown because "he was the one lonely Republican in my classes" (Edward J. Rozek, telephone interview by author, November 28, 1998).
58. Former Senator Hank Brown, telephone interview by author, September 21, 1998.
59. Brown, telephone interview, September 21, 1998.
60. *1996 CQ Almanac*, August 15, 1996, pp. 1815-16.
61. This information came from an extremely well-placed congressional staff member who requested anonymity.
62. "Other Defense Issues Considered in 1996," *1996 CQ Almanac*, pp. 8-16.
63. Had Nunn actively fought the legislation, proponents would have relied upon war heroes Dole and McCain to oppose the Georgian whose reputation as an authority on the armed forces raises hackles among some Washington security experts. They contend that Nunn's Coast Guard service did not

provide an adequate background for understanding the U.S. military and decry his having voted against Bush's dispatch of troops to the Persian Gulf in early 1991.

64. Former Senator Sam Nunn, telephone interview by author, December 14, 1998.

65. Brown, telephone interview, September 21, 1998.

66. Democratic Party Headquarters, "1996 Democratic National Platform," as adopted by the Democratic National Convention on August 27, 1996, p. 23, Internet.

67. "The Atlantic Alliance & Europe," *Congressional Quarterly*, August 17, 1996, p. 2332.

68. Clark, "How the East Was Won," p. 1.

Chapter 3

ℰℭ

Clinton's Decision to Support NATO Expansion

Introduction

Chapter 2 examined the role of influential scholars, senators, and German officials in advancing the argument for NATO's growth. This chapter shifts the analysis to the executive branch where a handful of foreign-policy advisers—aided by Central European leaders—worked with a new president to impel enlargement. Their task proved a cakewalk compared with maneuvering the bulk of the international affairs bureaucracy from opposition to support of alliance expansion.

Clinton's Challenges

Upon taking office, President Clinton, a neophyte in world affairs, encountered a global environment different from those faced by his predecessors. To begin with, the end of the cold war eliminated a rationale for activism abroad used by chief executives since President Truman sped aid to Greece and Turkey in 1947. No longer could the United States justify the commitment of money or manpower to an international hot spot on the grounds that failure to act would advance communism. For example, in the aftermath of a car bombing in Lebanon that killed 241 U.S. Marines, President Reagan dispatched 1,900 Marines, paratroopers, and rangers to the southeastern Caribbean island of Grenada in October 1983. To skeptics, the invasion seemed designed primarily to divert public attention from the Mideast tragedy.[1] Still, an overwhelming majority of Americans rallied behind the president, who claimed that leftist leaders on this small island had signed secret accords with the Soviet Union, Cuba, and North Korea. Reagan hailed the American dead-and-wounded as "heroes of freedom," adding that "[t]hey not only rescued our own citizens, but they saved the people of Grenada from repression and laid aside a potential threat to all the people of the Caribbean." After the UN General Assembly voted 108 to 9 (27 abstentions) to endorse a resolution "deeply deploring" the invasion, the president said airily: "One hundred nations in the United Nations have not agreed with us on just about everything that's come before them where we're involved, and it didn't upset my breakfast at all."[2]

At the same time, the collapse of the Soviet Union sharply reduced Russia's ability to maintain stability within its postwar sphere of influence. The breakup of Yugoslavia—complemented by Serbia's aggression toward its neighbors—illustrated the rebirth of turmoil in the Balkans where the USSR, bereft of superpower status, could no longer impose order.

Afflicted by internal problems, Russia saw its global role diminish. The People's Republic of China (PRC), by contrast, continued to emerge as an ever-more-powerful player on the world stage. While candidate Clinton deplored President Bush's pampering of the regime responsible for the 1989 Tiananmen Square massacre, President Clinton followed his predecessor's policy of engaging Chinese officials. China's huge population, vast territory, expanding market, trading potential, regional significance, and nuclear capability meant that no occupant of the Oval Office could turn his back on the PRC's authoritarian leadership.

Accelerating interdependence of national economies also complicates decision-making for Clinton and other contemporary heads of state. A vast country like the United States, whose global commerce totals less than five percent of Gross National Product, enjoys more freedom of action than smaller trade-dependent nations. Nevertheless, the meltdown of the Mexican peso, the collapse of the Japanese banking system, the Russian government's inability to secure reforms in tax law and collection, and other foreign economic crises amply threaten the jobs, savings, and investments of American citizens. But despite the authority of his office and his country's power, the American president can rarely make a decisive difference in such situations, unless he enlists other countries in joint rescue plans.

Additionally, trends caused by the cold war's passing and economic globalization have given rise to "intermesticity"—an interrelationship between internal and external affairs. This growing permeability between "inside" and "outside" spheres has emboldened domestic pressure groups to involve themselves in policy matters once outside, or tangential to, their political agendas. Thus, more and more political actors are now assigning a high priority to international issues. For instance, despite its emphatic Democratic leanings, the AFL-CIO—once a champion of free trade—has vigorously opposed Clinton's efforts to conclude and expand the North American Free Trade Agreement. And in 1994 the Congressional Black Caucus strongly encouraged the president to send twenty thousand U.S. troops to Haiti to restore Jean-Bertrand Aristide to his elected post.

The recent proliferation of all-news networks like CNN has helped mobilize public pressure on presidents to react rapidly to natural disasters, ethnic cleansing, and other calamities, even in remote areas where no direct threat to U.S. interests exists. Daily televised images of dying children with bony limbs and bloated bellies in Somalia and crude, ruthless violence in Bosnia contributed to American intervention in both countries.

Finally, the "deVaticanization" of Congress affects U.S. relations with other countries. Until the 1980s, a veritable "college of cardinals"— composed of chairmen and ranking minority members of committees responsible for international affairs, defense, and appropriations— dominated foreign policy-making on Capitol Hill. As detailed in Chapter 6, the escalating involvement of legislative back-benchers in international matters has multiplied the number of interlocutors with whom any chief executive must deal in crafting foreign initiatives. Legislators swept into the House of Representatives in the Republican triumph of 1994 have demonstrated marked resistance to any international commitments, even when advocated by party leaders.

The Bush Legacy on NATO Expansion

The Bush administration's European policy had concentrated on the fragmentation of the Soviet Union, German unification, the wars of secession that followed 1991 declarations of independence by Slovenia and Croatia from the former Yugoslavia, and assistance to Russia and its former satellites.

An example of the latter involved Tadeusz Mazowiecki, who jetted to Washington soon after becoming the first noncommunist head of government in the Eastern bloc in mid-1989. He stayed at the residence of his friend, Zbigniew Brzezinski. The former national security adviser arranged for him to meet with General Brent Scowcroft, Bush's NSC head, on September 26, 1989. Mazowiecki argued that without $1 billion in debt relief and assistance Poland's fledgling democracy would never stabilize its currency, the zloty. While having no plan in hand, Scowcroft promised that the United States would help the beleaguered country obtain sufficient resources. Washington worked with the International Monetary Fund, West Germany, and other governments to devise a sizable loan-package in December 1989. "Bush was fantastic as a fundraiser for Poland," according to an influential Polish American who attended Mazowiecki's meeting with Scowcroft.[3]

Although questions of assistance to the New Independent States found their way into the 1992 campaign, the president chose not to make NATO an issue in his bid for reelection.[4] Nevertheless, in the early 1990s, changes in the alliance's architecture precipitated discussions and policy papers within the State Department and NSC. Foreign-policy specialists realized that NATO would become irrelevant if it remained largely a mechanism for containing Russia. As a result, Secretary of State James A. Baker III authorized a European Strategic Steering Group (ESSG) to coordinate activities among the several agencies: Undersecretary for Economic and Agricultural Affairs Zoellick and Undersecretary for International Security Affairs Reginald Bartholomew represented the State Department; Undersecretary of Defense for Policy Paul D. Wolfowitz and Assistant Secretary of Defense for International Security Policy Steven J. Hadley sat in for the Pentagon; and European and Soviet Affairs Senior Director David C. Gompert and NATO specialist Barry Lowenkron attended for the National Security Council. This Group found itself paying increasing attention to how NATO might prevent the occurrence of future Balkan conflicts.

The Bush administration clearly understood the need to reshape NATO in accord with evolving challenges to trans-Atlantic security. The Soviet Union's disintegration had removed the danger of a full-scale attack on NATO's European fronts. The new threat arose from ethnic rivalries, border disputes, and socioeconomic inequalities plaguing Central and

Eastern Europe. Such conditions could engender armed struggles inimical to European stability. Zoellick, whose responsibilities included Europe and NATO, was "speculating about Polish . . . [and other Central European/East European] membership" from the time of German unification. As a result, he strongly advocated NATO outreach to former Warsaw Pact countries at the NATO London summit in mid-1991, while vigorously resisting limits on the movement of non-German alliance forces in the former German Democratic Republic, known as East Germany. In Zoellick's words,

> . . . the Bush Administration did take steps to prepare NATO for enlargement and new roles. Frankly, I have little doubt that, given Bush's inclinations toward Central Europe/East Europe, Baker would have moved Bush on this issue (if he needed moving) early in '93.[5]

The abortive coup in Moscow in August 1991 had hastened the collapse of the Soviet Union, which had plunged into disarray in previous years. President Gorbachev's bold promotion of simultaneous economic and political openings had spun out of control, sounding the death knell to communism's hegemony over an internal empire that spanned a dozen time zones. The State Department and U.S. officials at NATO proposed a qualitative change in the alliance: to institutionalize NATO's fledgling liaison with the former Warsaw Pact states to enhance the organization's effectiveness in confronting post-Soviet era challenges.[6] Washington consulted frequently about NATO's future with Germany, NATO's "front-line" state during the cold war. Undersecretary Zoellick reiterated this goal in conversations with Frank Elbe, his counterpart in the German Foreign Ministry. Their discussions laid the groundwork for the joint statement by Secretary of State Baker and German Foreign Minister Hans-Dietrich Genscher in early October 1991. This declaration foreshadowed the creation of the Partnership for Peace (PFP) two years later.

Although stressing the importance of the Conference on Security and Cooperation in Europe, the statesmen "agreed to work with their allied partners to develop a fresh institutional relationship between NATO and the new democracies of Central and Eastern Europe and the Soviet Union." They suggested that as a logical extension of decisions made at the London summit, the November 1991 NATO meeting in Rome might create a North Atlantic Cooperation Council (NACC) to formalize the "liaison relationship" between the sixteen NATO members and other European nations. The NACC, they hoped, would bring together NATO countries, successor states of the Soviet Union, and former members of the Warsaw Pact, which dissolved on the very day that the council held its first meeting. The new council could also provide a forum for implementing arms-control agreements and allowing ex-Soviet states—for instance, Armenia and Azerbaijan—to sort out their differences.[7] Congruent with the NACC concept, Baker and Genscher encouraged new civilian and military exchanges designed to promote Western approaches to civil-military relations, proposed opening NATO information offices in Eastern capitals, and suggested "[e]xamining on a priority basis the contribution that NATO can make to support efforts to convert defense industries in the emerging democracies to civilian production."[8]

In accord with the Baker-Genscher recommendation and as mentioned in Chapter 1, NATO members announced the North Atlantic Cooperation Council in the "Rome Declaration on Peace and Cooperation." This communiqué indicated that the foreign ministers of nine Central and Eastern European countries, including Poland, Hungary, Czechoslovakia, and the Soviet Union, would be invited to the December 1991 NATO ministerial meeting in Brussels.[9] Consultation and cooperation would concentrate on issues where allies could offer their experience and expertise: e.g., defense planning, democratic concepts of civilian-military relations, civil/military coordination of air traffic management, and the conversion of weapons factories to peacetime purposes. NACC activities would extend to the "Third Dimension" of scientific and environmental programs of the alliance.[10]

Policy Planning Staff (S/P)

In its seventh-floor precincts of the State Department, the Policy Planning Staff took seriously its function as an in-house think tank. The brainchild of Secretary of State Marshall in 1947, this office—known as S/P in bureaucratic shorthand—seeks to examine foreign policy as a whole, collecting and synthesizing the ideas and priorities of the disparate bureaus within the building. Rather than reacting to headlines like most of their colleagues, S/P's officials endeavor to anticipate problems that might arise not in the distant future, but beyond the vision of the operating officers caught in the smoke and crises of current battle; far enough ahead to see the emerging form of things to come and outline what should be done to meet or anticipate them.[11]

Until falling out of favor with Secretary Acheson, George Kennan served as policy planning's first director. The list of some of Kennan's successors reads like "a roll call from the Council of Foreign Relations": Paul H. Nitze, Robert Bowie, Winston Lord, Tony Lake, and Peter W. Rodman.[12]

In accord with this legacy and responsibility, in 1991 S/P's highly regarded director Dennis Ross and his principal deputy William Burns urged staff members to consider policy options for the Atlantic alliance and Central Europe. The NSC's Lowenkron also interested himself in the possible restructuring of NATO.

In contrast to their superiors, some mid-level U.S. policymakers had begun examining NATO's future even earlier. Officials in the Central Europe office of the State Department's European Bureau had echoed security concerns emanating from Warsaw, Budapest, Prague, and other Central European capitals after the fall of the Berlin Wall. However, proponents of adding members to the alliance—possibly on a probationary or "associate" basis—ran into a firestorm of opposition from other offices within the European Bureau, from the NSC, and from the military.

Most analysts worried that signaling NATO's readiness to open its door to the Visegrad states would spur Russia to postpone the removal of troops in its former satellites and demand that these nations agree to a neutral status, just as Austria had done after World War II. Carping by right-wing opponents in Poland that Walesa was procrastinating on Atlantic alliance membership infuriated the NSC's Gompert. "Such criticism shows only stupidity and irresponsibility," he told a prominent Polish American.[13]

Foes of enlargement advanced other arguments. With its own mutual-defense pact gone, Russia might interpret any eastward extension of the alliance as a lack of faith in its own fledgling democracy. Demagogic extremists in the former Soviet Union would decry expansion as provocative, a threat to their nation's independence, and grounds for voters to oust moderate reformers, who apparently could not persuade their "friends" in the West to spurn such menacing behavior. Enlargement would require the U.S. armed forces to assume new commitments during an era of declining resources. In addition, integrating Central and Eastern Europe's outdated militaries into NATO's technical, doctrinal, and procurement structures would impose a huge burden on the alliance and on member-state budgets. As one high-level Bush adviser said off the record: "Every time politicians decided to send more armaments to Israel, the cost came out of the Pentagon's hide. Supplying vast stores of equipment to Central Europe equaled Israel magnified by ten." Furthermore, with so many communists in key positions, how could the Central European nations keep intelligence flows confidential?

General Colin L. Powell, chairman of the Joint Chiefs of Staff, preferred to cultivate rather than antagonize Russia in its latest Time of Troubles. To this end, Powell not only encouraged traditional economic assistance to Moscow, but vigorously pushed the Military to Military Program (MTMP), begun by his predecessor, Admiral Crowe, in late 1990. MTMP stressed the exchange of junior- and middle-level officers between the United States and Russia, with a view to building personal and professional bonds that could obviate future cold or hot wars. Joint space activities dovetailed with MTMP.

Jan Nowak, an adviser to the NSC when Powell headed the council, recalls the general as "negative, negative, negative" with respect to Central Europe. "He opposed anything that had an element of risk," Nowak added.[14] Nevertheless, in May 1989, Powell predicted: "If tomorrow morning we opened NATO to new members we'd have several applications on our desk within a week—Poland, Hungary, Czechoslovakia, Yugoslavia, maybe Estonia, Latvia, Lithuania, and maybe even the Ukraine."[15] Although prescient about the likely interest in alliance membership, Powell did not champion NATO affiliation for the erstwhile Soviet satellites. Many of his Pentagon colleagues decried the quality of these nations' armed forces, dismissed the RAND troika's contention that a "security vacuum" surrounded a prostrate Russia, and emphasized that in the case of war in Central Europe only the United Kingdom and the United States could land divisions in the region.

The Vietnam experience had strengthened Powell's view that the United States should never again send eighteen-year-old foot soldiers into battle unless Washington articulated a clear political objective and backed that objective with overwhelming resources. This perspective ignited a heated exchange over Bosnia with UN Ambassador Albright, a powerful force in NATO expansion. "What's the point of having this superb military that you're always talking about if we can't use it?" she asked the general.

"I thought I would have an aneurysm," he wrote in his memoirs. "American GIs were not toy soldiers to be moved around on some sort of global game board." Then, the general patiently explained "that we had used our armed forces more than two dozen times in the preceding three years for war, peacekeeping, disaster relief, and humanitarian assistance. But in every one of those cases we had a clear goal and had matched our military commitment to the goal."[16] Six years later, Powell insisted the explosive disagreement was irrelevant to the NATO issue. "Even if I had opposed expanding NATO, what would that have to do with sending troops to Bosnia?" he asked.[17]

Flanagan's Article

During the last year of the Bush presidency, Stephen J. Flanagan, a European-security specialist on the Policy Planning Staff who had devised the NACC, braved the generally frigid atmosphere surrounding expansion to raise the issue in a paper prepared for a "Congressional-Executive Dialogue on the Future of NATO."[18]   Brad Roberts, editor of *The Washington Quarterly*, published by the Center for Strategic & International Studies (CSIS), attended the presentation. At the conclusion of the program, Roberts complimented Flanagan on the freshness of his ideas and inquired about the possibility of publishing a version of the talk in CSIS's journal. Flanagan got the green light from Ross to revise the paper for publication in hopes that it might stimulate discussion of the Atlantic community's most crucial post-cold war security issue.

In the article, Flanagan reiterated Secretary Baker's appeal for a new security "architecture" in order to achieve Bush's vision of a "Europe whole and free." The essay, an extension of ideas presented in a 1989 speech delivered by Secretary Baker in Berlin,[19] pointed to several organizations that could help achieve such an objective: the EU, NATO, and the OSCE.[20]

This last institution, which emerged from the Helsinki negotiations of the early 1970s, sought to promote democratic governments, respect for human and political rights, peaceful dispute resolution, and greater openness in military affairs among all European nations.

Flanagan repeated President Walesa's observation—made at a mid-1991 visit to NATO headquarters—that without "a secure Poland and a secure Central Europe, there is no secure and stable Europe."[21]

Walesa's statement, however, begged the question of who would stabilize Central Europe and how. One possibility lay in *"ententism"* — a system of mutual-security guarantees involving some or all of the allies and some or all of the former communist republics. "But such a web of incomplete and overlapping security guarantees in Central Europe could recreate a system not unlike the one that facilitated the outbreak of World War I," Flanagan observed.[22]   Another alternative rested with liaison programs between NATO members and the nations to the east. Indeed, Secretary Baker had enumerated five principles to guide such relations: building trust and reducing misunderstandings between former adversaries; improving understanding of parties' security concerns among all participant states; capitalizing on NATO's technical expertise to cope with common problems; responding appropriately to the changing societies based on their degree of democratization and demilitarization; and complementing activities of the EC, the OSCE, and other European organizations.[23]   Baker also pointed to the NACC as one potential home for a bold cooperative program; as such, he regarded the organization as a possible path to NATO membership.[24]

Although Flanagan had conceived the NACC, his essay emphasized that readiness for joint operations did not diminish several postcommunist states' eagerness to affiliate with NATO. In fact, then-NATO Secretary General Manfred Wörner had raised the membership issue in October 1991, when he called the alliance the "core" of the emerging European security system. Flanagan stopped short of recommending enlargement, but he did reiterate a set of expansion criteria for new alliance members proposed by Hans Binnendijk, who in 1993 became principal deputy director of policy planning under Director Samuel W. Lewis. In keeping with the Washington Treaty's provisions, Binnendijk had highlighted the need for candidate states to: (1) accept the rule of law; (2) renounce all disputed territorial claims; (3) support self-determination of subnational groups; (4) display willingness and capability to offer mutual assistance to other member states; and (5) accept phased integration into the alliance and acquisition of voting rights.[25]   Scrutinizing the rationale for a NATO with expanded size and revised scope, Flanagan concluded reflectively:

> Two years ago one could easily have dismissed these questions as of such remote possibility that they were not even worthy of consideration. As President Yeltsin noted, Russian membership is a long-term goal. It is a development difficult to imagine so long as Russia possesses so many nuclear weapons, which still pose an existential threat to Western

security. But we in the West should be chastened, however, by the pace and sweep of recent changes in the European landscape and begin to consider these difficult issues, which may well confront NATO governments sooner than they expect.[26]

At a North Atlantic Council meeting in Oslo in mid-1992, Deputy Secretary of State Lawrence S. Eagleburger, who filled in for Baker, argued that the time had come to make decisions on the future of NATO and Central Europe, and even referred to the possibility of Polish membership in the alliance—believed to be the first official reference to such a move.[27] Later, Eagleburger, who succeeded Baker as secretary of state, recalled that he "strongly favored some form of treaty arrangement with Central Europe," but believed it premature to decide on the specific elements of the relationship; he considered substantial changes in the Atlantic alliance a "problem." For example, he regarded as an "absurdity" the idea of Russia's membership in the pact.[28] The Europeans' inability to manage the Bosnian crisis combined with the exigencies of conducting a presidential campaign largely redirected the Bush administration's focus from international to domestic politics. Later, Gompert inserted a line reiterating Eagleburger's earlier comment about the desirability of NATO's door being open to new members in a speech President Bush would give to the Sejm, the Polish parliament, in July. Although the chief executive would not have mentioned any country by name, the city in which he delivered his remarks pointed unmistakably to Poland as a possible candidate-state. At the last minute, a top U.S. official outside the State Department succeeded in deleting this reference.[29]

Clinton in Office

President Clinton took office determined to give priority to domestic issues. Much to his dismay, Congress made mincemeat of his labyrinthine, 1,341-page "Health Security Act," which Republican Minority Leader Newt Gingrich ridiculed as a "bureaucratic monstrosity" that combined "German socialism and Italian corporatism."[30] In contrast to the health-care muddle, Clinton fared better when playing the centrist Democrat—as when he gained legislative support for international initiatives of the Bush years: NAFTA; U.S. affiliation with the World Trade Organization, successor to the General Agreement on Tariffs and Trade or GATT; participation in the Asia-Pacific Economic Cooperation program; and economic assistance for Russia and former Soviet-bloc states.

The new administration also confronted its share of problems: Bosnia continued to fester, the conversion of Bush's Somalian famine relief to "nation building" ended up a fiasco, and a commitment to restore President Aristide to power ensured the eventual need for military intervention in Haiti. After a year in office, Clinton's international-affairs advisers appeared as greenhorns at the poker table. They failed to define persuasively and pursue coherently their conception of the national interest and articulated no clear rationale for whether and how to commit American military force—a tendency still evident in mid-November 1998 when the White House aborted a missile strike against Iraq before launching "Operation Desert Fox" five weeks later. "In addition," wrote one careful observer,

> there has been a tendency to shift responsibility—crucial to successful leadership—away from the president and toward subordinates; away from the United States and to its allies, for example the Europeans on Bosnia or the Japanese and South Koreans on North Korea; and away from this administration and toward its predecessor with the rhetoric of "inherited crises."[31]

The president and his foreign-policy team groped for a unifying theme to capture the purpose for U.S. strategy in the post-cold-war era as "containment" had done during the cold war. Presidents Ronald Reagan ("Peace through Strength") and Bush ("New World Order") had failed to formulate a concept that resonated with foreign-affairs opinion leaders in academia, the media, and diplomatic circles. Thus, a student of the process suggested that the White House held a veritable "Kennan Sweepstakes" in its search for a compelling catchphrase.[32]

On September 21, 1993, Tony Lake captured the grand prize in an address delivered at the Johns Hopkins' Nitze School of Advanced International Studies. In this so-called "SAIS speech" written by Lake and Rosner, the national security adviser insisted that the successor to the containment doctrine must be a strategy of "democratic enlargement" or, that is to say, expanding "the world's free community of market democracies."[33] He employed a simplistic but effective metaphor to illustrate his point. "During the Cold War," he stated

> even children understood America's security mission; as they looked at those maps on their schoolroom walls, they knew we were trying to contain the creeping expansion of that big, red blob. Today, at great risk of oversimplification, we might visualize our security mission as

promoting the enlargement of the "blue areas" of market democracies. The difference, of course, is that we do not seek to expand the reach of our institutions by force, subversion or repression.[34]

How would America extend the "blue areas"? He recommended four steps. First, the United States should "strengthen the community of [existing] major market democracies" that forms the core of a global civil society. Second, Washington should undertake policies to "help foster and consolidate new democracies and market economies," concentrating on countries of special significance and opportunity. Third, Washington must counter aggression—and support liberalization—in "states hostile to democracy and [open] markets." Along these lines, Lake committed the Clinton administration to advancing a "humanitarian agenda" by providing aid, nurturing democracy, and encouraging market economies in states beginning to embrace pluralism, for example, in Latin America and Eastern Europe.[35]

Lake stressed that a successful foreign policy must marry principle to pragmatism. Rather than embark on a "democratic crusade," the NSC chief recommended that the United States focus on countries affecting its strategic interests—e.g., those with large economies, geostrategic significance, nuclear weapons, or the potential to generate refugee flows into America or its allies. As for working in league with other countries, Lake contended that "[w]e should act multilaterally where doing so advances our interests—and we should act unilaterally when *that* will serve our purpose. The simple question in each instance is this: what works best?"[36]

Six days later, in another Lake/Rosner speech, President Clinton reiterated the "democratic enlargement" message before the UN General Assembly. Although his speech ranged over more topics than Lake's had, the chief executive emphasized that

an expanded community of market democracies not only serves . . . [U.S.] security interests, it also advances the goals enshrined in this body's [the UN's] charter and its Universal Declaration of Human Rights. For broadly-based prosperity is clearly the strongest form of preventive diplomacy. And the habits of democracy are the habits of peace.[37]

Clinton also stressed that "[d]emocracies rarely wage war on one another." Instead, he noted that such states tend toward cooperation in commerce, diplomacy, and the stewardship of the world's environmental resources. Moreover, he added, "democracies with the rule of law and respect for political, religious, and cultural minorities are more responsive to their own people and to the protection of human rights."[38]

Clinton did not mention NATO in this address, and Lake's speech—which contained only a brief allusion to the Atlantic alliance—failed to chart a clear course for its future. Lake did, however, refer to "updating" the organization's functions. He went so far as to say that "[u]nless NATO is willing over time to assume a broader role, then it will lose public support, and all our nations will lose a vital bond of transatlantic and European security."[39]

In addition, Presidents Havel and Walesa—both passionate advocates of NATO enlargement—had greatly impressed Clinton when he met privately in the White House with each president after the dedication of the U.S. Holocaust Memorial Museum on April 22, 1993. The Czech leader made his case with the erudition of a playwright, stressing his belief in Atlantic Charter ideals and emphasizing the importance of seizing the historic moment to reunify the West—an objective best accomplished through NATO. Unable to summon Havel's poetic language, the self-educated Walesa nonetheless drove home the same message: Poland wanted a chance to rejoin the community whose ideals it venerates and shares; it would be a loyal ally to the United States and a contributor to trans-Atlantic security; and it could form an important link to Russia. Clinton's emotional encounter with the Central Europeans may have marked the first time that high officials had urged the president to augment the alliance.[40]

Meanwhile, the festering Bosnia crisis badly strained U.S.-European relations. The British and French, for example, considered the conflict a civil war, to be concluded as swiftly as possible even if Bosnia's Muslim government in Sarajevo emerged with the upper hand. In contrast, the Clinton administration berated President Slobodan Milosevic as a bloodthirsty tyrant and favored air assaults on the Serbian "aggressors." In hopes of overcoming the atmosphere of mutual distrust and recrimination, Secretary of State Christopher proposed a NATO summit, which would bring the heads of government together for the first time in three years. He made this suggestion at a June 1993 NATO ministerial session in Athens, just seven months before the high-level meeting would occur. This "bolt from the blue," in the words of one policymaker, required the White House's foreign-policy advisers to devise proposals that the president might present to America's fifteen Washington Treaty allies.

Intra-Administration Conflict

In preparation for Clinton's January 1994 address in Brussels, Christopher asked that Lynn E. Davis—undersecretary of state for Arms Control and International Security Affairs—Binnendijk, and Flanagan conduct a policy review that would lead to a plan for NATO's future. The secretary noted the existence of three broad possibilities: (1) disbanding an alliance that had fulfilled its cold war purpose; (2) maintaining the status quo without changing membership or mission; or (3) inviting nations to the east to join the organization.[41] Davis, Binnendijk, and Flanagan, all of whom favored the third option, enjoyed strong backing from Charles Gati, a highly respected, Hungarian-born scholar, who served briefly as the Policy Planning Staff's senior adviser on European and Russian affairs.[42]

In a September 1993 internal memorandum, Gati not only proved his astuteness, but also drew attention to Central Europe by predicting the communists would win the 1993 legislative contests in Poland. Thomas Donilon, Christopher's chief of staff, took the paper directly to his boss, who found the analysis impressive. "When the ex-Communists did win parliamentary elections in Poland weeks later, Gati's words carried even greater weight."[43] Later, he noted the likelihood that the Communist Party would stage a comeback in Hungary, which subsequently took place. Other supporters of NATO's growth—although marginal players on the issue—included Donilon, Policy Planning Director Lewis, and his predecessor Dennis Ross, who served as the Clinton administration's special Mideast envoy.

Pro-expansionists argued for maintaining, even accelerating, momentum for political and economic liberalization in Central Europe. They contended that EU members—occupied by the Maastricht Treaty, the advent of the European Monetary Union, and the prospect of cheap imports from the East—lacked motivation to open their ranks in the near- to medium-term to Poland, Hungary, the Czech Republic, and other former Soviet allies. Thus, NATO offered the only major institution that could selectively extend membership to its former enemies. But security would come only after aspiring states took steps to open their economies, democratize their political regimes, ensure civilian control of militaries, extend guarantees to ethnic and religious minorities, and resolve border conflicts with neighboring countries.[44] Should not the West at least provide entry criteria for NATO, so Central European states could know the rules of the game?

Jenonne Walker, the NSC's senior director for European Affairs, regarded setting forth NATO eligibility requirements as anathema. Walker also chaired an interagency working group (IWG) on NATO. Representing the State Department were Vershbow, Binnendijk, and Flanagan; sitting in for the Pentagon were General McCaffrey (assistant to the chairman of the JCS), Walter B. Slocombe, (deputy undersecretary of defense for Policy), and the late Joseph J. Kruzel (deputy assistant secretary of defense);[45] Lowenkron was present for the NSC; and Roger George attended from the Central Intelligence Agency (CIA).

Walker made no bones about Clinton's and Lake's wanting to pursue expansion. Although claiming not to have opposed NATO enlargement per se, she disagreed strenuously with

> those who, with the Cold War's end, were desperate (and I do not exaggerate) to preserve NATO's dominance of trans-Atlantic relations and saw both the then-CSCE and the European Union as threats to it that US policy should aim to keep as weak as possible. I believed (and still believe) that neither [organization] can threaten the core military role that all NATO members, on both sides of the Atlantic, will want to preserve—but that both can play critical roles that NATO cannot in the internal development of European states.[46]

Walker boasted a formidable ally in Strobe Talbott, whom Clinton had appointed ambassador-at-large and special adviser to the secretary of state on the New Independent States. Although destined to become one of the most effective proponents of NATO expansion, in 1993 Talbott vigorously resisted "fast-track for the V-4"—i.e., the Visegrad countries' quick admission to the alliance. Several factors shaped his position. First, he insisted that NATO assay each prospective member on "its own merits, not as part of a group or cluster." Second, he believed high stakes and complex issues dictated that "enlargement should be a deliberate process, not a quick one." Finally, he stressed the "Russia/Ukraine factor"—namely, that new members constituted only one element in a new NATO, which also had to consider prudently new missions and relationships with former adversaries.[47] A fluent Russian speaker, Talbott had translated former Soviet leader Nikita Khrushchev's writings, and authored a student thesis on nineteenth-century Russian poet-diplomat Fedor Tyutchev. As communism collapsed, Talbott said that the Soviet menace had never been as serious as alleged and that the "doves in the great debate of the past forty years were right all along."[48]

Other enlargement foes at the time included Thomas W. Simons, Jr., former ambassador to Poland and coordinator of U.S. assistance to the New Independent States (NIS); Steven Oxman, assistant secretary of state for European and Canadian Affairs; Thomas R. Pickering, U.S. ambassador to Russia; and most old hands at the State Department. Then-Secretary of Defense Les Aspin and the vast majority of Pentagon flag and general officers looked askance at expansion.

Although it appeared to Talbott that S/P was moving too fast, staff members themselves claimed they were only attempting to promote step-by-step progress toward enlargement. No advocate of expansion himself, Christopher asked Talbott and R. Nicholas Burns, the NSC's senior director for Russian, Ukraine, and Eurasia Affairs, to comment on the likely outcome of the alliance's accelerated growth. Both men cautioned Christopher and Lake that Russia would misinterpret a quick expansion, which could impair U.S.-Russian relations. In view of the domestic turmoil engulfing Moscow in late September and early October 1993, such a move might even shove Russia over the edge.[49]

Talbott privately referred to Russia's "Rodney Dangerfield syndrome," meaning that Moscow's leaders—eager to regain the status of "big boys"—bristled against the United States' and European countries' failure to accord them the respect they deserved. Christopher believed that, instead of rapidly altering NATO, Talbott preferred gradual changes in the organization, while strengthening linkages between the alliance and Russia and between the alliance and Ukraine.[50] In contrast, supporters of enlargement like Gati—who ultimately resigned over perceived efforts to thwart NATO expansion—believed that Talbott represented the State Department's dominant view on admitting new members: that is, "Delay, Postpone, Not Now, Forget!"[51] As a FOB ("Friend of Bill") since they roomed together at Oxford University, Talbott loomed as the potential eight-hundred-pound gorilla on this issue.

In mid-October 1993, when Talbott was out of Washington, Lynn Davis and several of her colleagues made a strong case to Christopher of the inadequacy of the NACC and Partnership for Peace (examined below) for advancing economic and political openings in Central Europe. Four years after the fall of the Berlin Wall, they maintained, the West had not brought the Central Europeans into the European family. Thus, the Atlantic community's allies to the east risked losing public support because they had promoted divisive economic and political reforms, but had little to show for their boldness in terms of enhanced security. Christopher remained unenthusiastic about adding nations to NATO and never became engaged in the question. Nevertheless, he seemed convinced of the need to broach alliance expansion during an upcoming trip to Central Europe, where he would brief regional leaders.

At that point, Talbott returned to Washington, learned of the luncheon, and wrote a four-and-a-half-page memorandum to the secretary and, in all likelihood, to the president. Among other things he stated that "[l]aying down criteria [for NATO membership] could be quite provocative, and badly timed with what is going on in Russia. Instead, he proposed, "[t]ake the one new idea that seems to be universally accepted, PFP, and make that the centerpiece of our NATO position." He also expressed opposition to Clinton's either naming prospective members or mentioning a time-table for affiliation in Brussels.[52] Across the Potomac, civilian and uniformed officials in the Defense Department shared Talbott's heartburn about rapid NATO enlargement.

Clinton, Aspin, and the Generals

The armed forces looked askance at President Clinton because of his draft avoidance, proposals to slash military spending, and advocacy of homosexuals openly serving in the military. Many officers voiced their misgivings to the press in off-the-record interviews, which Eisenhower once termed "legalized insubordination." However, its new commander in chief got off to a worse than anticipated start with the Pentagon over the gay issue. In a November 19 tête-à-tête, Powell had urged the president-elect to defer any policy changes regarding homosexuals for six months. "Give yourself some breathing space . . . . Don't make the gay issue the first horse out of the gate with the armed forces," he advised.[53] At their first meeting with the joint chiefs, Clinton, Secretary of Defense Aspin, and the president's and Aspin's top advisers ran into a firestorm of opposition to ending the ban on homosexuals serving in the military. The gay issue "entirely dominated" the session, one chief said. "At the end, we spent a few minutes on Iraq, Somalia and Bosnia."[54] Leaks of the White House exchange precipitated a spate of newspaper articles, editorials, and features, some of which depicted Powell as "the Rebellious General" and characterized the joint chiefs as "defiantly opposed [to removing the ban], almost to the point of insubordination."[55] Such bombasts infuriated Powell, who knew about discrimination first-hand and had grown accustomed to favorable press coverage. Deeply identified with the Reagan and Bush national-security policies, the chairman came to feel like "a skunk at a picnic" among Clinton's foreign-policy team.[56]

The JCS's concerns notwithstanding, Clinton advocated an end to discrimination against gays in the armed forces. Powell attributed this politically maladroit gambit to the new administration's having "already backed off from other campaign stands" like sending Haitian refugees back home. "I assume that some of his advisors must have told him," the general surmised later, 'Mr. President, you can't back down again. Just issue an executive order allowing gays to serve, and tell those generals to do it.'"[57] In the face of overwhelming congressional opposition to his ploy, Clinton retreated to a "Don't ask-Don't tell" policy—first suggested by Powell—that pleased neither the Pentagon nor the gay community. Powell disagrees with this conclusion, stating that the "Joint Chiefs of Staff supported it privately and publicly and testified in favor of it before Congress." After all, he added, "Consider the alternative we were facing six months earlier."[58]

Naming Aspin secretary of defense also raised hackles throughout the Pentagon's E-Ring, where the joint chiefs and their aides have offices. First, Aspin, deemed a "gadfly, capable of policy by one-liners and occasional cheap shots,"[59] had as chairman of the House Armed Services Committee continually backed sharp defense cuts since the USSR's demise. Once in the secretary's office, he launched a "Bottom Up Review" of the armed forces with a view to fulfilling Clinton's campaign pledge to cut forces by 200,000 troops and tens of billions of dollars below the Base Force level required to fight two aggressors at the same time. Aspin even floated a scheme about replacing this strategy with one predicated on undertaking just one major conflict combined with a holding action against a second enemy until completing the first engagement. The trial balloon gained neither altitude nor support.

Second, Aspin's reputation declined because of a ponderous decision-making style, a tendency to keep busy senior officers waiting an hour or two for appointments set by the secretary, a penchant for interminable meandering meetings, and an inability to manage a corporation with three million employees and a $300 billion budget.

Third, Aspin's rumpled suits, unironed shirts, shambling gait, and unpredictable schedule stood out like a sore thumb amid the spit-and-polish and razor-sharp creases of the military culture.

Fourth, Aspin suffered guilt by association with a White House that abounded with twenty- and thirty-somethings, who were indifferent, at times hostile, to men and women in uniform. On one occasion while walking through the West Wing, General McCaffrey said, "Hello, there," to a young female staffer, who reportedly replied in a haughty manner, "We don't talk to soldiers around here." Whether accurate or not, this alleged comment directed at the winner of three Silver Stars who commanded a crack division in Desert Storm and still bore disfiguring arm wounds from Vietnam "rocketed back to the Pentagon and whipped through the place like a free electron."[60]

Finally, in April 1993, Aspin angered senior officers by lifting the prohibition on women flying combat missions. "I'm sure some offices were angered," Powell wrote later, "but it must be noted that his [Aspin's] decision was supported by the Chiefs of the Air Force and the Navy, the two services affected."[61]

Although increasingly convinced that Aspin had fallen in over his head at the Defense Department, White House operatives had no love lost for Powell. His meteoric Bronx-to-four-star career, war hero status, reputation as a troops-friendly military intellectual, and loyalty to George Bush explained the general's independence and the Democrats' nightmare that he might wind up on the GOP national ticket in 1996.

Partnership for Peace (PFP)

In this complicated atmosphere, Pentagon officials sought to head off or delay expansion with an alternative of their own, rather than openly spurn opportunities for East-West cooperation in Europe. Undersecretary of Defense Frank Wisner, McCaffrey, Kori Schake,[62] and others helped to assemble and furnish proposals to Powell and, later, to General "Shali," a Powell protégé whom Clinton named as JCS chairman on August 11, 1993. As devised by Shalikashvili[63] —first as Supreme Allied Commander/Europe and then as head of the joint chiefs—PFP descended in a linear path from the North Atlantic Cooperation Council. Much like the NACC, the partnership would encourage military-to-military collaboration among current NATO members, former Warsaw Pact states, and European neutrals like Austria, Finland, Sweden, and Switzerland.

If the partnership were to be NACC-plus, why not simply revise the council? Kruzel astutely pointed out that the new administration wanted a program that carried its own brand name. Hence, the NACC metamorphosed into PFP.

Shalikashvili, whose grandfather had fought for czarist Russia in World War I and whose father had joined the *Wehrmacht* to combat Russia in World War II, was born in Warsaw. Still, he did not come across as a special pleader for Polish interests. He did, however, work hard to repair relations between the Pentagon and the Clinton administration. Although he and other top brass would suggest that the partnership might serve as a bridge to NATO, they actually treated the program as a dike to thwart the alliance's growth.

Many PFP proponents feared that Aspin, possessed of a short attention span, had not completely grasped the intent, much less the nuances, of the partnership. The chance for PFP's civilian and military advocates to fully discuss the initiative with the secretary came on September 11, 1993, at a dinner in the Brussels residence of Robert Hunter, U.S. ambassador to NATO. In addition to the secretary, those in attendance included Shalikashvili, Kruzel, Jenonne Walker, Joseph Nye, head of the National Intelligence Council, Admiral Jeremy M. Boorda, commander of NATO Forces/South Europe, and General Charles "Chuck" Boyd, deputy commander in chief of U.S. Forces in Europe.[64]

Back in Washington, Lake also attempted to "open channels of communication." The national security adviser began convening 7:30 a.m. breakfast meetings with Christopher, Albright, Shalikashvili, CIA Director John Deutsch, and William V. Perry, who had replaced Aspin as defense secretary in early 1994. At the same time, Lake "aggressively backgrounded reporters on the organic process that could lead to either the expansion of NATO or putting teeth in the OSCE."[65]

In his memoirs, Christopher avers that the administration's internal debate over NATO's future "crested" in October 1993: the cabinet-level Principals Committee embraced the general idea of augmenting the alliance after the conclusion of partnership agreements between NATO and states in Central and Eastern Europe.[66] Even Russia, though an unlikely candidate in the foreseeable future, might eventually apply for admission. Christopher later wrote that the proposal "struck the right balance, setting forth a gradual transparent process of offering reform-minded nations a chance to develop a partnership with NATO, holding out the prospect of full NATO membership, and not confronting Russia with an immediate fait accompli."[67]

Still, the ambiguity swirling around PFP left some observers thinking of the proposal as the utterance of a latter-day Oracle of Delphi: opaque plans left listeners to speculate self-servingly about their meaning. Although Christopher joined Talbott in rejecting swift enlargement of NATO, he flew to Budapest, Moscow, and four other Central European capitals in late October 1993 to inform his counterparts that the upcoming Brussels summit would spur the alliance's evolution.[68]   Meanwhile, Aspin jetted to Travemünde, Germany, where on October 20 he unveiled PFP to fellow NATO defense ministers. Even though the U.S. official explained that expansion would occur "sooner rather than later,"[69] he left the then-accurate impression that Washington was in no rush to seek enlargement. German Defense Minister Rühe sought to neutralize Aspin's comments by asserting that the partnership actually constituted a "step toward NATO expansion," and Secretary-General Wörner said, "We have reached a consensus to fundamentally open the gates of NATO."[70]

Immediate Reaction to PFP

Aspin's statement caught East European governments, U.S. embassies in the region, and the State Department off guard. In Warsaw, for instance, Polish leaders looked with jaundiced eyes at PFP, fearing that the initiative would exclude them from an integrated European security system. The unveiling of PFP just after tanks had shelled the Russian parliament building earlier that month exacerbated Polish paranoia about the West's intentions. "The [Polish] government called it 'Yalta II,'" said a U.S. foreign service officer serving in Warsaw at the time, who asked to remain anonymous. The Poles felt "we were almost there, but Talbott screwed us again," the diplomat added, referring to the ever-present belief by Central Europeans that Strobe Talbott stood between them and a seat on the NATO Council in Brussels.

In an effort to mollify the Central Europeans, the White House dispatched Albright, Gati, and Shalikashvili to Prague, Warsaw, and Budapest. The three officials assured their hosts that Washington backed their eventual inclusion in the Atlantic alliance. Albright repeatedly recited what was to become an administration mantra: "the question is no longer whether NATO will take on new members but when and how." Although polite to their guests, the hosts could see through Washington's transparent attempt to propitiate them by sending to their nations a Czech

American, a Hungarian American, and a Polish American. "The Poles, Czechs, and Hungarians were no fools; they knew they were being had," commented Gati.[71]

Brzezinski and Kissinger

In the United States, former Secretary of State Kissinger and Zbigniew Brzezinski inveighed against the partnership in opinion pieces and journal articles. Kissinger complained that PFP "would dilute what is left of the Atlantic alliance into a vague multilateralism," and urged admitting Poland, Hungary, and the Czech Republic into some form of "qualified membership."[72] He excoriated PFP as "a hybrid of the Wilsonian concept of collective security and of the Henry Wallace [FDR's liberal vice president and cabinet member] ideology of the 1940s"[73] —both, he said, reject the very concept of alliance. Underlining the central controversy respecting NATO expansion, Kissinger held that

> NATO was designed for security; its purpose was to resist a definable danger. The Partnership is designed not for defense but for reassurance. The joint military planning of the Partnership is an end in itself; it assumes no specific peril; it is undertaken unilaterally between NATO and each partner. But what common threat or purpose unites say, Uzbekistan and Spain?[74]

For his part, Brzezinski stressed the "flaws" marring any grand strategy that found Washington reaching out financially and diplomatically to Moscow at the expense of former Soviet satellites. "Particularly troubling," he wrote, "is the growing assertiveness of the Russian military in the effort to retain or regain control over the old Soviet empire." Thus, U.S. rapprochement with a "proto-imperial" Russia could legitimize the Kremlin's domination of its neighbors.[75] If PFP envisioned a security system stretching from Vancouver to Vladivostok, the result would be to attenuate the trans-Atlantic alliance, while enabling "a regionally hegemonic Russia, eventually revitalized under the umbrella of the American-Russian partnership, to become again the strongest power in Eurasia."[76] In addition, he cautioned

> [u]nlike the old centralized Soviet Union and its neighboring bloc of satellite states, the new arrangement would embrace Russia and its

satellite states (within the former Soviet Union) in some kind of confederation, with central Europe next door viewed by the West as Russia's sphere of influence.[77]

Such a Washington-Moscow "cooperative condominium" would alienate France, imperil prospects for German-Polish reconciliation, and tempt Germany to pursue its own interests, perhaps through a "separate accommodation" with Russia, he argued. The upshot would be to "forfeit the long-range fruits of the West's victory in the Cold War."[78]   As an alternate to the original PFP, Brzezinski advocated a "dual track"— namely, that the incremental enlargement of NATO proceed, while the alliance forged a special relationship with Moscow.

Clinton Moves to the Brink

On the eve of the January 1994 NATO meeting, Lake—encouraged by the president—shifted gears. In addition to launching PFP in Brussels, he worked to ensure the United States would push for a collective decision to open the door to NATO enlargement. This opportunity appeared in the summit's final communiqué, which stated, in part:

> We reaffirm that the Alliance, as proved for in *Article 10* of the Washington Treaty, remains open to membership of other European states in a position to further the principles of the Treaty and to contribute to the security of the North Atlantic area. We expect and would welcome NATO expansion that would reach to democratic states to our East, as part of an evolutionary process, taking into account political and security developments in the whole of Europe.[79]

Next the president flew to Prague to reassure Eastern European heads of state about U.S. objectives. At a January 12, 1994 news conference with Visegrad leaders at the American ambassador's residence, he embellished Albright's earlier message to the Central Europeans, promising that "[w]hile the Partnership is not NATO membership, neither is it a permanent holding room." Clinton added that "[i]t changes the entire NATO dialogue so that now the question is no longer whether NATO will take on new members but when and how." He insisted that PFP "leaves the door open to the best possible outcome for our region, democracy, markets, and security all across a broader Europe, while providing time and preparation to deal with a lesser outcome."[80] This statement reflected "the President's own strong interest in moving ahead with enlargement."[81]

"When" and "how" meant vastly different things to different people. In response to Clinton's comments, President Havel—who continuously reminded the U.S. leader of the "values of civilization" that the Visegrad countries shared with the West—said that for his country's part, "we want to do everything in our power in order that our partnership results in our full membership in the alliance. As we do not regard Partnership For Peace as a substitute for that but rather as a first step toward NATO."[82] The dramatist-turned-politician concluded that "[a]t one time, the city of Yalta went down in history as a symbol of the division of Europe. I would be happy if today the city of Prague emerged as a symbol of Europe's standing in alliance."[83]

Walesa, too, had shown a mistrust of promises that PFP cleared a path to NATO membership. Still, he had struggled too hard since 1980 to wind up with only the Finlandization of Poland. Above all, he sought a strong America presence in Europe to enable his nation to reach an accommodation with Russia. Thus, the hero of Solidarity agreed to participate in PFP, telling Clinton: "We welcome American generals in Europe: General Motors, General Electric . . . ."[84] This statement not only appealed to the president's sense of humor, but it also jibed with his belief in the interrelationship of democracy, economic openness, and security.

In the United States, the ethnic lobby continued to urge Clinton to identify potential candidates for NATO admission. Still, the chief executive temporized with the "not whether . . . but when and how" rhetoric for two reasons: first, it behooved his administration to give PFP a chance; and, second, presidential advisers could not guarantee that Secretary Perry and members of the JCS would unambiguously support alliance expansion before congressional committees.

The NSC's Own Troika: From Rhetoric to Action

In any case, the Brussels speech and Prague exchange temporarily took the pressure off the NATO issue as the unruly Bosnian crisis dominated Washington's international agenda. With respect to the Atlantic alliance, the president's one-line pronouncements at the top contrasted with widespread opposition throughout the upper and middle echelons of the bureaucracy. Most officials at the State Department and Pentagon assumed—and the Central Europeans feared—that the administration would not venture beyond rhetoric to action on NATO's growth. In March 1994, Lake and his deputy Sandy Berger summoned Central European expert Fried to a private meeting in Lake's West Wing office in the White House. Lake stressed that he was "serious" about advancing NATO enlargement and directed Fried to formulate a policy and action plan.

Fried believed that it would better to let the NATO initiative die than to carry it halfway forward and watch it fail. "That's all very well," Fried responded to Lake's intentions, "but the resistance in the bureaucracy is overwhelming. I can't get papers cleared through the bureaucracy. Will you really back me up all the way?" the aggressively charming diplomat inquired.

Lake responded, "I'm not without influence"—a clear reference to Clinton's endorsement of expansion. Berger made it clear that the president's pro-enlargement statements constituted policy; the time had come to press forward; and if Fried produced the paper, the White House would protect the policy.[85] The conspicuous absence of Fried's boss, anti-expansionist Walker, from the meeting further highlighted Lake's seriousness of purpose. Talbott, who joined the session midway, left the meeting extremely upset, saying "I thought we had put the [enlargement] issue on the back burner." Fried walked out of the session exuding optimism. For years, foreign-policy cognoscenti had wailed like Cassandras: Solidarity won't succeed; the Berlin Wall won't collapse; General Wojciech Jaruzelski won't yield power; opponents won't overthrow Soviet communism; Poland won't revitalize its economy; Germany won't reunite; a unified Germany won't be allowed into NATO. Now the president, Lake, and Berger were challenging the purveyors of received wisdom—and Fried could help them recast the map of Europe.

Fried immediately called upon two trusted colleagues to assist in drafting an action plan: Burns at the NSC and Vershbow in the State Department's European Bureau. Fried had known Burns since 1989 when he was the State Department's Polish desk officer, and Burns formally worked as a special assistant to Zoellick, with responsibility for Soviet and Eastern European Affairs. In fact, he functioned as the "gatekeeper to the gatekeeper" inasmuch as Zoellick was Secretary Baker's right-hand man. Fried numbered among a handful of U.S. officials who believed that the Poles would democratize their authoritarian polity and reform their near-bankrupt economy. Even his good friend Munter implied that Fried "resembled a slightly crazed eater of wild honey in the wilderness with prediction of the fall of communism and Solidarity's impending electoral triumph."[86] The articulate, personable Burns proved one of the few people in the building who would listen to his ideas: "Nick had a creative mind and a sense of history. And now we were at the NSC together." Fried later recounted:

> We talked, both of us struck by the enormity of the issue. This was the big one, and our strategy had to encompass European security as a whole, even beyond NATO enlargement. There must [also] be a place for Russia.[87]

Burns seemed to appreciate Fried's contacting him directly about his vision of European security rather than engaging in the bureaucratic trench warfare that abounds in Washington.

Fried and Burns knew Central Europe and Russia, but neither had a background in NATO affairs. Consequently, Fried turned to Vershbow, a Phi Beta Kappa graduate of Yale whom he had first met in Professor Marshal Shulman's arms-control seminar at Columbia University in the mid-1970s. Both men exhibited a passion for Central and Eastern Europe. In fact, Vershbow had begun studying Russian in the tenth grade, had participated in a language-study tour of Poland and the USSR while still in high school, and perfected his language skills when he and Fried served in the U.S. embassy in Moscow in the early 1980s. Interspersed with other assignments, Vershbow spent six years in the Office of Soviet Affairs, which he headed from 1988 to 1991. In this post, he participated in the Bush-Gorbachev summits. Next, the State Department sent Vershbow to Brussels as deputy permanent representative to NATO and chargé d'affaires of the U.S. mission. His late August 1991 arrival in Brussels coincided with the putsch in Moscow that foreshadowed Gorbachev's fall. This prospect gave impetus to the idea of institutionalized linkages between the USSR's former satellites and the North Atlantic Alliance, a subject Vershbow explored in his first cable from Brussels, "NATO in the Post-Soviet Era."[88] The young diplomat could turn theory into practice by taking part in the November 1991 NATO summit that established the North Atlantic Cooperation Council. Upon his return to Washington two years later, Vershbow worked as

principal deputy assistant secretary of state under Walker in the
department's European bureau. Vershbow was scheduled to move to the
NSC as senior director for Russia, Ukraine, and Eurasia Affairs in mid-
1994, thus ensuring him greater freedom of action. A low-keyed, self-
effacing style masked Vershbow's intellectual boldness and enabled him
to appear nonthreatening to policy rivals.

Fried, Burns, and Vershbow shared a balcony in the Old Executive
Office Building, overlooking the West Wing of the White House. When
any one of the men called "troika meeting now," the other two would
join him on their open-air porch. Our rules were simple, Fried recalls:

> no bureaucratic tricks or end runs (we were all too good at that game
> and each knew the others were just as good); keep the policy balanced
> (forward on NATO enlargement, but always reaching out to Russia);
> keep our eye on the substance (not the bureaucratic rivalries at State
> or Defense).[89]

Fried, Vershbow, and Burns faithfully adhered to these rules, thanks
to a growing personal affinity and respect for each other's bureaucratic
skills. If any member of the team took unfair advantage of the others, he
knew that retaliation would be swift, sure, and effective.[90] Rather than
descend into one-upmanship, they came to protect their colleagues' specific
interests when, for example, Fried was asked to draft a presidential letter
to Walesa or Burns was preparing talking points for Clinton to consider
during an upcoming phone conversation with Yeltsin.[91] Together, they
wrote the action plan for European security, which included a Brzezinski-
style two-track approach.[92] On one hand, NATO members would craft
an enlargement strategy. On the other hand, the alliance would strengthen
its ties to Moscow, thus assuring the Russian people of the West's desire
for friendship and cooperation. The three diplomats assembled their
ideas in the form of a "concept paper," not a decision memorandum,
which they forwarded to Lake and the president before the latter's trip to
Warsaw. Even though equivalent in rank to assistant secretaries of state,
the senior directors reported directly to the NSC head, obviating the
daunting task of percolating their ideas through encrusted layers of
middlemen. Their document, "Moving Toward NATO Expansion,"
which the authors revised in October 1994, largely established the
assumptions, procedures, and timing of U.S. policy. Fried credits
Assistant Secretary of Defense Kruzel with the idea to tie expansion to

NATO's fiftieth-anniversary celebration in 1999. The NSC troika's handiwork also served as the basis for the president's midyear speech in Poland.

The Fried-Vershbow-Burns paper envisioned the establishment of an "institutional partnership" between the Atlantic alliance and Russia as the principal means to contain Moscow's objections to expansion. This proposal crystallized in the NATO-Russia Founding Act in June 1997, an initiative whose success depended on Moscow's commitment and constructiveness.

In his July 7 address to the Sejm, the national parliament, Clinton praised Poland for having taken a "leading role" in the Partnership for Peace, noting that their nation would soon host the first PFP maneuvers on the territory of a former Warsaw Pact nation. "But the Partnership for Peace is only a beginning," he affirmed.

> Bringing new members into NATO . . . is no longer a question of whether, but when and how. . . . We are working with you in the Partnership for Peace in part because the United States believes that when NATO does expand as it will, a democratic Poland will have placed itself among those ready and able to join.[93]

These remarks and similar words at a Berlin press conference several days later constituted "instructions" to the bureaucracy to get moving on the "when and how" of NATO expansion.[94]

Evolution of Talbott's Position

Opponents of enlargement hoped that Talbott—the administration's most conspicuous and influential Russophile—would lead the charge against an eastbound alliance. However, Talbott gradually moved from the anti- to the pro-expansionist camp, giving the White House another powerful bureaucratic ally.

What accounted for Talbott's change of position? In addition to his stated reasons, he doubtless realized the futility of fighting to the bitter end, especially after the president had endorsed expansion. Rather than just fall on his sword, Talbott may have reasoned that by working with the expansionist group he would gain for himself a bigger role in shaping the pace and character of changes to NATO. He could also serve as the administration's interlocutor with Russia, keeping the Kremlin abreast of step-by-step developments concerning NATO. Others argued that Talbott's February 1994 elevation from coordinating the department's policy toward former communist states to deputy secretary of state forced him to scrutinize issues in a wider context and consider a broader spectrum of views. Less charitable observers report that Senator Dole and others harshly criticized Talbott at his early-1994 confirmation hearing, and that the evolution of his NATO position may have sprung from a prospective secretary of state's desire to improve his standing on Capitol Hill.[95]

No matter the explanation for his evolution, Talbott proved one of the most articulate, convincing, and forceful advocates of expansion. Indeed, Lake lauded him for doing "more than any other official to sell enlargement."[96]   Asmus agreed, stating that "Strobe Talbott was the key architect in this crucial diplomatic phase. He was more important than either the RAND or the NSC troika in actually implementing this [enlargement] strategy."[97]

In a lengthy article in the *New York Review of Books*,[98] Talbott referred to warnings and suspicions that reverberated across Russia. He noted that Russians tend to "point out that they have disbanded the Warsaw Pact, *their* military alliance, and ask why the West should not do the same." Furthermore,

> For [Russians], NATO's plan to take in new members looks like a Western vote of no confidence in the staying power of Russian reform. It makes them feel as though Russia is still on probation—still subject to a thinly disguised policy of containment. Beware, they say, the mistake that the victors at Versailles made in punishing the Weimar Republic: when Germany recovered in the Thirties, it was bent on military conquest and revenge.[99]

Talbott admitted that the rationale for NATO's continued existence included what Secretary Perry has called "a hedge against pessimistic outcomes." Still, he added, enlarging the alliance may serve Russia's geostrategic interests. Expansion could bring stability to Central Europe where turmoil precipitated two world wars that punished Russia in the twentieth century: "It should be seen as a process that has benefits for everyone and is not directed against any particular state."[100]

Enforcer Holbrooke Lays Down the Law

In mid-1994, Talbott urged Christopher to invite U.S. ambassador to Germany Holbrooke to assume the post of assistant secretary for European and Canadian Affairs.[101]   The longtime Democratic foreign-policy hand, who had experience as an editor and international banker, was then in his eighth month in Bonn. As a condition of taking the new position, Holbrooke insisted that he head the interagency group on NATO, a position usually reserved for a senior NSC staff member. In his role as IWG chief, Holbrooke became almost as influential as Talbott in advancing the alliance's growth.[102]   As discussed in Chapter 2, not wedded to the post-cold war map of Europe, Holbrooke had become an enthusiastic exponent of NATO expansion. Thus, the hard-charging, suffer-no-fools-gladly diplomat happily returned to Foggy Bottom not to preside over academic discussions of the pros and cons of expansion, but to bring closure to the debate. Reportedly, his ardor for the task mounted when, at a cocktail party, a senior Pentagon official brusquely cautioned Holbrooke that he would lose the battle.

In his July Warsaw speech, Clinton had reiterated his commitment to expanding NATO. Scholars have found no evidence of an NSC meeting that discussed and adopted the enlargement option; however, Lake informed Holbrooke that adding Central European members to NATO constituted administration policy based on presidential statements.

Although Lake dismissed the suggestion that Holbrooke served as the NATO "enforcer,"[103] this sobriquet captures the behavior of an intrepid, creative policymaker famous in Washington for his flamboyance and impatience with those blocking his path.

Washington Post writer Michael Dobbs, an expert on bureaucratic turf battles over NATO, avowed that, soon after taking office, Holbrooke confronted Pentagon foot-draggers at an Interagency Working Group meeting. General Clark—the IWG's senior representative from the joint chiefs—questioned the president's decision to move ahead with the "when" and "how" questions of NATO's growth. Anticipating such a query, Holbrooke immediately turned to Vershbow, the White House representative at the meeting, to corroborate that the president had, in fact, decided that the time had come to address these pivotal issues. Upon completing this choreographed exchange, the sharp-tongued Holbrooke shocked those in attendance by telling Clark, "[t]hat sounds like insubordination to me. Either you are on the president's program or you are not."[104]   One participant in the session, who asked not to be identified, remarked: "Following that confrontation, you could have heard a pin drop in the room."

After the rebuke to Clark, Secretary Perry—who contended that Holbrooke "presumed" the administration had formally decided on NATO's future[105]—met with Lake and Talbott to lay out his and the Defense Department's deep reservations about proceeding rapidly to admit the Central Europeans to the alliance.   Undaunted by the Pentagon's distress, Holbrooke seized upon the NSC troika document as the basis for consultations with allies.   These parleys laid the groundwork for the early December NATO decision to commence its own study of enlargement.

Perry's apprehensions mounted when the December 1, 1994 meeting of NATO foreign and defense ministers produced the Holbrooke-inspired communiqué, unveiling the alliance's plans for expansion. On December 5, Yeltsin got the chance to vent his anger at Clinton for this policy démarche. The president had jetted to Budapest to attend a CSCE meeting and sign a historic international arms treaty. Anticipating Yeltsin's ire, Clinton began making his case for expansion in remarks moments before the Russian leader's speech. "We must not allow the Iron Curtain to be replaced by a veil of indifference. We must not consign new democracies to a gray zone," he said.   "Instead we seek to increase the security of all—to erase the old lines without drawing arbitrary new ones."[106]

The American's words failed to mollify Yeltsin, who angrily warned the fifty-three-member CSCE that "Europe is in danger of plunging into a cold peace," adding, "Why sow the seeds of mistrust? After all, we are no longer enemies—we are partners now [and] . . . [i]t's too early to bury democracy in Russia! . . . For the first time in history, our continent has a real opportunity to achieve unity." he insisted. "To miss it means to forget the lessons of the past and to jeopardize our future."[107]

Former Secretary Perry believes the outburst caught the U.S. delegation off guard. After all, Washington had provided Yeltsin with generous financial, diplomatic, and political assistance.   Once aboard Air Force One, Clinton—a believer in forging personal ties with key statesmen like Yeltsin—expressed "concern and a state of perplexity about what the Russians were up to."[108]

A few days later, Russia's foreign-policy elite reiterated Yeltsin's sentiments at a Moscow gathering of the Gore-Chernomyrdin Commission, created in 1993 to promote U.S.-Russian cooperation in energy, space exploration, high technology, business development, defense conversion, the environment, and health. Incredulous that a firm decision had been taken, Perry reiterated his views on NATO at a meeting with Clinton in the president's personal White House study on December 21, 1994. Also present were Gore, Talbott, Christopher, Lake, and Berger. The defense secretary stressed the prudence of deferring enlargement until later in the decade to avoid, among other things, stirring distrust and dismay in Russia. Despite Perry's redoubtable powers of persuasion, Clinton politely informed him that the NATO die had been cast.[109]

Perry himself proved a model of loyalty to official policy. Back in the Pentagon, he called for (1) more Bilateral Working Group meetings with the Russian General Staff, (2) increased consultation via the hotline between Perry's office and its counterparts in Moscow, (3) more face-to-face meetings between Perry and Russian Defense Minister Pavel Grachev, and (4) greater cooperation between NATO and the Russian military. Despite Perry's commitment, some Pentagon officials continued to grouse about enlargement well into 1996. As a result, the Defense Department found itself marginalized in a decision-making process highlighted by increasingly less ambiguous pronouncements by the president, particularly in his 1996 reelection bid.

Also important for the administration's more assertive NATO policy was Walker's departure from the National Security Council in 1994, and Fried's promotion to special assistant to the president and the NSC's senior director for Central and East European Affairs in January 1995.

Few Press Leaks

Intra-administration conflicts notwithstanding, the NATO debate produced remarkably few press leaks and cases of backbiting in a city that has turned both from an art form to an exact science. Most insiders attribute this situation to the fact that many in Clinton's senior international affairs team had served under President Jimmy Carter (1976-80). The Carter years found Secretary of State Cyrus R. Vance frequently at odds with National Security Adviser Brzezinski—with the supporters of each rushing to the media to raise questions about, or even undermine, policies advocated by the other. Even zealots in this process realized by the end of Carter's term that their antics had weakened the president and his top two foreign-policy counselors. One State Department official, who asked to remain anonymous, suggested two additional factors militating against sub rosa press contacts: first, the cohesion derived from the growing number of political appointees occupying key international affairs positions; and second, the breakdown of the eastern establishment old-boy network. The latter meant that by the 1990s few diplomats had personal fortunes that afforded them the luxury of risking jobs by whispering in journalists' ears about the missteps of their colleagues or the White House.

Walker exemplified the administration's pulling together when she became ambassador to the Czech Republic in mid-1995. In that post, she suppressed her earlier reservations and actively supported Czech membership in the alliance. Nevertheless, some U.S. Information Agency officials in Washington complained that she gave her USIA team in Prague much less latitude in publicizing NATO expansion than its counterparts in Warsaw and Budapest. Administration insiders call the criticism of Walker a "cheap shot," and correctly point out the eagerness of enlargement promoters to share credit with colleagues for the successful venture—an unusual occurrence among the Type-A personalities who seek recognition in the nation's capital.

The 1996 Presidential Campaign

In their 1994 "Contract With America," GOP candidates for the House of Representatives had committed themselves to adding Central European countries to NATO. Senate Republican Leader Dole had spoken and voted for this objective in the years before he secured his party's nomination to oppose Clinton. The Kansas lawmaker had reiterated his emphatic stand in meetings with Central European leaders in Washington and abroad. Consequently, he readily agreed to emphasize NATO expansion in his campaign during a Capitol Hill breakfast with American ethnic-group leaders in early June 1996. The executive committee of the Central and East European Coalition (CEEC), created in late 1993 and composed of nineteen organizations ranging from the Armenian Assembly of America to the Ukrainian National Association, suggested Detroit as a logical site for the GOP standard-bearer to deliver a ringing policy speech on the subject, given the city's relative convenience for their members living in the midwest and the northeast.

An opportunity for such an address presented itself on July 17 when Senator and Mrs. Dole attended the Republican National Leadership

Award Dinner in Detroit to honor automobile-industry legend Max Fisher. Coincidentally, a large group of Americans of Central European ancestry were assembled in a location near mammoth Cobo Hall, site of the GOP conclave. Astute activists like Julie Finley, the party's District of Columbia State Chairman and co-chairman of Dole's Finance Committee, had urged that the candidate take a half-hour or so from the Fisher event to speak to the ethnic Americans about NATO and Central Europe. The campaign's political operatives vetoed this proposal. As a result Dole rubbed elbows for some three hours with the party faithful when he could have been broadening his support among a constituency that had given more than forty percent of its vote to Clinton in 1992. The failure of the candidate's staff to seize upon this obvious bridge-strengthening opportunity reflected a "complete breakdown in advance work, scheduling, and political judgment," observed Finley.[110]

After the missed chance in Detroit, Paula Dobriansky, the candidate's foreign-policy coordinator, continued to press for a NATO event. Yet weeks—then months—passed without the Dole campaign confirming a place and date with the CEEC.[111] The modus operandi of the 1996 Dole-Kemp campaign strongly suggests that either Dole himself or campaign manager Scott Reed made the final decision on not scheduling a major NATO-focused rally.

Clinton found himself constrained by his bureaucracy until Lake and Holbrooke broke the logjam in 1994. After that, his enthusiasm for expansion became increasingly evident. In a mid-January 1995 speech in Cleveland, drafted by Fried and NSC speech writer Tony Blinken, the president emphasized that PFP had blazed the trail for NATO enlargement. "In just a year," he said, "the Partnership For Peace has become a dynamic forum for practical military and political cooperation among its members . . . . [and f]or some countries, the partnership will be the path to full NATO membership." Nevertheless, he warned that nations "with repressive political systems, countries with designs on their neighbors, countries with militaries unchecked by civilian control or with closed economic systems need not apply."[112]

The president embellished these remarks two weeks before the 1996 election. In mid-October, the Clinton camp alerted the Central and East European Coalition to its candidate's plans for a "major address" on NATO in Detroit on October 22. Could the CEEC help round up a crowd for this speech? Not surprisingly, hundreds of Americans of Central European descent helped pack the 2,400-seat Fisher Theater in downtown Detroit. In remarks prepared by Lake, Clinton claimed credit for promoting NATO enlargement, having raised the idea at the NATO summit in 1994. In that speech, the president demanded that a "gray zone of insecurity must not re-emerge in Europe," adding that the West must not "allow the Iron Curtain to be replaced by a veil of indifference."[113]

While not mentioning specific countries, Clinton affirmed that NATO would take in "the first group" of new members in 1999, in time for the fiftieth anniversary of the Washington Treaty and ten years after the fall of the Berlin Wall. He urged Kremlin leaders not to "look at NATO through a Cold War prism," but rather to see the alliance as a partner contributing to Russia's own security, "reducing rivalry and fear" in Eastern Europe and "strengthening peace and cooperation." In a further effort to soothe Russian fears, the chief executive emphasized that "NATO enlargement is not directed against anyone," and called for a "regular mechanism for NATO-Russia meetings at all levels." In case anyone missed candidate Clinton's overture to ethnic voters, he followed his speech with a lunchtime visit to the Polish Village Cafe in Hamtramck, a blue-collar Detroit suburb.[114]

The Detroit address—one of only a handful delivered on foreign policy during the 1996 campaign—allowed the president to portray himself as a defender of Central Europe, a friend of Russia, an advocate of a strong defense posture, and a future-oriented leader of the world's greatest power. Moreover, his call for a NATO summit in 1997 moved the alliance debate from a dialogue over enlargement to the issuance of invitations. In contrast, Senator Dole, initially the more ardent champion of NATO expansion, could only sputter that he would "move faster" on admitting new members, and that President Clinton was "still waffling and still unwilling to assert American leadership in NATO." In his written release, the Republican candidate concluded that "[u]nder Bill Clinton NATO enlargement will never happen."[115]

When rhetoric finally gave way to casting ballots, Polish Americans awarded Clinton nearly half their votes, up from 44 percent in 1992 and 42.3 percent for Dukakis in 1988.[116] The absence of specific questions relating candidate preference to his stand on expanding the Atlantic alliance prevents political scientists from knowing whether the Democrat's stronger showing in 1996 sprang from Clinton's NATO position or from other factors like economic growth, job creation, and his promises to reform health-care delivery.

Conclusion

Congress-watchers could not believe that Clinton had successfully appropriated the NATO issue from the GOP standard-bearer. Indeed, as early as 1993, while savage infighting raged within the executive branch, Senator Lugar—animated by the RAND troika's article—had begun declaiming the merits of alliance enlargement. Senators Biden, Brown, Dole, Lieberman, Mikulski, Simon, Roth, and others soon followed suit. In dozens of interviews conducted on Capitol Hill in 1998 and early 1999, legislators and their staffs accentuated a single message: "NATO expansion emanated from the legislative branch of government!"

While the RAND scholars and key lawmakers manifested the earliest comprehensive vision for NATO's growth, the dogged determination of key players overcame formidable bureaucratic obstacles to accomplish this historic change in the alliance. The moral considerations articulated by Havel and Walesa helped bring the president into the pro-enlargement camp. Lake and the NSC troika furnished the chief executive with an action plan; Holbrooke steamrolled Pentagon resistance; Albright and Talbott spearheaded diplomatic activity; and NATO's December 1994 communiqué smoothed the way for dialogues with individual candidate countries one year later and, ultimately, the mid-1997 decision at Madrid to extend invitations to Poland, Hungary, and the Czech Republic.

Throughout the process, altruism coincided with electoral benefits for Clinton, who had raised permanent campaigning to a new dimension. The next chapter illuminates the executive branch's "rapid-response capabilities" embodied in the NATO Enlargement Ratification Office, which worked hand-in-glove with State Department, NSC, and Pentagon experts. By detailing the office's organization and activities—as well as the NERO staff's exploits in the thrust-and-parry of policy debate, Chapter 4 allows insights into the mobilization of grass-roots and elite support for NATO expansion.

Notes

1. Speaker of the House Thomas "Tip" O'Neill said of the operation: "To be perfectly truthful, his policy scares me. We can't go the way of gunboat diplomacy. His policy is wrong. His policy is frightening" (*Facts on File*, November 4, 1983, p. 830).
2. Quoted in *Facts on File*, November 11, 1983, p. 830.
3. Nowak, telephone interview, November 16, 1998.
4. In fact, no reference to NATO expansion appears in the index to George Bush and Brent Scowcroft, *A World Transformed* (New York: Alfred A. Knopf, 1998).
5. Former Undersecretary of State Robert B. Zoellick, letter to author, December 19, 1998. Zoellick also pointed out that most early advocates of NATO expansion in the Clinton administration were recently retired Bush appointees.
6. Vershbow, electronic mail, December 10, 1998.
7. Archer, *Organizing Europe*, p. 38.
8. Secretary Baker and Foreign Minister Gencher, "US-German Joint Statement on Transatlantic Community," *US Department of State Dispatch*, October 7, 1991, p. 736.
9. NATO also invited "at this stage of the process" the foreign ministers of Bulgaria, Estonia, Latvia, Lithuania, and Romania.
10. NATO, "Rome Declaration on Peace and Cooperation," Press Communiqué S-1(91)86, November 8, 1991, Internet.
11. General Marshall's concept of S/P's function according to Acheson, *Present at the Creation*, p. 214.
12. Quoted in Susan Ellingwood, "Unplanned: Bureaucratic Decay at State; U.S. State Dept. Policy Planning Office," *The New Republic*, October 6, 1997, p. 16.
13. Nowak, telephone interview, November 16, 1998.
14. Nowak, telephone interview, January 10, 1999.
15. Colin L. Powell, with Joseph E. Persico, *My American Journey* (New York: Random House, 1995), pp. 402-3.
16. Powell, *My American Journey*, pp. 576-77.
17. Colin L. Powell, former chairman of the Joint Chiefs of Staff, letter to the author, January 4, 1999. The general added: "I fear you have overreached to provide some excitement to your readers."
18. The Congressional Research Service and the U.S. Information Agency sponsored this symposium on October 10, 1991; Flanagan's paper later appeared as "NATO and Central and Eastern Europe: From Liaison to Security Partnership," *Washington Quarterly* 15, no. 2 (spring 1992): 141-51.

19. Among other things, Baker called for adapting the "instruments of Western cooperation." NATO, he stated, must create a new military security structure and move more actively into political and economic tasks in Western Europe, with the East and beyond. See, "America's Ideas, Europe's Future," *Washington Post*, December 15, 1989, p. A-24.

20. Flanagan, "NATO and Central and Eastern Europe," p. 142.

21. "Address by President Lech Walesa of Poland on the Occasion of His Visit to NATO July 3, 1991," Press Release, Republic of Poland, Brussels.

22. Flanagan, "NATO and Central and Eastern Europe," pp. 143-44.

23. U.S. Department of State, Office of the assistant secretary/spokesman, "Intervention by Secretary of State James A. Baker, III at the North Atlantic Council, June 6, 1991," Press Release, Copenhagen, June 7, 1991.

24. Zoellick, letter to author, December 19, 1998.

25. Hans Binnendijk, "NATO Can't Be Vague About Commitment to Eastern Europe," *International Herald Tribune* (Paris), November 8, 1991, p. 6; while not "original" with him, former Secretary Perry said that "I seemed to be the only senior official willing to articulate them to candidate nations, and so my name came to be attached to them" (letter to author, November 30, 1998).

26. Flanagan, "NATO and Central and Eastern Europe," p. 150.

27. Zoellick, letter, December 19, 1998.

28. Former Secretary of State Lawrence S. Eagleburger, telephone interview by author, December 11, 1998.

29. David C. Gompert, former senior director for European and Soviet Affairs, National Security Council, telephone interview by author, January 4, 1999.

30. Quoted in *Facts on File*, November 4, 1993, p. 823.

31. Paul D. Wolfowitz, "Clinton's First Year," *Foreign Affairs* 73, no. 1 (January/February 1994): 30.

32. Jeremy Rosner, *The New Tug-of-War: Congress, the Executive Branch, and National Security* (Washington, D.C.: Carnegie Endowment for International Peace, 1995), p. 11.

33. Lake, "From Containment to Enlargement," *Vital Speeches of the Day* 60 (October 15, 1993): 15.

34. Lake, "From Containment to Enlargement," p. 15.

35. Lake, "From Containment to Enlargement," p. 15.

36. Lake, "From Containment to Enlargement," pp. 18-19.

37. Speech by Bill Clinton, "Reforming the United Nations," Academic Universe, LEXIS-NEXIS, September 27, 1993, p. 4.

38. "Reforming the United Nations," p. 4.

39. Lake, "From Containment to Enlargement," p. 16.

40. W. Anthony Lake, former national security adviser, interview by author, Washington, D.C., August 24, 1998; Lake conveyed the importance of the meetings, not the substance of the conversations.

41. Christopher, *In the Stream of History*, pp. 128-29.
42. From 1989 to 1992, Gati had worked as a consultant to the Policy Planning Staff. He fled Budapest shortly after the Soviet Union crushed the 1956 Hungarian uprising, earned three degrees from Indian University, taught at Columbia, Yale, Georgetown, Kansas, and other universities, and was honored as the first recipient of the Marshall Shulman Prize (1987) for his book, *Hungary and the Soviet Bloc* (Durham: Duke University Press, 1986).
43. Goldgeier, "NATO Expansion," p. 89.
44. These five criteria—which, in September 1995, became the "Perry Principles" for admission to NATO—appear to derive in part from the provisions embedded in Binnendijk's *International Herald-Tribute* article. While agreeing that similarities exist, Binnendijk says he has no basis for accepting paternity for the Perry Principles (Hans Binnendijk, director of the Institute for National Strategic Studies, National Defense University, interview by author, Washington, D.C., November 6, 1998).
45. Kruzel, Samuel Nelson Drew of the NSC, and special envoy Robert Frasure died in Bosnia when their armored vehicle slipped off a narrow road near Sarajevo and rolled several hundred yards down a mountainside on August 25, 1995.
46. Jenonne Walker, former director of European Affairs, National Security Council, facsimile to author, January 8, 1999.
47. Strobe Talbott, deputy secretary of state, facsimile to author, January 8, 1999.
48. Quoted in "American Survey; Lexington," *The Economist*, March 12, 1994, p. 36.
49. Goldgeier, "NATO Expansion," p. 90.
50. Christopher, *In the Stream of History*, p. 229; Richard C. Holbrooke, *To End a War* (New York: Random House, 1998), p. 117.
51. Charles Gati, interview, November 6, 1998. While disapproving of the ambassador-at-large's position in 1994, Gati later "came to respect Talbott's expert handling of the implementation and enlargement [of NATO]" (Gati, written communication to author, November 30, 1998).
52. Quotations from the Talbott memorandum appear in Michael Dobbs, "Wider Alliance Would Increase U.S. Commitments," *Washington Post*, July 5, 1995, pp. A-1, A-16; Michael R. Gordon, "U.S. Opposes Move to Rapidly Expand NATO Membership," *New York Times*, January 2, 1994, pp. A-1, A-7; and Goldgeier, "NATO Expansion," p. 90.
53. Powell, *My American Journey*, p. 564.
54. Quotations from the *New York Times*, which appear in *Facts on File*, January 28, 1993, p. 47.
55. See, for example, "Ego and Error on Gay Issue," *New York Times*, January 29, 1993, p. 26; and Mary McGrory, "For Whom the Phone Tolls," *Washington Post*, January 31, 1993, p. C-1.

56. Powell, *My American Journey*, p. 575.

57. Powell, *My American Journey*, p. 572.

58. Powell, letter, January 4, 1999.

59. Powell, *My American Journey*, p. 566.

60. Powell, *My American Journey*, p. 581.

61. Powell, letter, January 4, 1999. The general added: "By the way, I really don't know what gay admission and women pilot policies have to do with NATO expansion. We [the military] really could clap and chew gum at the same time."

62. Although a young staff member, civilian Schake increasingly became a conduit for exchanges between the Defense and State departments. She worked first in the Pentagon's J-5 European Division and, beginning in early 1994, as a special assistant to the assistant secretary of defense for strategy and requirements. She now teaches at the University of Maryland and holds the post of senior research professor, Institute for National Strategic Studies, National Defense University.

63. Although most policymakers with whom I have spoken lay PFP's birth at the door of the Pentagon and Jenonne Walker, Henry Kissinger has named Strobe Talbott as the program's "architect" ("It's an Alliance, Not a Relic," *Washington Post*, August 16, 1994, p. A-19).

64. Robert Hunter, former U.S. ambassador to NATO, Washington, D.C., interview by author, October 21, 1998.

65. Lake, interview, August 24, 1998.

66. The president, vice president, national security adviser, CIA director, chairman of the Joint Chiefs of Staff, and secretaries of State and Defense comprise this committee.

67. Christopher, *In the Stream of History*, p. 130.

68. On the flight to Hungary, State Department official Stephen Oxman briefed reporters on PFP. While walking down the aisle of the aircraft, Gati stopped to chat with *New York Times* correspondent Elaine Sciolino, who was writing an article based on Oxman's background statements. "What's your lead?" the kindly Gati asked. In response, Sciolino showed him her first paragraph, which emphasized that the Budapest meeting would advance NATO enlargement. "Are you sure that's what he said?," Gati inquired before continuing down the aisle. The Hungarian expert immediately told Talbott what Sciolino intended to transmit to her editors. Alarmed by the erroneous lead, Talbott urged Gati to set her straight. Gati demurred, saying, "this policy is your baby, you take care of it." As a result Talbott, accompanied by Gati, attempted to impress upon Sciolino the centrality of PFP to Christopher's message to the Central Europeans (Gati, interview, November 6, 1998).

69. Quoted in *Facts on File*, October 28, 1993, p. 802.

70. Asmus, interview, October 1, 1998; and *Facts on File*, October 28, 1993, p. 803. Wörner and Aspin disliked each other, possibly because, as a Defense Department analyst told me, "Wörner believed he would have made a superb American secretary of defense and resented the fact that Aspin made such a lousy one."

71. Gati, interview, November 6, 1998.

72. Kissinger, "NOT This Partnership," *Washington Post*, November 24, 1993, p. 17.

73. A progressive who advocated world-federalist views, Wallace urged cooperation rather than confrontation with Moscow. He ultimately broke with Truman and ran unsuccessfully as a "Progressive" candidate in the 1948 presidential contest.

74. Kissinger, "It's an Alliance, Not a Relic," p. A-19.

75. Brzezinski, "The Premature Partnership," *Foreign Affairs* 73, no. 2 (March/April 1994): 76. This article provides the most comprehensive statement of Brzezinski's views.

76. Brzezinski, "Premature Partnership," p. 77.

77. Brzezinski, "Premature Partnership," p. 77.

78. Brzezinski, "Premature Partnership," p. 78.

79. NATO, *Declaration of the Heads of State and Government*, Ministerial Meeting of the North Atlantic Council/North Atlantic Cooperation Council, NATO Headquarters, Brussels, January 10-11, 1994, Press Communiqué M-1(94)3, Internet, p. 4.

80. U.S. Government, *Public Papers of the President, William J. Clinton*, "The President's News Conference with Visegrad Leaders in Prague," VI (Washington, D.C.: Office of the Federal Register, National Archives and Records Administration, 1994), p. 39.

81. Vershbow, electronic mail to author, December 10, 1998.

82. Quoted in "The President's News Conference with Visegrad Leaders in Prague," p. 40.

83. Quoted in "The President's News Conference with Visegrad Leaders in Prague," p. 41.

84. Fried, interview, December 28, 1998.

85. Fried, electronic mail, December 15, 1998.

86. Fried, electronic mail to author, December 16, 1998. Although not recalling having used such flowery language to describe Fried, Munter said that he agreed with the sentiment—with the removal of "slightly" as a modifier for "crazed" (telephone interview, December 21, 1998).

87. Fried, electronic mail, December 15, 1998.

88. Vershbow, electronic mail, December 30, 1998.

89. Fried, electronic mail, December 15, 1998.

90. Fried was born on September 19, 1952 (New York City); Vershbow on July 3, 1952 (Boston); and Burns on January 28, 1956 (Buffalo).

91. Fried, interview, December 28, 1998.

92. Even as Fried and Vershbow continued to design policy, Burns left the NSC in 1995 to become spokesman of the Department of State and acting assistant secretary for Public Affairs. In 1997, President Clinton named him ambassador to Greece. Replacing Burns as collaborator with the two remaining troika members were Coit D. "Chip" Blacker, a Stanford professor (1995-96), and later, Steven Pifer (1996-97), whom the president subsequently appointed ambassador to Ukraine.

93. Quoted in "Remarks by President Clinton to the Polish Parliament July 7," *U.S. Newswire, Inc.*, LEXIS-NEXIS, July 8, 1998, p. 4.

94. Vershbow, electronic mail, December 13, 1998.

95. Even more than raising his reputation as a Russophile, critics bored in on Talbott's allegedly "anti-Israel" writings during his tenure at *Time* magazine ("Testimony February 8, 1994/ Strobe Talbott Nominee Deputy Secretary of State/Senate Foreign Relations State Department, Federal Document Clearing House, Inc., Academic Universe, pp. 1-6). Ultimately, the committee sent the nominee's name to the full Senate for confirmation on a 17 to 2 vote. Helms and Brown were the dissenters.

96. Lake, interview, August 24, 1998.

97. Asmus, electronic mail, January 3, 1999.

98. Talbott, "Why NATO Should Grow," *New York Review of Books*, August 10, 1995, pp. 27-30.

99. Talbott, "Why NATO Should Grow," p. 29.

100. Talbott, "Why NATO Should Grow," p. 30.

101. Asmus, interview, October 1, 1998.

102. State Department Central Europeanists sometimes referred to their division as the "Africa of the European Bureau" because other geographic areas— Western Europe and Russia—commanded more attention. To reflect the priority he assigned to Central Europe, Holbrooke abolished the "outdated" Office of Eastern European Affairs on his first day in office, replacing it with three new offices that "reflected the post-Cold War realities of Europe." He also banished the phrase "Eastern Europe" from the "official vocabulary," replacing it with the historically and geographically more accurate "Central Europe." See, Holbrooke, *To End a War*, p. 8 fn.

103. Lake, interview, August 24, 1998.

104. Quoted in Dobbs, "Wider Alliance Would Increase U.S. Commitments," pp. A-1, A-16; and Goldgeier, "NATO Expansion," p. 98.

105. Goldgeier, "NATO Expansion," p. 98.

106. Quoted in Ron Fournier, "Russian Opposition to NATO Expansion Another Problem for Clinton," *Associated Press*, December 6, 1994, Internet edition.

107. Fournier, "Russian Opposition," p. 1; and Martin Sieff, "Yeltsin Fears 'Cold Peace' in Europe; at Odds with U.S. on NATO, Bosnia," *Washington Times*, December 6, 1994, p. A-1.

108. An anonymous administration official quoted by the AP's Ron Fournier, "Russian Opposition," p. 1.

109. Perry, letter to author, November 30, 1998.

110. Julie Finley, District of Columbia Republican State Chairman, telephone interview by author, December 17, 1998.

111. Frank Koszorus, Jr., executive-director, Hungarian American Coalition, interview by author, Washington, D.C., July 14, 1998.

112. "Remarks in Cleveland, Ohio, at the White House Conference on Trade and Investment in Central and Eastern Europe, January 13, 1995," *Administration of William J. Clinton*, 1995, p. 44.

113. For the text of the speech, see "Remarks by President Bill Clinton at Fisher Theater, Detroit, Michigan," *Federal News Service*, LEXIS-NEXIS, October 22, 1996.

114. John F. Harris, "Clinton Vows Wider NATO in 3 Years," *Washington Post*, October 23, 1996, p. A-1; and "NATO and the Campaign," *Washington Post* (editorial), October 23, 1996, p. A-22.

115. Harris, "Clinton Vows Wider NATO," p. A-1.

116. I am indebted to my William & Mary colleague Ronald Rapoport, John Marshall professor of Government, for extracting these percentages from a data bank of the National Opinion Research Center at the University of Chicago.

Chapter 4

ℰᏠ ⅭᏒ

"Fudge Factory" Versus Ben & Jerry's

Introduction

In preceding chapters, I noted how NATO-enlargement deliberations sprang in large measure from innovative scholarship and the sustained commitment of key American legislators, German officials, distinguished intellectuals, and certain interest groups focused on post-cold war security issues. A core of experts within the executive branch—the NSC troika— ultimately converted alliance expansion from anathema to doctrine within the foreign-affairs bureaucracy. This chapter illustrates how the NATO Enlargement Ratification Office and other U.S. policymakers kept control of deliberations once underway. By means of vigilant and decisive effort, Jeremy Rosner and the Clinton administration helped frame public discourse in terms favorable to their perspective, worked closely with allies on Capitol Hill, gained inexorable momentum for their cause, and overwhelmed a disparate coalition of opponents as the final ratification vote neared.

Captain Waters to the Rescue

On July 3, 1997, President Clinton, Secretary Albright, and other notables planned to welcome to the White House's East and Blue Rooms representatives of the American Legion, the Reserve Officers Association, and other veterans' organizations for a highly publicized endorsement of NATO expansion. Seeking a dramatic twist, Rosner hoped to highlight the session by having an American veteran speak fervently of fighting side-by-side with the Poles long before the fall of the Berlin Wall. Did such cooperation between U.S. and Polish units actually take place? And, if so, could the Pentagon locate an American participant prepared to sing the praises of his Polish comrades?

After several expeditions down blind alleys, Rosner turned to John Keegan's *Six Armies in Normandy*, a book that had provided him with source material for Clinton speeches commemorating the Allied landing at Omaha Beach. Keegan described the exploits of the Polish First Armored Division, which landed in Normandy and helped close the Falaise Gap in August 1944, preventing thousands of German soldiers from fleeing eastward. During late-night fighting, Keegan reported, leaders of this unit saw the silhouetted helmets of the U.S. 90th Infantry. Second Lieutenant Jan Karcz, a troop leader in the Dragoons' 4th Squadron, recalled the scene as follows:

> An American captain ran towards me, and, still running, caught hold of me and lifted me in the air as if I had been a child . . . . That was the precise moment when the Falaise Pocket was closed. It was nearly 1800 hours and the American's name was L.E. Waters.[1]

As it turned out, Keegan, relying on a secondary source, erred in reporting this incident, for Karcz and Waters had never met. However, Rosner's colleague, Lieutenant Colonel Roger Kaplan, found another reference to Waters in John Colby's *War from the Ground Up: The Nineteenth Division in WWII*. This study accurately described Captain Laughlin E. Waters as commanding Company "G," 359th Infantry, 90th Division. In fact, he was the first American to establish contact with Polish troops. Company G was attacking through Fel to Chambois and carried the right flank of that attack. At the conclusion of the battle, Waters encountered Major W. Zgorzelski of the 10th Polish Dragoons. They saluted each other, shook hands, and extended greetings on behalf of their respective commanding generals and countries. The Waters-Zgorzelski meeting constituted the event that closed the Falaise Gap.

The Pentagon's Public Affairs Office set about the task of tracking down Waters. They found him in Los Angeles, where he serves as a senior federal judge. "Do you support NATO's expansion?" asked Kaplan, the liaison officer for veterans, bands and special events. "Well, yes," answered Waters. "That's good," the colonel answered. "If you'd said no our conversation would be over now."

Waters next received a call from Rosner, who asked if he could come to Washington to express his views on the NATO issue. At this point, the eighty-two-year-old judge—convinced that someone was putting him on—said he was getting up in years, did not travel much, and wasn't sure about a cross-country journey. He also emphasized that his judicial post prevented his taking positions on political matters.

Countering this diffidence, Rosner inquired if Waters would consider flying to the nation's capital to introduce the president of the United States at 1600 Pennsylvania Avenue. In response to Waters' question, "What should I say?" Rosner replied, "Anything you want, as long as you don't trespass on the president's time." "That's a fairly broad invitation to extend to a Republican!" chuckled Waters. Partisan considerations aside, he agreed to come east, provided that NERO cover the cost of plane tickets for him and his wife.

After Judge and Mrs. Waters had settled into a downtown Marriott, Rosner dropped by for a get-acquainted call, during which he hoped to review the judge's "three-minute" introduction of Clinton. At first Waters resisted showing Rosner his text, which he was still revising. The jurist teasingly reminded his host of the separation of powers between the executive and judicial arms of government. Despite Mrs. Waters' continued misgivings, the judge finally relented and read Rosner a roughly hewn copy of his remarks. Not only did Waters refer to an animal's derrière in his lengthy comments, but he refused to say a word about NATO's growth, lest he plunge into the political thicket from which he was ethically excluded. Upon hearing the material, Rosner commented, "Very Eloquent."

No matter how much Rosner pleaded and cajoled, Judge Waters remained noncommittal on the length of his statement, showed no inclination to delete earthy references, and simply did not have a final text to pass along to the White House as requested by the chief of staff's office. Waters did, however, delete certain portions of his notes at Rosner's request.[2]

Just before the festivities began, the usually unflappable Rosner found himself on pins and needles. He had cooked up the big idea for the unknown, unpredictable Waters to introduce the chief executive; his neck would be in a noose if the judge embarrassed the dignitaries, the audience, and the leader of the free world—with C-SPAN cameras recording every word.

"I saw my career in Washington going up in flames," Rosner laughingly recalled.[3]   Fried, seated next to Rosner, said "Jeremy was sweating bullets."[4]

Vice President Gore commenced the program, which eventually led to the president of the Reserve Officers Association delivering an extremely laudatory presentation of Waters. Once at the microphone, the dignified judge winged his remarks when light from the television cameras obscured his yellow foolscap text. Waters duly observed that the U.S. government hadn't always said such nice things about him, and went on to recount his unit's participation in closing and sealing the Falaise Gap.

After "G" Company was relieved following the successful battle, the unit came upon horses that German soldiers had released from a nearby stud farm. Because the men—most of whom hailed from Texas and Oklahoma—deserved a treat, Waters allowed them to ride to their bivouac area on horseback. The captain noticed that his own steed had suffered a shrapnel wound in its right hip, prompting him to ask Lieutenant Colonel Murray Franklin, a medical officer, to treat the wound. After animated exchanges of salty words, the colonel—who maintained that he was "not a horse doctor"—grudgingly sprinkled sulfur powder on the animal's wound. To show his pique, he instructed his medical orderly to scrawl on the official report of the incident: "Captain L.E. Waters—horse's ass."

While the president doubled up with laughter, Waters concluded that, if ever again faced with enemy forces, he would want Polish troops at his side in view of their determination, toughness, and bravery. After the proceedings concluded, Rosner called Waters to commend him for being the hit of the program.[5]

The initiative, creativity, and attention to detail that Rosner devoted to the veterans' event illustrated the reason why policymakers like Asmus and others congratulated themselves for having selected Rosner to head the NATO Expansion Ratification Office, which had begun functioning four months earlier.

I. NERO's Goals and Strategy

Soon after his appointment, Rosner sent a memorandum to Secretary Albright, National Security Adviser Berger, and other top officials conveying his "initial thoughts" on the strategy for enlarging NATO in particular, and for advancing U.S. foreign policy goals in general.[6] As noted in the Introduction, Rosner focused not on squeaking by with sixty-seven votes in the Senate, but registering a "good" win for the NATO protocols. He defined such a victory as one which demonstrated "broad, enthusiastic US support, both to make our new security guarantees meaningful, and to strengthen the US as it pursues other goals in Europe and elsewhere." Furthermore, Rosner underscored the importance of gaining ratification "in a way that does not harm, and hopefully advances, other US objectives, such as constructive relations with Russia." He called for a concerted effort to tone down anti-Russian rhetoric and accentuated the desirability of an outcome that served as a "showcase of bipartisanship," given the need to strengthen the political base for future development of internationalist policies and because of the impossibility of achieving ratification without GOP votes.

In the same document, Rosner outlined a strategy that included four elements:

* **Take nothing for granted:** Several factors augured well for ratification: eighty percent support for recent NATO-related votes in Congress; bipartisan backing; strong administration leadership; favorable polling figures; and focused ethnic constituencies. Yet increased assertiveness, partisanship, and volatility have characterized congressional behavior on foreign policy since the end of the cold war. Thus, don't assume that past supporters will remain on board; don't assume that past opponents lie beyond conversion. "Especially if this is to be a 'good' win . . . we must pursue the ratification effort aggressively, broadly, and doggedly."

* **Manage the Pro-Enlargement Coalition**. Success required spreading credit for achieving enlargement in a bipartisan manner: Thus, administration pronouncements would have to balance costs and force structures, and avoid either excessive antagonism or conciliation toward Russia. "While most of the votes we need to pick up . . . are from Democrats

on the left, the most serious prospect for defeat entails a broad defection by Republicans on the right."

* **Lay the Groundwork Now for the National (and International) Effort Later**. Between mid-winter and the July 1997 NATO summit in Madrid, the lack of attention focused on the alliance suggested that the administration should downplay "retail" persuasion of the public and Congress in favor of forging a strong, bipartisan consensus on Capitol Hill; coordinating ratification and sequencing strategies within Washington and between Washington and U.S. allies; and building support among the narrow interest groups which themselves declaimed the virtues of enlargement.

* **Define the Issue in the Broadest Terms, and with the Highest Stakes**. Advocates of expansion must stress not only the importance of the Senate vote with respect to adding signatories to the Washington Treaty, but also the vote's impact on NATO's prestige, the future of Europe, and U.S. internationalism writ large. "Although 'isolationist' epithets should be held in reserve, the broader the lens and the higher the stakes, the stronger the President's hand on the Hill."

Finally, Rosner detailed the early steps that NERO and the rest of the executive branch should take to achieve enlargement. First, he stressed the need to: signal to Congress the high priority that the administration assigned to this issue; convince lawmakers that inclusiveness and bipartisanship would characterize the White House's ratification drive; encourage creation of a Senate leadership group to meet regularly with the president's foreign-policy team and to attend the alliance's upcoming summit in Madrid; and organize meals and meetings between legislators and members of the executive branch, including the president.

Second, before the mid-1997 NATO gathering in Madrid, the administration should forge an agreement with alliance allies, formalizing the ratification process for new members and the order in which countries would receive invitations for affiliation. The sequencing should convey a "maximum sense" of momentum and alliance cohesion.

Third, NERO should reach out to a wide variety of business, labor, veterans', religious, and artistic/intellectual groups so that observers would not perceive NATO expansion as solely a priority for Polish Americans and other ethnic constituencies.

Fourth, the memo noted that while the *New York Times* and some foreign-policy notables adamantly opposed enlargement, a 1994 Chicago Council on Foreign Relations survey showed that a higher percentage of elites (59-37) than members of the general public (42-32) backed expansion, pointing to the need to mobilize elite opinion as part of creating a sense of momentum.[7]

Fifth, Rosner recommended complementing regular meetings with selected reporters and columnists by strengthening "our rapid response capability to attacks and adverse events, nurturing 'niche' coverage on various sub-issues, and working with local editorial boards."

Finally, he proposed setting expectations about a "sufficient" level of public attention to the issue, lest critics continue to decry the absence of a national debate on NATO's growth. After all, "a 'good win' . . . must include a sense of broad public support after a full debate." Nevertheless, Rosner cautioned that expansion advocates keep their expectation realistic, inasmuch as forty-seven percent of the public claimed to have heard "nothing" about NATO on the eve of the Senate's vote in 1949.[8]

Organizing NERO

As mentioned earlier, NERO suffered chronically from a lack of staff. By recruiting Munter, the office gained a bright, dynamic Foreign Service professional, familiar with the State Department's inner workings and conversant with, and personally committed to, U.S. interests in Central Europe. After all, Munter's service at the U.S. embassies in Prague and Warsaw had given him intimate knowledge of the region. Despite his diplomatic bearing and penchant for order, Munter also brought a keen sense of humor to the office.

Although job descriptions remained flexible, Rosner became NERO's "Mr. Outside," while Munter assumed the role of "Mr. Inside"—or, as Munter amusingly described their division of labor, "Jeremy went out and broke the china; I followed behind, sweeping up the shards." In a typically self-deprecating manner, Munter also described himself as "Jeremy's sherpa."[9] For the year beginning in March 1997, Rosner usually concentrated on Capitol Hill and personal contacts with the print and electronic media. Then for the three months before the final vote, he benefitted from having Mary Daly as his legislative right-hand: A thirty-seven-year-old graduate of the University of Virginia who had also studied

Three Zones Theory[1]

Munter established rapport with audiences from Savannah to Salt Lake City by advancing his satirical "three zone" explanation for political behavior in Central Europe. In elaborating why Czechoslovakia had split into the Czech and Slovak Republics, Munter posited the existence of three zones—"vodka," "wine," and "beer"—in Central Europe where the people take on the attributes of their given drink. Familiarity breeds contempt, and one country cannot form part of two regions, which explains Czechoslovakia's breakup. The Poles, he argued, are fiery and prone to self-destruction, like the vodka they imbibe. As a result, they have always been at the throats of the Russians and vice versa because Russia also occupies the vodka zone. For their part, the Czechs are stolid and filling like the beer that characterizes their zone. Thus, relations between the Czechs and beer-zone Germans have been troubled for years. And the Slovaks and Hungarians are smooth, romantic, and sometimes even duplicitous like the wine they drink. Consequently, these two people labor under heavy historical baggage. Had Czechoslovakia remained a single entity, which spilled over into two zones, its number of adversaries would have doubled.

In promoting NATO expansion, Munter used the three-zone hypothesis to set audiences up for his "-ia" theory on the number of countries an enlarged NATO should admit. Not one of the names of the current sixteen members of NATO in English—Britain, France, Germany, Holland, etc.—carries the suffix "-ia." Now, among the five countries under consideration, two—Romania and Slovenia—bear the "-ia" suffix. The others—Poland, Hungary, the Czech Republic—do not. To keep the alliance coherent, he argued, admit only the Poles, Czechs, and Hungarians.

1.   Munter, facsimile to author, December 16, 1998.

theology at Yale, Daly had amassed numerous awards since joining the Foreign Service in 1984. Having worked for Senator James M. Jeffords (R-VT), she knew her way around the Capitol. Thus, she gave and arranged briefings for congressional staffers, responded to questions from legislators' offices, and kept NERO's secret scorecard on each lawmaker's stance on NATO's future. Daly's training as a postulant in the Episcopal Church afforded her the calm and perspective required to perform such a key role in the hectic run-up to ratification.

Munter frequently reached the State Department at 6:30 a.m. to get a head start on the day's challenges and to be in the office for more of Europe's work day. He took care of organizing and equipping the office, monitored the cable traffic to keep Rosner up to date on relevant diplomatic developments, directed an outreach program to constituencies who resonated with the issue, maintained contact with the "virtual office" of dozens of specialists spread throughout executive agencies, and sent dispatches including the weekly *NATO Enlargement News Alert* to supporters, potential supporters, and the press.

Despite the demands of Washington, Rosner and Munter traveled extensively, at least during the first few months after NERO opened its doors. They often following an ad hoc agenda. For example, Rosner remembers one appearance on a Fairfax County public-access TV show that aired on the same night as the Academy Awards, reaching, at best, a highly motivated audience. (The effort paid dividends, however, because one the viewers—perhaps the only one—turned out to be SFRC staff member Steve Biegun, who noted the unusually ambitious outreach effort in behalf of the alliance's growth.) The administration's NATO point man also flew to Portland State University in Oregon, only to find just five people on hand to hear him.[10] On one occasion, Munter scrambled from Salt Lake City to Omaha to Indianapolis to countless other locations, briefing business leaders, editorial boards, and academic audiences. The office also sent him to Bonn, Brussels, Bucharest, and Prague to propagate the enlargement message. In addition, he flew to Madrid to plan the arrival of the congressional delegation that would accompany the president to the summit there in mid-1997. Ambassador Rey's arrival in November 1997 provided NERO a deft public speaker whose ambitious schedule allowed Rosner and Munter to concentrate on inside-the-beltway priorities.

From May to December 1997, Christine Wormuth joined NERO as a presidential management intern.[11] A 1991 Williams College graduate who had earned an M.A. in Public Affairs at the University of Maryland

and served a year as a Congressional Fellow, Wormuth began her stint as a "foot soldier" before assuming ever-greater responsibilities involving legislative and media relations. Her comparative advantage lay in her knowledge of NATO-related cost questions, security issues, and the labyrinthine Pentagon, where she had worked before coming to NERO.[12] While in the office, she also designed and wrote the *NATO Enlargement Alerts*, tracked newspaper editorials, drafted speeches, researched and wrote background papers for Rosner's meetings on Capitol Hill, prepared editorial boards for Rosner's visits, ran the interagency working group that coordinated congressional testimony, and led a contingent of veterans', religious, and ethnic organizations to examine the Visegrad countries' militaries in October 1997. Although funding constraints prevented her continuing on the NATO project, Rosner and Munter called her a "terrific catch" for NERO during her tenure.[13]

The United States Information Agency (USIA) detailed Andrew Koss to work in the office beginning in September 1997. Koss, a graduate of Colby College, proved a splendid writer. He produced a fact-laden twenty-four-page booklet on the alliance's future titled *The Enlargement of NATO: Why Adding Poland, Hungary, and the Czech Republic to NATO Strengthens American National Security*.[14] Although Federal law prohibits USIA personnel from trying to influence domestic public opinion, Koss remained extremely busy monitoring the overseas' press, interacting with foreign reporters, coordinating with delegations from throughout Europe, gathering polling data collected by the USIA in Russia and Central Europe, and undertaking special projects.

For a month, NERO also received a helping hand from Captain Walter Steiner, on leave from NATO headquarters in Brussels. Steiner assisted in arranging the February 11, 1998 event that brought the three Visegrad countries' foreign ministers to the State Department's ornate Franklin Room for a meeting with the chief executive, cabinet members, the chairman of the Joint Chiefs of Staff, senators Roth and Biden, and a chorus of the faithful. On this occasion, President Clinton signed the transmittal documents to the Senate that proposed the addition of Poland, Hungary, and the Czech Republic to NATO, describing his initiative as "a major stride forward for America, the Alliance, and the stability and unity of all of Europe."[15]

Even before Rosner had assembled his staff, he had spent months both at the Carnegie Endowment for Peace and then the State Department immersing himself in the literature concerning Senate treaty-making, beginning with Professor W. Stull Holt's classic study of *Treaties Defeated by the Senate*.[16] He also pored over information concerning each of the one hundred senators' biographies, voting records, constituencies, NATO statements, public utterances about the alliance, and foreign-policy advisers. Rosner's voracious reading enabled him to determine where senators stood on ratification and which amendments each senator would likely offer. Slightly more than four months after creating NERO, Rosner predicted that the Senate would vote 82 to 18 to expand NATO—just one vote off the mark.[17] When, early in 1998, Daly heard from a committee staff member that the majority leader planned to delay the NATO vote, Rosner quizzed her thoroughly about the source. This information enabled him to determine accurately the motivation underlying the postponement.[18]

But despite the conclusion of Rosner's astute assessment, he would not allow NERO to slip into complacency. Colleagues joked that by adopting an office name that reduced to the acronym NERO, Rosner really sought to imply that "the administration will not fiddle while NATO burns."[19]

Rosner realized that the end of the cold war presaged an entirely new era in foreign affairs, one that could prove inhospitable to NATO expansion if certain groups coalesced to oppose the change. Although liberals had expressed more skepticism, Rosner concluded that their internationalism and support for the president would lead the great majority of Democrats to vote in favor, though reluctantly so in some cases. Rosner's study of history convinced him that conservative Republicans posed the greatest threat to ratification, given the deep enmity between Clinton and the GOP's congressional leadership.

A new period in international affairs may have dawned, but the aftermath of the cold war also exhibited similarities to 1919, when the Senate rejected the Versailles Treaty. As noted earlier, both periods featured conservative, highly partisan Republicans chairing the Foreign Relations Committee; and just as Senator Henry Cabot Lodge loathed Woodrow Wilson, Jesse Helms cherished a profound contempt for Bill Clinton. Then, as now, the Republicans sought to recapture the White House, which it had held for many years before losing to an upstart incumbent. Finally, the resolution of a protracted international crisis in both eras heightened the public's desire for attention to domestic issues.

At the time NERO opened its door, Secretary Albright told Rosner and Munter that congressional Democrats were complaining to her that

the United States was "strangling Russia's infant democracy in its crib."[20]
Rosner reiterated his belief, derived from voracious reading about the
Senate, that conservatives, not liberal internationalists, eviscerate treaties.
In particular, ratification could become extremely problematic if conser-
vatives wary of foreign entanglements should align with two, mostly
Republican, groups: military hawks, who believed that the addition of
states would weaken the alliance, and Russophobes, who feared that
Moscow might gain influence over NATO as a quid pro quo for
acquiescing in new members.[21]

To assuage such suspicions, he stressed the imperative of addressing
their three major concerns, namely, that (1) Russia receive neither a veto
nor a major voice in NATO's transformation; (2) Washington not bear a
disproportionate share of enlargement costs; and (3) expansion not dilute
the alliance's central mission of collective territorial defense

Russian Question

NATO confronted the Russian question in the spring of 1997. On
May 27, NATO Secretary General Javier Solana and Foreign Minister
Yevgeny Primakov signed the "Founding Act on Mutual Relations,
Cooperation and Security between NATO and the Russia Federation."[22]
Section I of the accord commits the signatories to the norms of international
behavior reflected in the UN Charter and the Helsinki Final Act, while
stressing respect for the sovereignty of states, their independence, and
the peaceful resolution of conflicts. Both parties agreed that states enjoy
the inherent right to choose the means to ensure their security, and that
they should work to fortify the OSCE, with the aim of creating a common
zone of security and stability in Europe. Although couched in general
terms, Section I represented Russia's tacit acceptance of the Visegrad
countries' joining the alliance.[23] Section II of the Act established a
NATO-Russia Joint Permanent Council as a forum to discuss political
and security issues, to develop common initiatives and, "once consensus
has been reached, make joint decisions, if appropriate, and take joint
actions on a case-by-case basis." Such cooperation could include
peacekeeping operations under UN Security Council or OSCE
responsibility.

Section III keyed on appropriate topics for consultation and
cooperation, including conflict resolution, peacekeeping, preventing

proliferation of weapons of mass destruction, conversion of defense industries, defense-related environmental concerns, and civil-emergency preparedness.

Section IV reiterated NATO's statement, issued on December 10, 1996, that the alliance had no intention, no plan, and no reason to deploy nuclear weapons on the territory of new members. In addition, this section restated NATO's goal, articulated in mid-March 1997, "to carry out its collective defense and other missions by ensuring the necessary interoperability, integration and capability for reinforcement rather than by additional permanent stationing of substantial combat forces." In this pledge, NATO signaled to Moscow that it did not expect to station troops in Central Europe except in emergencies.[24] Moreover, the two parties reaffirmed their intention to further reduce armaments under the treaty governing Conventional Forces in Europe.[25]

Secretary Albright's Appearance

Foreign Relations Committee Chairman Helms worried that under this ostensibly benign "Founding Act," dogs in the Kremlin might wind up wagging NATO's tail. On the eve of Secretary Albright's early October 1997 appearance before his committee, avid expansion proponents on Helms's staff asked Rosner if he would like to know the line of questioning the North Carolina Republican would pursue. In fact, they provided NERO with an advance copy of the question that Helms would ask Albright with respect to his fear that Russia might enjoy a veto over new NATO members. Rosner tested various responses on Helms's aides before the secretary's appearance.

The hearing unfolded according to script, except that—much to the delight of NERO—Albright hugged Helms in the committee room while waiting to testify.[26] After the chairman's crisp introduction cum questions, the secretary deftly wove the following statement into her presentation:

> I know that some are concerned that this relationship with Russia may actually go too far. You have asked me for an affirmation, Mr. Chairman, that the North Atlantic Council remains NATO's supreme decisionmaking body. Let me say it clearly: It docs and it will. The NATO-Russia Founding Act gives Russia no opportunity to dilute, delay, or block NATO decisions.[27]

Born in Czechoslovakia and twice a refugee from Europe's conflicts, Albright could credibly remind Senators that

> . . . there are dangers of Europe's past. It is easy to forget this, but for centuries, virtually every European nation treated virtually every other as a military threat. That pattern was broken only when NATO was born and only in the half of Europe NATO covered. With NATO, each member's security came to depend on cooperation with others, not competition. It is also one reason why we need a larger NATO which extends its positive influence to Europe's other half.[28]

One month later, the placated foreign relations chairman along with Senator Biden circulated a "Dear Colleague" letter, asserting that "enlargement is squarely in the American national interest." The missive also showed that Albright had satisfied Helms's concerns about Russia.[29] Indeed, throughout the drive toward ratification, the secretary's ability to speak convincingly the idiom of "captive nations" and "Yalta betrayal" endeared her to conservative Republicans who had cut their eye teeth on such invective. The Stetson hat she wore also conveyed the message, "I'm no effete intellectual; I mean business!"

Albright's appearance before Helms's committee pleased Rosner on another count. The secretary of state had garnered substantially more press coverage than a second hearing, held two days later, on the pros (Brzezinski and former UN Ambassador Jeane Kirkpatrick) and cons (Johns Hopkins scholar Mandelbaum and Ambassador Jonathan Dean). In a memorandum to the National Security Council's front office, Rosner indicated that NERO was "coordinating interagency prep" for nine more Senate committee hearings in October and November scheduled by the Foreign Relations, Appropriations, and Budget panels.[30] Pro-expansions also took comfort in meager concern about adding several countries to NATO voiced to pollsters by voters during the last parliamentary elections in Russia.[31]

With respect to expansion costs, in early 1997 the Pentagon estimated that the first round of enlargement would carry a price tag of $27 to $35 billion over a thirteen-year period, with the U.S. share totaling $1.5 to $2 billion spread over a decade. This study included costs that would be borne by each nation's own defense budgets—particularly the Visegrad states, should they earmark billions of dollars to modernize their armed forces. In the fall of 1997, NATO authorities released an estimate of $1.5 billion, with the U.S. share falling to $400 million over ten years.

The sharply lower figure arose after on-site visits convinced specialists that the military facilities of the three prospective members were better than previously assumed. More fundamentally, the $1.5 billion amount only described what the alliance would incur as an organization, to be funded by the member states with the United States picking up approximately one-quarter of the bill.

Critics jumped on the new, lower estimate as evidence that proponents of enlargement would stoop to distorting the facts so as to strengthen their case. Throughout the process, however, NERO strove to explain the methodological differences underlying the two figures, and to introduce lawmakers to the arcana of NATO budgeting. Rosner insisted that the administration not downplay or "low ball" the expected costs, lest lawmakers later claim they had been duped on the financial implications of expansion. The administration sought to remain objective, continuing to disseminate the Pentagon's number as well as NATO's. He feared that legislators would react negatively toward future rounds of expansion if they felt deceived over the costs of accession for Poland, Hungary, and the Czech Republic.[32]

Among perspective members, the Poles helped to allay fears that accepting the Visegrad nations would undermine NATO's effectiveness. NATO's Partnership for Peace involved joint operations between member-state forces and the militaries of Central Europe. The Polish contingents distinguished themselves as well-trained, highly motivated professionals who would, in Albright's words, prove themselves "security producers" rather than "security consumers." The Hungarian and Czech units performed adequately, but these countries also helped their case for membership by raising their defense budgets to two percent of GDP—enough to meet their commitments for military modernization.

Intra-Bureaucratic Hurdles

Although established with the blessing of the secretary, NERO needed to win over, or learn to work with, several State Department offices: the Bureau of European and Canadian Affairs, some of whose leaders initially voiced profound skepticism about enlargement; the Office of New Independent States, where "Russia-firsters" continued to display reservations about the impact of expansion; and the Bureau of Legislative Affairs—known as "H" for "Hill" in bureaucratic argot—where NERO's need to work with legislators might conflict with the broad congressional agenda of other parts of the department. Rosner recalls that Assistant Secretary Barbara Mills Larkin had weighed in against NERO's creation, fearful that the new office might attempt to monopolize administration-Capitol Hill communications over NATO.[33]

In contrast, Assistant Secretary for Public Affairs Nicholas Burns, a former member of the NSC troika and an NSC colleague of Rosner's, phoned the NERO office as soon as it began operations to offer his "complete cooperation." Rosner's and Munter's inclusion of the spokesman's office in their activities—particularly in lending a hand with NATO-related speaking engagements and publications—helped to nurture even warmer relations between NERO and State's Bureau of Public Affairs. In keeping with overall administration policy, Rosner agreed to present himself as only an unnamed source in "background" briefings to the press, leaving major pronouncements on NATO to Albright and her spokesmen—first Burns and later James Rubin.

As months passed, NERO learned to work with most other Foggy Bottom offices and vice versa. NERO's relations with the European Bureau warmed as soon as Marc Grossman became assistant secretary. The former ambassador to Turkey shared a warm friendship with Asmus, who became his deputy assistant secretary. Both Clinton's close relationship with Yeltsin and the NATO-Russia Founding Act reduced friction with officials who worried that augmenting the alliance would antagonize Moscow. In addition, the Poles, Hungarians, and Czechs had made a concerted effort to improve ties with Russia.

NERO's relationship with the Bureau of Legislative Affairs had its trials and tribulations. According to several observers, Larkin never made her peace with Rosner. An Albright confidant who had held key posts with Senators Dianne Feinstein (D-CA) and the late Terry Sanford (D-NC) before coming to the department, the legislative affairs chief fought tenaciously to manage all exchanges between the State Department and Congress. After all, myriad headaches figured on her agenda, including attacks on the agency's budget, legislation to constrict the foreign-affairs bureaucracy, hostility toward funding for international financial institutions, and demands for UN restructuring. Losing control over any single issue, especially NATO, might impair the lawyer-bureaucrat's ability to negotiate with legislators. While understanding her territoriality, Rosner doubted that Larkin would devote sufficient time and personnel to alliance enlargement inasmuch as she believed the Senate would approve the protocols easily. Moreover, the "H" bureau, like most government agencies, had to respond to the crisis of the moment.[34]   Even worse from NERO's perspective, Larkin underlined the importance of concentrating on liberal Democrats, not the conservative Republicans whom Rosner felt held the key to victory. Above all, Rosner strenuously insisted that only one executive branch official should make final decisions concerning approaches to Congress about NATO. Otherwise, the administration's message could become garbled, with lawmakers seizing upon any perceived division in the executive's ranks to pursue political horse-trading.

In 1993, Clinton had gained approval of the North American Free Trade Agreement—considered a "near-death experience" by White House insiders—only after showering both personal attention and legislative concessions on grasping lawmakers. Chastened by this every-legislator-for-himself episode that Rosner had seen first-hand while at the NSC, the NERO head endeavored to instill a sense of inevitability about NATO's future, thereby preventing any senator from believing that he or she alone could provide the marginal vote required for passage. Such an approach, the NERO chief argued, "avoided heartburn for the staff, squandering the president's time, and frittering away resources [needed for deal-making]."[35]

In addition, pro-expansionists' continual stress on the West's moral obligation to Central Europe—for example, lawmakers responded to the theme of Poland's "betrayal" at Yalta—cast the debate as one that transcended petty politics. "Even [Senator] Al D'Amato and [Senator] Bob Byrd who are always on the prowl to cut deals for their states would have had a hard time squeezing the White House for a bridge or federal office building in exchange for voting to add these countries to NATO," said a congressional staff member who asked that his name not be used.

Rosner invited legislative affairs representatives to take part in strategy meetings. While Larkin sent representatives Michael Clausen, Thomas Wolfson, and James Hamilton to these sessions, she continued to bristle at NERO's perceived intrusion into her bailiwick. She went so far as to gain authority for the "H" bureau to sign off on any memoranda between Rosner's team and the secretary of state, waiting an unheard-of seven months to clear an innocuous March/April 1996 communication that urged the administration to back an early Senate vote on expansion.[36]

In late March 1998, the SFRC began preparing the final version of the NATO protocols before the floor vote. Larkin insisted on attending this "mark-up" session, telling Rosner that she would present him at the appropriate time during the committee meeting. After all, she knew the senators better; Rosner had worked mainly with their key lieutenants.

Instead of making an introduction, the assistant secretary took her place with the senators and their staff aides, even though she possessed no expertise in "out-of-area" missions and other issues under discussion. Only when Rosner made it clear that he was about to speak up with or without her invitation did Larkin reluctantly ask him to join her at the witness table.[37]

Outreach Activities

Debate over NATO expansion burgeoned in government and the academy, but the issue failed to precipitate interest among rank-and-file citizens. Consequently, NERO feared that if only foreign-policy elites engaged this issue, opponents might take a populist tack in persuading thirty-four senators to turn thumbs-down on enlargement. Thus, Rosner and Munter sought as many endorsements as possible so that, when challenged about the breadth of support for the protocols, Senators backing expansion could brandish a list of sympathetic organizations and individuals.

Reflecting upon NERO's strategy, Rosner recalled the story that former Speaker of the House Thomas "Tip" O'Neill recounted about his first race for elective office, a seat on the Cambridge City Council. The night before the vote, one of his high school teachers, who lived across the street, told him, "Tom, I'm going to vote for you tomorrow even though you didn't ask me to."

"I was shocked," he wrote later. "Why, Mrs. O'Brien, I've lived across from you for eighteen years. I cut your grass in the summer. I shovel your walk in the winter. I didn't think I had to ask for your vote."

"Tom," she replied, "let me tell you something: people like to be asked."

Although he failed to win the council post, O'Neill took this advice to heart: in the future, he never failed to ask and he never lost another election.[38]

A tale about Franklin Roosevelt also reflected Rosner's leave-nothing-to-chance outlook. After a member of his brain trust had expounded a bright idea to the canny FDR, the president reportedly responded: "Well, you've convinced me. Now go out and convince everyone else, so I'll have no choice in the matter."[39]

Thus, Rosner, Munter, and their allies resolved to ask early and often for support from dozens of groups in hopes of leaving the Senate with no choice in the matter. When necessary, they would tender the request in person; when possible, they would rely upon a highly respected figure among the target populations to do their bidding. In keeping with this approach, they persuaded Generals Shalikashvili and Robert "Tip" Osterthaler to address veterans' groups. NERO tapped Detroit Mayor Dennis W. Archer to present their case before the U.S. Conference of Mayors.[40] The Polish American Congress and other ethnic groups pitched in to obtain the backing of state legislators and governors. And John T. "Jack" Joyce, president of the International Union of Bricklayers, pursued an endorsement from the AFL-CIO. Even more important, Defense Secretary Cohen and Secretary Albright held one-on-one sessions with AFL-CIO president John Sweeney, while Polish President Walesa made a direct telephone appeal to the union leader.[41]

As illustrated in Table 2, NERO helped obtain endorsements from fifteen state legislatures, more than one hundred top foreign-policy experts, and thirty-three political, retired-military, and ethnic organizations.[42] At NERO's behest, the departments of State and Defense jointly sponsored a trip so that representatives of veterans' groups, as well as religious and ethnic nongovernmental organizations, could tour military bases in Poland, Hungary, and the Czech Republic.[43]

The New Atlantic Initiative (NAI)—headquartered in Washington's conservative American Enterprise Institute—did yeoman's work in mustering elite support for the NATO legislation. Partially in response to the so-called "Experts' Letter" disseminated by expansion foes in June 1997, four NAI staff members, including Executive Director Jeffrey Gedmin and AEI resident scholar Joshua Muravchik, drafted a statement for signing by distinguished individuals supportive of extending the alliance to Central Europe. This effort, which began in early August, bore fruit on September 9 when the Initiative released a letter bearing signatures of 136 prominent foreign-policy experts, businessmen, scholars, and former government officials,[44] representing a "Who's Who" of the Washington establishment. Among the ranks of notables appeared the names of every living former secretary of state, five former national security advisers, six former secretaries of defense, eight former senators, and six former representatives, as well as former vice presidents Walter Mondale and Dan Quayle. At a press conference sponsored by the New Atlantic Initiative on September 9, 1997, Lake, Kirkpatrick, Holbrooke, and

Table 2: Key Groups, Organizations, and Individuals Endorsing NATO Expansion

Category	Date	Number	Composition
Former Presidents	Various	3	Ford, Bush, and Carter
Former Vice Presidents	9/9/97	2	Quayle, Mondale
Former Secretaries of State	9/9/97	8	Baker, Christopher, Eagleburger, Haig, Kissinger, Rogers, Shultz, and Vance
Former members of the Senate	9/9/97	12	Bentsen, Boren, Brown, DeConcini, Dole, Exon, Huddleston, Melcher, Packwood, Percy, Sasser, Simon
Former National Security Advisers	9/9/97	5	Allen, Brzezinski, Lake, McFarlane, and Powell
Former Secretaries of Defense	9/9/97	6	Carlucci, Cheney, Clifford, Laird, Perry, and Rumsfeld
Former CIA Directors	9/9/97	2	Webster and Woolsey
Former UN Representatives	9/9/97	1	Kirkpatrick
Senior Military Officers	2/3/98	60	
Organized Labor	1/30/98	1	AFL-CIO
Ethnic Action by House	Various	20	Central and East European Coalition, including 17 affiliated organizations (9/17/97); American Latvian Association (9/17/97); Armenian Assembly of America (9/17/97); Belarussian Congress Committee of America (9/17/97); Bulgarian Institute for Research and Analysis (9/17/97); Congress of Romanian Americans, Inc. (9/17/97); Czechoslovak National Council of America (9/17/97); Estonian National Council of America (9/17/97); Georgian Association in the U.S.A., Inc. (9/17/97); Hungarian American Coalition (11/5/97); Joint Baltic American National Committee (9/17/97); Lithuanian American Community, Inc. (9/17/97); National Federation of American Hungarians (9/17/97); Polish American Congress (5/2/97); Slovak League of America (9/17/97); Ukrainian Congress Committee of America, Inc. (9/17/97); Ukrainian National Association, Inc. (9/17/97); US-Baltic Foundation (9/17/97); American Coalition for Central and Eastern Europe (2/1/98); and Federation of Polish Americans

Table 2: Key Groups, Organizations, and Individuals Endorsing NATO Expansion (Contd.)

Category		Number	Members
Veterans		9	AMVETS (9/9/97), the American G.I. Forum (8/10/97), The American Legion (9/4/97), Association of the U.S. Army (2/3/98), Jewish War Veterans of America (8/28/97), Marine Corps League (2/18/97), National Guard Association of the U.S. (12/7/97), Reserve Officers Association of the U.S. (6/21/97), and Veterans of Foreign Wars (8/21/97)
Governors' offices	Various	6	Florida (11/24/97), Illinois (10/28/97), Michigan (3/24/97), New Mexico (3/13/97), Ohio (6/11/97), and Puerto Rico (1/16/98)
State Senates	Various	11	California (7/11/97), Connecticut (2/15/96), Delaware (1/28/97), Georgia (3/11/97), Illinois (5/22/97), Massachusetts (10/16/95), Michigan (4/30/97), New Jersey (2/5/96), Pennsylvania (10/7/96), Rhode Island (2/6/97), and South Carolina (4/2/97)
State Legislatures	Various	4	Colorado (3/20/97), Illinois (5/22/97), Michigan (3/19/97), and New Jersey (6/26/96)
Civic, Policy, and Political		3	Council of State Governments (12/1/97), National Governor's Association (2/24/98), and U.S. Conference of Mayors (6/24/97)
Religious/Human Rights		4	American Jewish Committee (6/26/97), Anti-Defamation League of B'nai B'rith (2/13/98), Hungarian Human Rights Foundation (9/17/97), and Jewish Institute for National Security Affairs (1/30/98)

Source: NERO, "NATO Enlargement Fact Sheet," NATO Enlargement Ratification Office, U.S. Department of State, Washington, D.C. (mimeo.).

Wolfowitz released the endorsements at the Andrew Mellon Auditorium where representatives of twelve countries had signed the Washington Treaty forty-eight years before.[45]

NERO and the administration also homed in on former presidents. While George Bush and Gerald Ford readily agreed to back NATO expansion, former President Carter appeared less likely to come aboard. To begin with, he was worried about the impact on Russia, and was impressed by the criticisms offered by fellow Georgian Sam Nunn, an outspoken opponent of expansion. In addition, Carter seldom lent his name to policy matters in which he had no direct involvement.

Undaunted, Rosner contacted an associate at the Carter Center in Atlanta, who expressed doubts over the ex-chief executive's willingness to endorse NATO's admission of new members, but suggested that a personal visit and briefing by Secretary Albright might bring Carter around. In December 1997, Albright wrote the former president, emphasizing the importance of NATO enlargement for the Clinton administration, laying out their reasons for seeking this goal, and stressing how much she and the president valued his counsel. She also indicated a readiness to meet with Carter in Washington or to dispatch a top aide to Atlanta, whichever would prove more convenient.

Before Rosner could explore the possibility of sending an official to Atlanta, he received word that the former president would visit Washington for appointments with Clinton and Albright on January 24, 1998. Rosner ensured that NATO appeared on the agenda in both meetings. After the Oval Office session, Carter sent letters to five key senators endorsing expansion. Upon Rosner's request to Carter's staff, the ex-president also agreed to the public release of these communications. Two factors contributed to this unexpected action: first, Carter realized that the Senate would probably approve the protocols with or without additional endorsements; and, second, his concerns about a damaging adverse reaction in Russia were assuaged. On the same visit to Washington, he wanted a favor—namely, for President Clinton to name him as special U.S. negotiator with North Korea, whose Stalinist regime had resumed its provocative behavior after agreeing to shut down its entire plutonium production during Carter's personal visit to Pyongyang in June 1994.[46] Ultimately, Clinton bestowed the diplomatic assignment on former Defense Secretary Perry.[47]

U.S. Committee to Expand NATO

In October 1996, Fried was in his office at the Old Executive Office Building, having just talked with Blinken, the NSC's chief speech writer, about the president's imminent Detroit address on NATO expansion. Fried's secretary notified him that he had a call from "a Bruce Jackson," whom the NSC official could not have picked out of a crowd of one. When Fried came on the line, Jackson immediately identified himself as a Republican and, curiously, on the eve of the presidential election, as a Dole fundraiser. This introduction, the "most unusual of the year" in Fried's words, got the NSC official's attention, although he wondered whether the caller didn't "have better prospects for donations than from the Clinton White House?"

Jackson hurried to explain that he had obtained Fried's name from their mutual friends, ambassadors Kozminski of Poland and Gyorgy Banlaki of Hungary and that he meant business about NATO expansion. He then expressed hope that Republicans and Democrats could work together for the common cause. Promising that "no tricks and no partisan advantage" figured in his overture, Jackson asked Fried to have lunch with him. Over a meal at the power meisters' Metropolitan Club, Jackson outlined his well-developed plans to create the "U.S. Committee to Expand NATO." Still cautious, Fried waited until after Clinton's reelection to consult others about Jackson's overture. Rosner had also heard about Jackson, and Jan Nowak could not say enough good things about the suave, assertive Republican.

As a World War II undercover agent, Nowak had met Bruce's father, William Harding Jackson. The older Jackson had distinguished himself as a liaison between U.S. Army Intelligence (G-2) and Lieutenant General Walter Bedell Smith who, in turn, reported to General Omar Bradley, Eisenhower's right-hand man. Jackson had managerial responsibilities for the code-breaking, intelligence-gathering Ultra project. After the war, William Jackson helped General Smith create the Central Intelligence Agency, becoming the CIA's first deputy director. In 1952 Eisenhower named Jackson special assistant to the president for foreign affairs, a post that evolved into national security adviser. Bruce Jackson's mother, Mary Pitcairn Keating, had arrived on Omaha Beach forty-eight hours after the D-Day landing. A Red Cross staff member, she distributed coffee, doughnuts, and smiles to American troops locked in fierce combat with German units.

Central Europeans hold the Jackson family in particularly high regard because William Jackson, then in private business, opened his Princeton estate to Hungarian freedom fighters whom he had helped spirit out of Budapest in 1956. When four-year-old Bruce inquired about the identity of the new people living in the Jackson's garage, his father replied that they were recently hired chauffeurs. "We must be quite rich to have six drivers," the younger Jackson responded.[48]

After Berger flashed the green light, Rosner and Jackson got down to organizational brass tacks. "We had always intended NATO enlargement as bipartisan," Fried said, "and now we had a basis to put it in practice."[49]

The U.S. Committee to Expand NATO (USCEN) helped NERO round up support for enlarging the alliance. Incorporated in November 1996 as a nonprofit corporation located in AEI's Washington offices, USCEN described itself as a bipartisan effort to achieve the "admission of additional European nations to membership in NATO as a way to strengthen democratic institutions and market economies in these nations."[50]

Hollywood could have cast Jackson, USCEN's president, and Rosner as *The Odd Couple*. Director for Strategic Planning for Lockheed Martin, Jackson yields to few in his Republican sympathies, having served as cochairman of Dole's National Finance Committee in 1996. Raised in Princeton, New Jersey, the forty-five-year-old Jackson prepped at St. Marks School in Southborough, Massachusetts, before entering Princeton University. There he majored in literature and went on to pursue doctoral studies at Johns Hopkins. His personal tastes run to Brooks Brothers suits, playing eighteen holes at the Chevy Chase Club, and wielding a mean squash racket. Rosner, five years younger than Jackson, was born in Youngstown, Ohio, and grew up in Seattle, where he attended public schools before enrolling at Brandeis. A "Yellow-Dog Democrat" who identifies with the realism and compassion of Harry Truman, Rosner worked for Clinton's election, prefers neat but casual attire, and relaxes by hunching over a poker table.

Personal styles aside, the two men worked effectively in tandem. A moral commitment conveyed by his parents explains Jackson's devotion to trans-Atlanticism. Although a relative newcomer to the intricacies of NATO, Rosner views the alliance as the foundation upon which to construct a new, broad security system featuring democratic states.

The two men promoted bipartisanship. Rosner had superb contacts with Democrats in Washington, and Jackson—a Republican insider's insider—engrafted NATO expansion into the GOP's 1996 platform. They cooperated in crafting and implementing a "freeze-the-wing-nuts" strategy based on two elements: first, working from the center outward to capture a broad swath of backers, extending to Biden and Lieberman among Democrats and to Lott, Helms, and Don Nickles (R-OK) among Republicans; second, building up such a head of steam that ultraconservatives like James M. Inhofe (R-OK) and extreme liberals like Paul D. Wellstone (D-MN) would find themselves marginalized and thus offer only token opposition to the expansion legislation. In carrying out this plan, USCEN focused its appeals on senators, veterans' groups, editorial boards, and trade unions.

The issue of U.S.-European security arrangements appeals primarily to international affairs experts. Predictably, former high-level state and defense department executives who had gravitated to the private sector signed on to USCEN's fourteen-member board of directors. Jackson had himself served as a staff officer in the Office of the Secretary of Defense, working on nuclear forces and arms-control policy; USCEN's cofounder Gregory Craig is a liberal lawyer-lobbyist who worked for congressional sanctions on South Africa in the mid-1980s and later became the head of the Policy Planning Staff and the State Department's resident Tibet expert; Julie Finley, another cofounder, is an indefatigable GOP activist, whose interest in security matters traces to influence exerted by former Senator "Scoop" Jackson (D-WA); Steven Hadley, a former assistant secretary of defense, practiced law at Shea and Gardner, which has done some work for Lockheed Martin; David J. Gribben, Bush's assistant secretary of defense for Legislative Affairs, had become The Halliburton Company's vice president for government relations; Gregory F. Treverton, vice chairman of the National Intelligence Council and a member of the National Security Council staff during the Carter years, had gone on to head the Center of International Security and Defense Policy at RAND; and Landon Butler, president of the Polish American Enterprise Fund, which astutely invests union monies in Central Europe, was close to the AFL-CIO leadership.

Two criteria guided Jackson, Craig, and Finley in selecting USCEN's board. Given reasonable notice, each member had to be willing at his own expense to hop a cab to meet with senators or staff members on Capitol Hill. In addition, each had to exhibit strong links to top officials in recent administrations. Craig, the president's movie-star-handsome counsel in his Senate impeachment trial, first met the Clintons when studying at Yale; Gribben and Hadley had served under George Bush;

Jackson enjoyed especially good ties to Reagan's foreign-policy team; and Butler, who negotiated the Panama Canal treaties, and Treverton boasted excellent contacts with Carter's chief lieutenants.[51]

Such contacts enabled USCEN's Hadley to organize the collection of signatures of sixty retired U.S. generals and admirals on a letter endorsing NATO expansion, released by USCEN on February 3, 1998 and quickly disseminated by NERO. The signers included five former chairmen of the Joint Chiefs of Staff: Generals David C. Jones, Colin Powell, Shalikashvili, and John W. Vessey, Jr., along with Admiral Crowe.[52]

Committee members' excellent contacts enabled USCEN to attract Washington movers-and-shakers to dinners at the Metropolitan Club and Finley's home near Embassy Row. These events afforded senators an opportunity to chat informally with Albright, Brzezinski, Holbrooke, Wolfowitz, Zoellick, and other establishment luminaries about the wisdom of enlarging the alliance. The lawmakers particularly enjoyed hobnobbing with Central European notables like the pipe-smoking Bronislaw Geremek, a Jewish History professor who had survived the Warsaw ghetto, provided brain power to the Solidarity movement, and gained appointment as Poland's foreign minister. Bon vivant Adam Michnik, who survived six years in a communist prison to become editor of *Gazeta Wyborcza* which claims 500,000 readers, also fascinated the legislators. "He exudes a passion for life despite his lengthy incarceration," observed Finley, whom Jackson called the "catalyst" for the social events.[53]

"If a senator is wavering, we arrange for a meeting between that senator and a member of our committee," said USCEN director Cece Boyer.[54] For example, when Senator Biden worried that the United States had forsworn NATO's enlargement in the "Two Plus Four" scheme reuniting Germany, Jackson requested—via USCEN board member Zoellick—that the agreement's negotiator, former Secretary of State Baker, phone the legislator to assuage his concerns.

The committee helped convey to lawmakers the fact that highly respected conservatives and international-affairs experts across the spectrum supported NATO's moving eastward. When a hard-core Republican senator said he would "never" vote for anything pushed by that expletive-deleted Arkansan, Bruce Jackson tactfully reminded him that "you may be shooting at Clinton but you are hitting Reagan"—a reference to the former chief executive's bullishness on European defense. Another Republican participant, who asked not to be quoted, confided that "the presence at the dinners of men like Wolfowitz and Zoellick whom the military trusted showed that the [expansion] campaign wasn't just a Holbrooke publicity venture." Although a moderate Republican, Jackson successfully obtained the quiet backing of Ralph Reed and the Christian Coalition on the basis that NATO enlargement broadened and strengthened the community of shared Western values.[55]

Despite administration discouragement of budget-busting purchases of high-tech weapons by the three would-be NATO members, the Central Europeans exaggerated their readiness to buy armaments. To bolster their support on Capitol Hill and elsewhere in Washington, they even implied that NATO expansion marked a high-stakes gambit for American technology exporters. In fact, the United States sent approximately $53 million in direct military aid to Eastern European countries in 1996—a figure that rose to $67 million in 1997, when Washington also made available $240 million in loans. The Clinton administration sought $70 million in fiscal year 1998, as well as $400 million in guaranteed loans.[56]

In a move to upgrade its armed forces, Poland expressed hope that it could purchase one hundred to one hundred and fifty fighter planes, and held talks with Lockheed, Boeing, and companies in Britain, France, and Russia. A single F-16, manufactured by Lockheed Martin, carries a price tag of $20 million, although a used model runs only several million dollars; a Boeing-made F/A-18 costs $35 to 40 million. The Pentagon had already awarded one contract to Lockheed Martin—through the Foreign Military Financing program—to integrate systems for a series of Air Sovereignty Operations Centers designed to help the Eastern Europeans modernize their military and civilian air traffic-control systems. Reportedly, the company had the "inside track" on the sale of FPS-117 radar to Hungary, a deal that never materialized. Such opportunities prompted Senator Tom Harkin (D-IW), an opponent of the protocols, to deride expansion as "a Marshall Plan for defense contractors who are chomping at the bit to sell weapons and make profits." A top GOP Senate aide joked that the arms makers' eagerness for NATO enlargement means "we'll probably be giving landlocked Hungary a new navy."[57] Indeed, Jackson, who never mentioned his Lockheed Martin connection when participating in USCEN functions, put the annual cost of expansion in perspective by telling the *Wall Street Journal* that it would be equivalent to "buying a candy bar for every American taxpayer."[58]

As fashionable as it may be to lambast the "merchants of death," a careful account must note several other points. First, defense sales to

Central Europe constitute only a pittance compared with these Fortune 500 corporations' multi-billion-dollar annual revenues. Moreover, regardless of their relationship to NATO, the Visegrad states and other former satellites wished to replace their Russian-made armaments in part because of obsolescence, and in part because of their negative historical connotation. In addition, the sales-promotion program under which American firms have sold aircraft and other weapons preceded the NATO-enlargement debate. Finally, some observers insisted that Poland, for example, would feel more vulnerable and so procure even more defense matériel if excluded from the Atlantic alliance. One Polish defense official even cautioned that rejection by the West might force his government to explore the possibility of acquiring its own nuclear capability.[59] As it turned out, executives and lobbyists from aerospace and defense firms rarely participated in USCEN activities, and the industry's lobbyists were virtual no-shows in lobbying the Hill on the issue. Finally, USCEN, which funded its projects entirely with individual contributions, accepted no financial support from arms producers and other corporations.

Ironically, the business community showed little interest in USCEN. Weapons manufacturers had other channels through which to pursue the modest contracts that Central European militaries were likely to sign in the short to medium term. And corporations like Procter & Gamble, Office Depot, and McDonald's restaurants had already established beachheads, if not major presences, in the region.

In an examination of the contributions of major ethnic groups to ratification, Chapter 5 will discuss how USCEN joined forces with the Polish American Congress, the Hungarian American Coalition, and other organizations that had long advocated alliance membership for Central European states. Throughout the process, however, the committee emphasized the importance of NATO expansion to all U.S. citizens, not just to ethnic groups.

The Press

NERO's assiduous cultivation of the press paid off in a remarkably large number of articles about the NATO expansion, even though the issue never generated a groundswell of public interest: while sixty-three percent of respondents to a Pew Research Center poll favored enlargement of the alliance, few could name the candidate-states seeking entry. As depicted in Table 3, of sixty-eight North American newspapers that took editorial positions on the issue, thirty-four opposed enlargement, twenty-one supported adding new members to NATO, and thirteen (eleven of which opposed expansion) favored delaying the vote. The major newspapers inveighing against expansion included the *New York Times*, the *Boston Globe*, the *Los Angeles Times*, and *Newsday*, while the *Washington Post*, the *Wall Street Journal*, and the *Chicago Tribune* numbered among the proponents.

Rosner took great pride in his office's work with the *Chicago Tribune*, which originally stood against NATO's growth. He asked both U.S. ambassador to NATO Vershbow and General Shalikashvili to meet with the paper's editorial board. When the NERO chief heard that editorial writers, including one from the *Tribune*, would visit Eastern Europe, he encouraged American embassies in the region to roll out the red carpet for them. Of course, virtual-office paladins like Vershbow in Brussels and Fried in Warsaw needed no instruction on how to win the hearts and minds of the Fourth Estate. Fried, for instance, credits Foreign Minister Geremek for selling the Chicago journalists on the merits of expansion. On March 13, 1998, the *Tribune* averred that it is not "a small thing for a newspaper to change its mind on an issue as momentous as NATO expansion [but] that is what we do today." Rosner wasted no time in distributing copies of the editorial to Democratic Senate staffers to rebut concerns raised about antagonizing Russia.[60]

Expansion Opponents

In March 1997, five organizations opposed to enlarging the Atlantic alliance formed the NATO Working Group. Chaired by Alistair I. Millar, then-assistant to the director and European-security analyst for the British American Security Information Council, the loosely structured Group also embraced The Center for Defense Analysis, the Council for a Livable World, the Union of Concerned Scientists, and the Federation of American Scientists. Several objectives linked the NATO Working Group members: curbing wasteful military spending, converting nonessential outlays on armed forces to social priorities, and reducing the threat of nuclear warfare. The group, which often met at the Dupont Circle offices of The Center for Defense Analysis, tracked developments in the U.S. Senate on the NATO issue, coordinated the writing and placement of op-ed essays in leading publications, and organized events on European security in Washington, D.C.[61]

Table 3: Editorial Positions of North American Newspapers on NATO Enlargement

Pro-Enlargement	Anti-Enlargement	Delay Vote*
Charleston (W VA) Gazette	Albany Times-Union	Albuquerque Journal
Chicago Tribune	Albuquerque Journal	Arizona Daily Star
Christian Science Monitor	Arizona Daily Star	Atlanta Constitution
Dallas Morning News	Bangor Daily News	Boston Herald
Fort Worth Star-Telegram	Boston Globe	Lima (OH) News
Harrisburg Patriot	Boston Herald	Los Angeles Times
Harrisburg Patriot-News	Buffalo News	Milwaukee
Houston Chronicle	Chicago Sun-Times	Journal-Sentinel
Kansas City Star	Defense News	New York Times
Minneapolis Star-Tribune	Detroit News	Newsday
New York Post	Edmonton Journal	Orlando Sentinel
Peoria Journal Star	Financial Times**	Sacramento Bee
Portland (ME) Press Herald	Fort Lauderdale Sun-Sentinel	San Diego Union-
Providence Journal-Bulletin	Fort Worth Star-Telegram	Tribune
San Francisco Chronicle	The Gazette (Montreal)	Tampa Tribune
San Francisco Examiner	Hartford Courant	
USA Today	Indianapolis News	
Wall Street Journal	Keene (NH) Sentinel	
Washington Post	Lima (OH) News	
Washington Times	Manchester Union-Leader	
Wyoming Tribune-Eagle	Milwaukee Journal-Sentinel	
	New Haven Register	
	New York Times	
	Newsday	
	Orlando Sentinel	
	Philadelphia Inquirer	
	Rocky Mountain News	
	Sacramento Bee	
	Salt Lake Tribune	
	San Diego Union-Tribune	
	Sarasota Herald-Tribune	
	St. Petersburg Times	
	Syracuse Post-Standard	
	Tampa Tribune	
Total 21	34	13

*Except for the *Atlanta Constitution*, newspapers editorializing for delaying the vote opposed enlargement.

**Although London-based, the *Financial Times* boasts a substantial North American readership.

Source: Public affairs consultant Scott Cohen, former staff director, Senate Foreign Relations Committee, and former Senior Foreign Affairs Adviser to Senator Charles Percy. Although Cohen opposed expansion, his data proved the most objective and comprehensive available.

Only in mid-1997, however, did the NATO Working Group and other foes of expansion begin to register their dissent in a well-publicized fashion. Their initial salvo took the form of "An Open Letter to President Clinton," released on June 26, 1997.[62] In this communication, forty-eight intellectuals, policymakers, and former high-level government officials, including presidential granddaughter and Russia expert Susan Eisenhower, former Senators Bill Bradley (D-NJ), Gary Hart (D-CO), Gordon Humphrey (R-NH), Bennett Johnston (D-LA), and Sam Nunn called NATO enlargement "a policy error of historic proportions." They argued that adding new countries to the alliance would: (1) give the impression of an encirclement, strengthening the nondemocratic opposition in Russia; (2) draw a new line dividing Europe between "ins" and "outs"; (3) degrade NATO's ability to carry out its primary mission of collective territorial defense; and (4) threaten the U.S. government's ability to remain engaged with the alliance, chiefly because of the expense of enlargement.[63]

In lieu of admitting new countries to NATO, the signatories to what some referred to as the "Nunn-Eisenhower" or "Experts' Letter," advocated the European Union's admission of Central and East European countries, development of an enhanced Partnership for Peace program, support for cooperative NATO-Russian relations, and continued reductions in stockpiles of nuclear weapons and conventional forces.

In conclusion, the writers argued that

> Russia does not now pose a threat to its western neighbors and the nations of Central and Eastern Europe are not in danger. For this reason, and the others cited above, we believe that NATO expansion is neither necessary nor desirable and that this ill-conceived policy can and should be put on hold.[64]

Nevertheless, expansion opponents allowed seven months to elapse before converting their rhetoric into an organized drive against enlargement. They took this step in late January 1998 with the formation of the "Coalition Against NATO Expansion" (CANE), also known as the "Left-Right Coalition" because members ranged from the liberal Americans for Democratic Action to the libertarian Cato Institute to Phyllis Schlaffley's ultraconservative Eagle Forum.[65] In fact, John Isaacs of the Council for a Livable World and Bill Lind of the Free Congress Foundation—college roommates at Dartmouth forty years earlier—devised CANE to accentuate the breadth of hostility to NATO's growth. They succeeded in bringing together a full spectrum of groups, including arms-control advocates, business leaders, UN-bashers, and foreign-policy wonks. The group's "founding declaration"[66] warned that precipitous action on the alliance would constitute "a Tonkin Gulf Resolution" for Central and East Europe—a reference to the August 1964 blank check that Congress handed President Lyndon Johnson to prosecute the Vietnam war. CANE insisted that NATO's growth would offend three kinds of American interests: strategic, political, and financial.

From a strategic perspective, CANE's messages noted that enlargement would impede reintegrating Russia with the West. "Today, Russia is too weak to oppose NATO expansion effectively, so she has chosen to remain officially silent. But Russia understands. She will remember, and ultimately, she will react, either from a position of renewed strength or out of desperation."[67]

In political terms, the coalition asserted that NATO expansion would exacerbate the growing split between ordinary Americans and Washington power brokers, contending that "NATO offers Washington insiders a cornucopia of opportunities for career advancement and prestige." Explaining elite support for expansion, CANE affiliates avowed that the capital's officialdom had encouragement from defense-industry lobbyists seeking "multi-billion dollar weapons contracts." CANE indicted enlargement as a classic example of insider politics as usual:

> Outside of the beltway, however, it is difficult to find much enthusiasm for additional foreign military commitments. America has grown tired of 'cabinet wars,' of conflicts and commitments to conflict . . . to serve the interests of Washington gameplayers. By quickly ratifying the treaty, the Senate would deliver a blow to the very system of participatory government that should be at the heart of American democracy.[68]

Finally, CANE predicted that increasing NATO membership would impose "a new and potentially heavy burden on the American taxpayer," to the tune of $125 billion. "The new planes, tanks and other equipment the lobbyists are hawking on Capitol Hill must be paid for. Who will pay? Inevitably, the American people."

CANE called for both houses of Congress to hold exhaustive hearings on expansion, with equal time allocated to foes and advocates. The anti-enlargement coalition favored an extensive floor debate in the Senate, with no action before mid-1998, charging that any plans for an "earlier vote is railroading the issue." Finally, CANE recommended a series of public debates in major cities throughout the country pitting its spokesmen against those of the State Department: "By debating NATO expansion across America, instead of treating the matter as a Washington beltway 'insider deal,' the advocates of expansion can answer the objection that the American people are not being consulted on a matter of overwhelming importance to their interests."[69]

At CANE's inaugural session, Ted Galen Carpenter, a prominent foreign-policy analyst on the organization's twelve-member advisory council, uttered the most memorable *bon mot* of the NATO debate. In an opinion-page publication, Albright had used a line from Ambassador Rey about the United States' readiness to aid Gdansk in case of an attack on the Polish Baltic port. The secretary replied that the issue was not Gdansk, but strengthening NATO "to protect Gdover, Gdenver, and Gdallas." When reminded of her riposte, Carpenter said the "Secretary is Gdumb!"[70]

Only *New Yorker* essayist Calvin Trillin came close to matching Carpenter's repartee, publishing the following poem:

> *U.S. Policy on NATO Expansion*
>
> At last a NATO policy
> That makes some sense to me:
> Reject two former Red-bloc states[1]
> But take the other three.[2]
>
> So why can't NATO take all five,
> If three would be all right?
> My theory is that NATO needs
> Some countries left to fight.
>
> The cost of soldiers, tanks and planes
> Will then seem rather teeny—a
> Mere trifle for protection from
> Romania and Slovenia.[71]

Not even Carpenter's Dorothy Parker-style thrusts could unify the disparate coalition-fighting expansion. Although remaining in desultory

---

1. A reference to Romania and Slovakia.
2. A reference to Poland, Hungary, and the Czech Republic.

contact and sharing some information, CANE organizations functioned mainly on a free-lance basis. Despite loose coordination, CANE affiliates sent speakers to Capitol Hill, newspaper editorial boards, open forums, public debates, radio talk shows, and television interviews. As the Senate NATO debate began in late spring, the Left-Right Coalition sponsored "electronic town meetings" on talk-radio shows in more than twenty cities, including Raleigh, North Carolina, and Concord, New Hampshire.[72] Carpenter, Ambassador Dean, former Senator Humphrey, Russian specialist Eisenhower, and Johns Hopkins Professor Mandelbaum came across as especially articulate opponents of NATO's growth.

Most observers viewed Mandelbaum as the driving intellectual force behind the opposition. A close friend of Deputy Secretary of State Talbott, with whom he had authored a book, and a former Clinton adviser who had publicly backed enlarging the alliance in 1993,[73] Mandelbaum argued his newfound, anti-enlargement case with the zeal of the converted. He wrote opinion articles in major newspapers, scored points against Holbrooke in a debate sponsored by the Council on Foreign Relations, made numerous television appearances on the *Newshour with Jim Lehrer* and major network programs, and churned out ideas that found their way into the columns of top journalists like *New York Times* editorialist Thomas Friedman, a Pulitzer Prize winner and an unrelenting critic of expansion.

In an essay titled "Foreign Policy as Social Work," Mandelbaum pilloried Clinton's foreign policy for incoherence, inconstancy, and an inability to define American interests.[74] He reserved his harshest invective for the administration's European policy:

> NATO expansion had the potential to alienate Russia from the post-Cold War settlement in Europe and make the goal of overturning that settlement central to Russian foreign policy, even as the infamous Clause 231 of the Versailles Treaty, assigning guilt for World War I to Germany, helped set the Germans on the course that led to World War II. In that worst case, the Clinton policy would rank with America's two greatest twentieth-century foreign policy blunders: the failure to remain politically engaged in Europe after World War I and the Vietnam war.[75]

Mandelbaum attributed the perceived maladroitness in international affairs to: "doubt about whether he measured up to the job of chief executive and commander in chief" well enough to advance his all-important political agenda at home.[76]

The Johns Hopkins scholar came in for his own share of brickbats. Although lacking evidence, detractors claimed that Mandelbaum's change of heart resulted from Clinton's failure to name him national security adviser. At least one USCEN board member puckishly proposed to nominate Mandelbaum for the "Charles Lindbergh Award"—bestowed on a promising and talented young man who makes one career-shattering mistake.[77]

Accustomed to the dangers of Washington's fast lane, Mandelbaum offered five explanations for his turnabout. First, he endorsed expansion when, following the Yeltsin-Walesa August 1993 dinner in Warsaw, it appeared that Russia approved the gambit. Second, he conditioned his initial support on a successful U.S. policy toward Ukraine, which has not materialized, he claims. Third, his *Washington Post* essay attracted critical letters from major international-affairs experts like William Maynes, former editor of *Foreign Policy*, whose views prompted him to rethink his stance. Fourth, he bristled at the failure of Holbrooke and the RAND troika to make a "strategic rationale" during the lunch sessions at the Monocle Restaurant, leading him to conclude that domestic and bureaucratic politics motivated these expansion supporters. "They acted as if NATO enlargement were a fait accompli and displayed impatience toward those of us who criticized adding Central European states to the alliance," he said. Finally, the inability to determine subconscious motivations demands the evaluation of ideas on their merits, not on *ad hominem* grounds, and he believes events have demonstrated the correctness of his position.

In response to Senator Helms's question about Mandelbaum's change of heart, the scholar said:

> This is one of those issues that sounds good at first glance. When you first hear about it, you think why not? Let's be inclusive. Who could object to that? But then, when you look further into it, you discover all the snares and pitfalls and disadvantages. So I changed my mind. If I can change my mind, Senator, so can others . . . .[78]

With respect to the putative Lindbergh Award, Mandelbaum emphasized that

> I am a career academic. My job is to think clearly and write and speak honestly about foreign policy. Therefore, to have rolled over for a dangerous policy like NATO expansion simply, as Bill Clinton

once said, to protect my 'political viability,' would have constituted a real career shattering mistake.[79]

Despite the intellectual firepower and fervor that Mandelbaum and other opponents mustered in the United States, few trans-Atlantic groups actively opposed NATO's growth. In fact, the legislatures of Canada, Denmark, Norway, and Germany ratified expansion before the U.S. Senate acted.[80] Nevertheless, CANE did arrange for a "No to NATO Expansion Speakers Tour," which included retired British General Sir Hugh Beach, who had joined other retired officers and defense experts in warning U.K. Prime Minister Tony Blair against the dangers of enlargement, and Dr. Rob de Wijk, who had served as an adviser to the Netherlands Ministry of Defense.[81]

Table 4: Coalition Against NATO Expansion

Member Organizations	Advisory Council
American Defense Institute	Dr. Ted Galen Carpenter
Americans for Democratic Action	Ambassador Jonathan Dean
Center for Defense Information	Senator Gary Hart
Council for a Livable World Education Fund	Senator Gordon Humphrey
Eagle Forum	Dr. Fred Ikle
Free Congress Foundation	Ambassador Jack Matlock
Media Research Center	Professor Richard Pipes
National Traditionalist Coalition	
Peace Action	
Union of Concerned Scientists	

Source: Council for a Livable World, website <http:www.clw.org>

Ben & Jerry's Weighs In

In addition to the problems inherent in heterogeneity, anti-expansion forces lacked adequate resources until a few weeks before the Senate vote. Then, Ben Cohen, cofounder of Ben & Jerry's ice cream empire and president of Business Leaders for Sensible Priorities (BLSP), entered the fray with a $150,000 commitment. "Ben's belief is that NATO's expansion will soak up billions of taxpayers dollars that could be better spent on our domestic agenda, such as education," said Gary Ferdman, the BLSP's executive director.[82]

Committed to shifting government spending from unnecessary military ventures to internal priorities, BLSP hired Washington, D.C.-based Fenton Communications, known for its advocacy of environmental and liberal causes, to craft a three-pronged campaign.[83] CEO David Fenton, jokingly dubbed the "Pitchman for the Politically Correct,"[84] produced television commercials warning that NATO expansion would alienate Russia and rekindle cold-war tensions. These thirty-second spots, featuring footage of mushroom clouds, ran during *Face the Nation, Meet the Press, Nightline, Good Morning America*, and major news programs.

In addition, Fenton broadcast these ads primarily in five states where senators had yet to announce their position on the NATO vote—Iowa, Oklahoma, Montana, Rhode Island, and Vermont. Fenton publicist Elizabeth Buchanan phoned and faxed information about the wrongheadedness of enlarging NATO to some four hundred journalists. The public-relations firm also prepared a full-page advertisement for the *New York Times*. This ad, which appeared on April 20, 1998 at a cost of $60,000, carried a screaming headline, "Hey, let's scare the Russians!" Underneath, the bold-type text stated in tongue-in-cheek fashion:

> Let's take NATO and expand it toward Russia's very borders. We'll assure the Russians we come in peace. We'll explain that the Russian people should feel more secure knowing that Poland, Hungary and the Czech Republic are in a military alliance with the United States.[85]

The ad went on to claim that such an expansion would stir "the same feeling of peace and security Americans would have if Russia were in a military alliance with Canada and Mexico, armed to the teeth, and excluding the United States."

In smaller type, the advertisement made a half-dozen arguments against increasing NATO's size. First, this "unfriendly expansion" would pose "serious threats to peace" by possibly delaying Russian approval of the Start II Treaty, which, if ratified by Russia, would eliminate many nuclear weapons. After all, the Russians had already "step[ped] back" from their promise not to launch a first nuclear strike. Second, adding the Visegrad nations to the alliance would mean that the U.S. government would break promises made to President Gorbachev when he dismantled the Soviet Union. Third, enlargement would constitute a "$60 billion boondoggle," benefitting big defense contractors who had lobbied so actively for the opportunity to increase their sales in Central Europe. Fourth, admitting Hungary to NATO might require U.S. troops to settle simmering border disputes between Hungary and Romania over Hungarians living in Transylvania. Fifth, foreign-policy experts like former Secretary of Defense Robert McNamara, ex-CIA Director Stansfield Turner, and former NSC head Brent Scowcroft have opposed or expressed grave reservations about the administration's policy. Finally, BLSP asked why policymakers should rush to judgment: "Before we reintroduce our children to the threat of nuclear war, there should be a broad public discussion."

Although only four senators in the five targeted states voted "nay" on the successful ratification resolution, Ferdman claims that the media blitz helped pull a total of eleven senators into the anti-expansion column.[86] He laments that his organization failed to become involved earlier in the effort, that BLSP had too little time to recruit other socially conscious business interests, and that they neglected to reach out to ethnic groups like Russian Americans who might have lobbied against the NATO protocols.[87]

While admitting that his firm entered the struggle late, Fenton said, "at least we had a good time." In reaction to the news that Ben & Jerry's had lined up against him on the NATO issue, Jackson, confusing ice cream companies, scoffed: "We've got 77 generals; they've only got thirty-six flavors."[88]

Conclusion

In the "inside" and "outside" struggles surrounding NATO expansion, NERO and other enlargement advocates clearly outclassed anti-enlargement forces. First, as mentioned in Chapter 2, Congress took a proprietary interest in NATO, dating to the Senate's constitutional role in adopting the 1949 Washington Treaty. Rosner and the administration did everything possible to reinforce this sentiment. They involved as many senators and house members as possible in the ratification venture. Second, the president commands a decided advantage in treaty-making, all the more so because most observers believe that the Senate erred in defeating the Versailles Treaty. The executive branch sometimes loses battles—Helms and other senators forced Clinton to temporarily withdraw the Chemical Weapons Convention, for example—but the chief executive generally enjoys the benefit of the doubt in negotiating major international accords. Secretary Albright magnified the White House's influence through her tireless cultivation of senators, her special bond with Senator Helms, the complete trust she enjoyed among Central European leaders, and her acumen in handling the media.

Third, although beset by bureaucratic infighting, Rosner managed to keep a firm rein on pro-enlargement forces. In contrast, anti-expansionists had no leader, never reconciled their divergent ideological beliefs, appeared uncomfortable working with each other, and could unite for little else than media events. The coalition's behavior confirmed the adage that when everyone is in charge, no one is in charge.

Fourth, NERO reached across the country to marshal backing for ratification. Superficial knowledge of the subject may have preceded some endorsements, but the sources of support turned out to be as varied as they were numerous. In contrast, most opposition lay principally within the Cambridge-New York-Washington corridor and, even there, advocates of enlargement held their own in debates with foes. Elements of the eastern establishment had grown complacent during the cold war, when they could glibly marshal anticommunist rhetoric to justify U.S. activities abroad. As a result, these foreign-policy elites lacked ties to grass-roots organizations and came either to take Congress for granted, or to show disdain for the ever-more parochial collection of lawmakers on Capitol Hill. CANE concentrated on the east coast; NERO took its message directly to forty states. In addition, pro-ratificationists included Europeans, largely absent from the opposition's ranks.

Fifth, Rosner and his team satisfied the concerns of most potential conservative opponents with respect to "costs" (the raft of figures proved mind-numbing), "NATO's mission"(Poland sold itself as a worthy ally and the administration stressed the centrality of collective defense), and "Russia" (thanks to Albright's unambiguous response to Helms). The administration helped neutralize fears that expansion would unify and radicalize Russia by extending the olive branch in the form of various aid packages, and bringing Moscow into the "Russia-NATO Founding Act"— an initiative deftly managed by Strobe Talbott.

At the same time, various developments diminished sympathy for the Kremlin, including Yeltsin's erratic behavior, Russia's invasion of Chechnya, and the absence of credible Russian spokesmen in Washington. While Poles, Hungarians, Czechs, and other Central and East-European ethnic groups roamed the corridors of Senate office buildings in search of votes, Russian diplomats remained inert. They did visit Capitol Hill to talk with Senator Paul Wellstone, but the lawmaker's staff, not the

Russian embassy, arranged the meeting. "We really didn't want them to get involved because their activism might have proven counter-productive," said a CANE leader.[89]

Above all, NERO kept banging the ratification drum—with announcements of new proponents, the circulation of "Dear Colleague" letters among legislators, and high-level media events transpiring every several weeks. For their part, critics of expansion acted sporadically, as evidenced by the time lag between the "Experts' Letter" and the unveiling of the Coalition Against NATO Expansion: CANE appeared irresolute, balkanized, ideologically divided, and underfunded, while the administration, through NERO, projected an image of decisiveness, cohesion, and economic wherewithal. Rosner and his colleagues conveyed a sense of momentum and inevitability that not only furthered their cause, but dissuaded potential adversaries from committing time and resources to the battle. As detailed in the account in Chapter 6 of final legislative action, no prominent senator became invested in defeating the protocols amending the Washington Treaty; and there was a dearth of anti-expansionists to provide testimony to Senate committees.

Chapter 5 will analyze how the Warsaw government and its European and American supporters promoted international, political, military, and social policies that placed Poland in the front of the queue when the NATO ministers, assembled in Madrid in July 1997, opened the doors of the Atlantic alliance to new members. I will complement an examination of actions spearheaded in behalf of Poland by furnishing examples of those undertaken for Hungary and the Czech Republic.

Notes

1. John Keegan, *Six Armies in Normandy: From D-Day to the Liberation of Paris* (New York: Viking, 1982), p. 275.
2. Waters, facsimile to author, January 12, 1999.
3. Rosner, interview, August 5, 1998.
4. Fried, interview, December 28, 1998.
5. Rosner, interview, August 5, 1998; Waters, telephone interview, December 28, 1998; and Waters, facsimile to author, January 12, 1999.
6. Rosner, Memorandum on "Initial Thoughts on NATO Enlargement Ratification Strategy" to Secretary Albright, Deputy Secretary Talbott, APNSA Berger, and DAPNSA Steinberg, February 26, 1997.
7. Cited in Jeremy D. Rosner, "NATO's Enlargement's American Hurdle: The Perils of Misjudging Our Political Will," *Foreign Affairs* 75, no. 4 (July/August 1996): 12-13. Another survey found that respondents favoring expansion (45-46 percent) barely exceeded those who believed it should not grow (39-40 percent). See, The Pew Research Center, *Public Indifference about NATO Expansion*, News Release, Washington, D.C., January 24, 1997.
8. Rosner, interview, August 5, 1998.
9. Munter, interview, July 21, 1998. "Sherpa" has become a diplomatic term of art: Like Western mountain climbers' sherpa guides in the Himalayas, lower-ranking staff wrangle out consensus positions with counterparts, then ensure logistics for principals to meet and conclude agreements. Diplomatic "sherpas," like the eponymous mountaineers in Nepal, go first to test a passage's safety, then help leaders reach the summit.
10. Dana Milbank, "SNOG Job," *The New Republic*, May 25, 1998, p. 14.
11. This prestigious program typically allows young professionals inclined toward public service to spend two years rotating through several federal agencies.
12. Christine Wormuth, assistant to the Special Adviser for Public and Legislative Affairs, NERO, interview by author, Arlington, VA, August 24, 1998.
13. Munter, telephone interview, September 1, 1998.
14. Bureau of Public Affairs, U.S. Department of State, *The Enlargement of NATO: Why Adding Poland, Hungary, and the Czech Republic to NATO Strengthens American National Security* (Washington, D.C.: U.S. Department of State, 1998). The Department distributed 10,000 copies of this pamphlet in the United States and abroad (Andrew Koss, telephone interview by author, September 23, 1998).
15. Quoted in The White House, "President Transmits Accession Protocols to Senate," *NATO Enlargement News Alert*, no. 15, February 11, 1998, p. 1.

16. Holt, *Treaties Defeated by the Senate* (Baltimore: Johns Hopkins University Press, 1933).

17. Policymaker Daniel Fried, who succeeded Rey as ambassador to Poland, witnessed Rosner's "Final NATO Enlargement Vote Prediction: As of 7/14/97." Several of Rosner's putative opponents—Ben Nighthorse Campbell (R-CO), D. M. Faircloth (R-NC), Ted Stevens (R-AK), Craig Thomas (R-WY), Barbara Boxer (D-CA), Wendell Ford (D-KY), Ernest F. Hollings (D-SC), and Patty Murray (D-WA)—wound up backing expansion, but the prediction proved amazingly accurate inasmuch as the final vote was 80-19, with one proponent absent.

18. Daly, interview, October 2, 1998.

19. Rosner, telephone interview, September 30, 1998.

20. Rosner, interview, August 5, 1998.

21. Rosner, "NATO Enlargement's American Hurdle," pp. 9-10.

22. For the text of this Act, see NATO, *Founding Act on Mutual Relations, Cooperation and Security between NATO and the Russia Federation*, Internet.

23. Rosner, telephone interview, October 12, 1998.

24. Rosner, telephone interview, October 12, 1998.

25. NATO, "The Partnership between NATO and Russia," NATO Basic Fact Sheet No. 20, July 1997, Internet.

26. Wormuth, facsimile to author, November 6, 1998.

27. Quoted in U.S. Senate, Committee on Foreign Relations, *The Debate on NATO Enlargement: Hearings before the Committee on Foreign Relations, United States Senate, 105th Congress, October 7, 9, 22, 28, 30 and November 5, 1997* (Washington, D.C.: U.S. Government Printing Office, 1998), p. 11.

28. Quoted in U.S. Senate, *The Debate on NATO Enlargement*, p. 8.

29. Milbank, "SNOG Job," p. 15.

30. Rosner, "Weekly Update on NATO Enlargement Ratification," Memorandum to Rob Malley, dated October 10, 1997.

31. Munter, interview, July 21, 1998.

32. Rosner, interview, August 5, 1998.

33. Rosner, telephone interview, October 12, 1998.

34. In a 1996 "decision memo" on NATO, the State Department included only a fleeting reference to potential political problems facing the initiative.

35. Rosner, telephone interview, July 31, 1998.

36. In order to communicate with Albright, NERO sent her off-line, private communications (Rosner, telephone interview, October 12, 1998).

37. Rosner, interview, Washington, D.C., August 5, 1998.

38. Speaker Tip O'Neill with William Novak, *Man of the House: The Life and Political Memoirs of Speaker Tip O'Neill* (New York: Random House, 1987), p. 26.

39. Rosner, interview, August 5, 1998.
40. Munter attended the U.S. Conference of Mayors' convention in San Francisco. When the diplomat asked the mayor of Ft. Lauderdale, who chaired the organization, if he backed NATO expansion, the politician countered, "Does the President support NATO enlargement?" After Munter replied "absolutely, that's who sent me here," the chairman said, "I like it, too." The Conference unanimously endorsed expansion in June 1997.
41. The AFL-CIO took more than six months to reach a decision on NATO's expansion, possibly because Sweeney sought to avoid criticism directed at his predecessor Lane Kirkland that the labor movement devoted too much attention to foreign rather than domestic affairs. Ultimately, the AFL-CIO threw its weight behind enlargement in January 1998.
42. NERO, *NATO Enlargement News Alert*, no. 13, January 30, 1998, p. 1.
43. Rosner, "Weekly Update on NATO Enlargement Ratification," Memorandum to Rob Malley, executive assistant to National Security Adviser Sandy Berger, October 10, 1997.
44. Amanda Schnetzer, research assistant, New Atlantic Initiative, telephone interview by author, October 9, 1998.
45. American Enterprise Institute, "NAI Releases Statement in Support of NATO Enlargement," Internet.
46. President James Carter, electronic mail communicated through his biographer, Steven H. Hochman, November 16, 1998. Clinton embraced the Carter-brokered accord on June 22, 1994: under its terms, the United States would resume high-level talks with North Korea, broken off in mid-1993; in exchange, then-President Kim Il Sung pledged to shut down his country's Yongbyon nuclear complex while parleys proceeded. See, *Facts on File*, June 23, 1994, pp. 437-39.
47. Thomas W. Lippman, "Perry May be Named to Try to Salvage Pact with N. Korea," *Washington Post*, October 4, 1998, p. A-27.
48. Bruce Jackson, cochairman, U.S. Committee to Expand NATO, telephone interview by author, January 11, 1999.
49. Fried, electronic mail, December 16, 1998.
50. U.S. Committee to Expand NATO, "U.S. Committee to Expand NATO," letter that recites the organization's mission and provides brief biographies of the members of its board of directors, Washington, D.C., n.d.
51. Jackson, telephone interview, December 21, 1998.
52. "NATO Enlargement Ratification Endorsement by 60 Retired U.S. Generals and Admirals," February 3, 1998, photocopied and distributed by NERO.
53. Julie Finley, telephone interview by author, January 6, 1999; Jackson, telephone interview, January 11, 1998.
54. Bill Mesler, "NATO's New Arms Bazaar," *The Nation*, July 21, 1997, p. 3.
55. Jackson, telephone interview, December 21, 1998.

56. Mesler, "NATO's New Arms Bazaar," p. 6.

57. Katharine Q. Seelye, "Arms Contractors Spend to Promote an Expanded NATO," *New York Times*, March 30, 1998, p. A-6.

58. Quoted in Bill Mesler, "NATO's Stealth Costs," *The Nation*, July 21, 1997, p. 21. Kugler actually came up with the candy-bar estimate for Americans; he also calculated the costs for West Europeans (a McDonald's hamburger) and for Central Europeans (a restaurant dinner); see, "Costs of NATO Enlargement: Moderate and Affordable," *Strategic Forum,* no. 128 (October 1997): 3.

59. No post-cold war Polish government has recommended this action, which the official only mentioned in a brainstorming session with an employee of the U.S. Department of Defense, who insisted on anonymity.

60. Milbank, "SNOG Job," p. 14.

61. Tomas Valasek, research analyst, Center for Defense Information, interview by author, Washington, D.C., July 21, 1998; Alistair I. Millar, program director and director of Washington, D.C. Office, Fourth Freedom Forum, telephone interview by author, December 7, 1998; and Millar, electronic mail to author, December 9, 1998.

62. "An Open Letter to President Clinton," in Council for a Livable World Education Fund, *Briefing Book on NATO Enlargement* (Washington, D.C.: Council for a Livable World Education Fund, April 1998), pp. 59-62.

63. "An Open Letter to President Clinton," p. 59.

64. "An Open Letter to President Clinton," p. 59.

65. CANE members were: American Cause, American Defense Institute, Americans for Democratic Action, America's Survival, Center for Defense Information, Council for a Livable World Educational Fund, Eagle Forum, Free Congress Foundation, Media Research Center, National Traditionalist Coalition, Peace Action, Taxpayers for Common Sense, Union of Concerned Scientists, and Women's Action for New Directions.

66. "Founding Declaration of the Coalition against NATO Expansion," Council for a Livable World Education Fund, *Briefing Book on NATO Enlargement* (Washington, D.C.: Council for a Livable World Education Fund, April 1998), pp. 69-72.

67. "Founding Declaration," p. 69.

68. "Founding Declaration," p. 70.

69. "Founding Declaration," p. 71.

70. Ted Galen Carpenter, vice president, CATO Institute, interview by author, Washington, D.C., July 13, 1998.

71. Published in *The Nation*, July 28, 1997, p. 6.

72. Eric Schmitt, "NATO Opponents Vocal, Diverse and Active," *New York Times*, April 21, 1998, Internet Edition.

73. He wrote: "The idea [of expansion] is a good one. The inclusion of Poland— and of Hungary and the Czech Republic, the two other formerly Communist

countries most firmly com.*itted to democracy and free markets—would be good for them, good for the West and good for Russia too, provided that it is accompanied by a clear definition of a new NATO policy toward the former Soviet Union ("Open the Ranks to Eastern Europe," *Washington Post*, September 6, 1993, p. A-23).

74. Mandelbaum, "Foreign Policy as Social Work," *Foreign Affairs* 75, no. 1 (January/February 1996): 16-32. He also extended his views on U.S. foreign policy in the post-cold war period in *The Dawn of Peace in Europe* (New York: The Twentieth Century Fund Press, 1996), and in a monograph, *NATO Expansion: A Bridge to the Nineteenth Century* (Washington, D.C.: Center for Political and Strategic Studies, 1997).

75. Mandelbaum, "Foreign Policy as Social Work," pp. 31-32.

76. Mandelbaum, "Foreign Policy as Social Work," p. 32.

77. Jackson, telephone interview, January 11, 1999.

78. Quoted in U.S. Senate, Committee on Foreign Relations, *The Debate on NATO Enlargement*, p. 80; and Mandelbaum, telephone interview with author, December 22, 1998.

79. Mandelbaum, telephone interview, January 8, 1999. He stressed that he harbored "no resentment" toward the Clinton administration, which had offered him the post of director of the Policy Planning Staff.

80. Their dates of ratification were: Canada (February 4, 1998), Denmark (February 17, 1998), Germany (April 24, 1998), and Norway (March 17, 1998); see NATO, "Status of Ratification of Accession Protocols," *NATO Fact Sheet*, August 26, 1998, Internet.

81. Valasek, interview, July 21, 1998.

82. Quoted in Schmitt, "NATO Opponents Vocal, Diverse and Active," Internet Edition.

83. Elizabeth Buchanan, publicist, Fenton Communications, telephone interview by author, September 30, 1998.

84. David Daley, "Pitchman for the Politically Correct," *National Journal* 40 (October 3, 1992): 2266.

85. *New York Times*, April 20, 1998, p. A-11.

86. Tom Harkin (D-IW), James M. Inhofe (R-OK), and the two senators from Vermont, home of Ben & Jerry's corporate offices, James M. Jeffords (R) and Patrick J. Leahy (D).

87. Gary Ferdman, executive-director, Business Leaders for Sensible Priorities, telephone interview by author, October 5, 1998.

88. Jackson, telephone interview, December 21, 1998.

89. Valasek, interview, July 21, 1998.

Chapter 5

ഇൗരു

Poland, Inc.

Introduction

Thus far, this account of an evolving U.S. policy favoring NATO expansion has concentrated on leading figures in think tanks, the executive branch, Congress, the business community, and other political/ opinion elites. But American foreign policy will always depend substantially on popular interests and attitudes. In previous chapters, analysis of policy deliberations has touched in passing on foreign and American-ethnic advocacy groups. This chapter focuses on such actors, chiefly, the Polish government and Americans of Polish descent.

As in real estate, the heart of *Realpolitik* is "location, location, location." From 1795 on, Poland had suffered invasions, occupations, and partitions at the hands of Germany from the west, Austria from the south, or Russia from the east. As soon as the Berlin Wall fell, Central European statesmen began minting strategies to reintegrate their countries with the West. Officials in virtually all former Soviet satellites looked forward to affiliating with a united Europe, but Polish leaders demonstrated the strongest commitment to this goal. The dedication of groups across the social and political spectrum to joining NATO prompted former Ambassador Rey to label the collective effort "Poland, Inc.," the title chosen for this chapter.[1]   Additional reasons for the attention to this country lie in its strategic importance to NATO, its leadership in PFP (which diminished Pentagon opposition to extending the alliance eastward), and its astute lobbying of Congress (which other nations of the region sought to emulate).   However, one of the loudest cries for Senate action came from neither a Central European foreign office nor an interest-group headquarters, but from the kitchen of the Polish embassy.

On the morning of Tuesday, April 28, 1998, Poland's ambassador to the United States, Jerzy Kozminski, had just presided over his weekly staff meeting.   The agenda had included a discussion among the envoy and his advisers of probable dates of the Senate vote on NATO enlargement.   "We concluded that three possible timing scenarios existed: this week, next week, or even next month," Kozminski said.

No sooner had the ambassador returned to his office when Arek Darkowski, the embassy's cherubic twenty-nine-year-old chef, anxiously sent him word that "[t]he Senate has to vote this week; I've already ordered dozens of chickens for the victory party, and we don't have enough refrigerator space to keep them fresh!"[2]

The portly young man, renowned throughout Washington for his elegant food designs and delectable blintzes, reflected the suspense felt by millions of Poles, Polish Americans, and their allies in seeking swift action on the admission of the Visegrad countries to NATO.   Not only would this vote allow Chef Darkowski to display his mastery of the culinary arts, but it would provide the Polish government an opportunity to celebrate its achievements in statesmanship, economics, politics, and coalition-building.

The Warsaw Government

Until Walesa's election in December 1990, communists still held Poland's presidency, which limited the pace at which a progressive government could bolster its ties with the West.   A more imposing constraint lay in Russia's slowness in fixing a date for the removal of its troops from Polish soil.

This situation prompted Poland's defense minister, Vice-Admiral Piotr Kolodziejczyk, to propose that his country remain militarily neutral, forming a bridge between East and West.   In the same vein, Deputy Defense Minister Janusz Onyszkiewicz—a former spokesman for the

Solidarity trade-union movement—feared rejection by the West, giving rise to his advocacy of a policy in which Poland

> does not plan to join NATO or to get into some sort of military alliance with the Soviet Union that would make it impossible for Poland to keep close [ties] both to the West and the East.[3]

Polish pronouncements began to shift in early 1991, when Foreign Minister Krzysztof Skubiszewski indicated that NATO might play a role in stabilizing East Europe.[4] An icy reception to Czech President Havel's March 1991 call for Czechoslovakian "associate membership" in the Atlantic pact cooled such rhetoric for the remainder of the year. Polish leaders contemplated entering the European Union; however, the EU's wide-ranging requirements for economic, legal, and political reforms obviated this possibility, at least in the short to medium term. Thus, President Walesa and a growing segment of Poland's elite viewed affiliation with the North Atlantic Treaty Organization as a much more promising opportunity. Their conclusion reflected what would later become a popular aphorism: "EU membership was politically easier to achieve, but practically difficult; NATO membership was politically difficult to accomplish but practically easier."

Decades of bilateral conflict aside, Poland and Germany undertook a dramatic rapprochement. German President Richard von Weizsäcker gave impulse to this new era of friendship during a visit to Warsaw in May 1990, when he renounced all German territorial claims on his host's country. This change in policy, reportedly opposed until the eleventh hour by Chancellor Kohl,[5] ensured that the Oder-Neisse line would remain Poland's westernmost boundary, thereby removing a source of bilateral friction.

Beginning in 1992, Warsaw governments, regardless of political hue, began making alliance affiliation the centerpiece of their domestic and foreign agenda, a decision that enjoyed overwhelming support across the political landscape. Central to this policy change was the elevation of Onyszkiewicz, a top security specialist, to the post of defense minister. Although pro-NATO, Onyszkiewicz pragmatically stated in an August 1992 interview: "There is no point in kicking at a door that is firmly closed for the time being."[6]

Rather than attempting to crash through the door, the Polish government persisted in knocking at NATO's portal so as to convince the allies of their *bona fides* for admittance. Ambassador Rey stressed that the Warsaw regime's external niceties masked an internal commitment to figure out, "[h]ow we can embarrass the living daylights out of the United States and the West to gain admission to NATO."[7] Even before beginning their quest for alliance membership, Polish officials had demonstrated their geostrategic solidarity with the West in general and the United States in particular through several courses of action:

* The Polish Intelligence Service, an arm of the State Protection Office (UOP), facilitated the escape of seven CIA and military-intelligence officers from Baghdad in October 1990, just before the Gulf War erupted. The Poles provided fake passports, hiding places, and transportation to the Americans. Warsaw had excellent contacts in, and good maps of, the city because Polish construction companies had completed several major projects in the Iraqi capital. The CIA later presented a medal to General Gromoslaw Czempinski, commander of the operation, for outstanding intelligence service.[8]
* The Polish government sent medical personnel to assist the anti-Hussein forces in Desert Storm/Desert Shield.
* Polish diplomats staff the U.S. "interest section" in Poland's embassy in Baghdad.

Once Warsaw fixed its sights on joining the Atlantic pact, its cooperation with NATO states became even more pronounced. The following acts epitomized Poland's determination to earn a place at the NATO table.

* In mid-October 1994, the Polish Interior Ministry dispatched a fifty-one-member antiterrorist GROM unit to protect VIPs during Operation Restore Democracy, when a U.S.-led UN Multilateral Force landed 20,000 troops on Haiti to return Father Aristide to the island republic's presidency in mid-October 1994.
* Under the auspices of NATO's Partnership for Peace, Poland sent a mechanized infantry battalion to Bosnia to join the alliance's "Implementation Force" (IFOR), established under the Dayton Accords to separate combatants and to facilitate a peaceful transition. Even though this commitment far

outstripped Poland's 1995-96 budgetary reserves, the government also ensured that Polish forces participated in the follow-on "Stabilization Force" (SFOR).

* Despite Poland's desperate need for new sources of hard currency, the government halted arms shipments to Iran—including the sale of one hundred Soviet-designed tanks—after expiration of these lucrative contracts signed at the beginning of the 1990s.

* Even while fearing that the program signified an alternative to NATO affiliation, the Polish military took part in more than fifty PFP exercises to underscore the contribution it could make to NATO.

While not as assertive as Poland, Hungary took steps of its own to gain credibility with the West.

* In September 1989, before East Germany had opened its borders, the Budapest government broke with its German communist allies to allow more than some thirty thousand "vacationing" East Germans to slip across its border with Austria in order to enter West Germany.

* On June 8, 1990, Prime Minister Jozsef Antall, head of the first freely elected government since the fall of communism, called for dissolution of the Warsaw Pact, even though the Soviet troops continued to occupy his country.

* During the Balkan crisis, the Budapest government permitted NATO to fly Advanced Warning and Control System aircraft over its nation in order to monitor Bosnian airspace and, later, to enforce the no-fly zone over the region. These flights represented NATO forces' first out-of-area joint operations in Europe.[9]

* Hungary's postcommunist regime authorized NATO forces to utilize the nation's bases at Tazar as staging points for the alliance's deployment to Bosnia.

* The Hungarian armed forces dispatched more than 550 personnel to Bosnia.

* To facilitate the U.S. presence in its country, Hungary agreed to a bilateral supplement to the NATO PFP Status of Forces Agreement, granting addition privileges and immunities to U.S. troops and contractors.

* Hungary's armed forces participated in more than fifty PFP exercises.

Possessed of one of the smallest and least respected militaries in the region, the Czech Republic showed less activism. Nevertheless, it embarked on the following initiatives:

* A Czech chemical-warfare-defense unit joined the U.S.-led coalition in the 1991 Persian Gulf conflict.
* Prague dispatched a battalion of more than six hundred personnel to Bosnia.
* The Czech Republic contributed forces to the peacekeeping mission in Croatia.
* The Czech armed forces participated in twenty-seven PFP missions.

Six Stages

In retrospect, Polish leaders pointed to six stages of the process that culminated in their winning approval to join NATO.[10]

Stage 1: Summer/Fall 1993 to January 1994

Until mid-1993, mainly high-ranking government officials, analysts, and other Polish elites had discussed NATO expansion. The public began to pay greater attention to the question during Senator Lugar's August 1993 visit to Warsaw, when he openly and enthusiastically supported Poland's entering the alliance. Shortly afterwards, following the widely reported marathon dinner with Walesa, Russian President Yeltsin raised the salience of the issue even more by placing his imprimatur on Polish membership. Two events—Russia's subsequent rejection of Poland's accession and the unveiling of Partnership for Peace—activated the Warsaw government and its backers in the United States. President Walesa communicated his strong misgivings about PFP to NATO members, dispatching the new foreign minister, Andrzej Olechowski, to reiterate this sentiment in Washington.[11] Poland's government also welcomed Brzezinski's proposing the "dual-track" formula—later adopted by the NSC troika—whereby NATO would both open its doors to new members and formalize its relationship with Russia.

At the same time, the Polish government kept in constant touch with the Polish American Congress (PAC), an organization that assists and lobbies for the ten million American citizens of Polish ancestry. The PAC sprang to life following the November 1943 Teheran Conference involving Roosevelt, Churchill, and Stalin. There, the "Big Three" called for a Russian invasion of Germany from the east, which meant that Soviet troops would have the ability to occupy Poland at war's end. Thus, in May 1944, fifteen thousand delegates representing three thousand organizations swarmed into Buffalo, New York, creating the PAC as an organization committed to the struggle for a free and independent Poland. On Pulaski Day, October 11, 1945,

> [The] American Polonia learned a very bitter lesson . . . when at a meeting in the White House, President Roosevelt deceived it by creating the impression that Poland would be free within its pre-war borders. In actuality, months earlier he and Churchill had already conceded Poland's eastern territories to Stalin. The February 1945 Yalta Agreement, signed by the three war-time allies, was later violated by the Soviet Union.[12]

Senator Barbara Mikulski remembers that her great-grandmother turned FDR's picture to the wall to protest his "betrayal at Yalta," where Stalin's allies consented to a Soviet condominium in Central and Eastern Europe. For the next half-century, the Polish American Congress devoted itself to reversing that diplomatic setback. Termination of the cold war inspired PAC members with the hope they might finally achieve their goal. Myra Lenard, executive director of the PAC's Washington office since 1980, led the organization's effort to persuade the U.S. Congress to establish the Oder-Neisse line as Poland's western border. In mid-1991, the congress's Council of National Directors urged the U.S. government to demand the cessation of Soviet occupation of their homeland, declaring that "any economic aid to the Soviet Union should be closely linked to the removal without further delay of all Soviet . . . military forces from Poland."[13] In September, the PAC's Northern California Division passed a resolution calling for NATO membership for Poland, Hungary, and Czechoslovakia. The following month, the congress's national vice president included this request in a petition to President Bush. On October 28, 1993, in response to anxiety in Warsaw over the Partnership for Peace, the Polish American Congress resolved to urge President Clinton and "the Government of the United States to ensure that Poland become a full member of NATO as soon as possible."[14]

Like the Polish government, the PAC worried when the Democratic administration unveiled PFP, ridiculed in some circles as "NATO lite" or the "Partnership for Procrastination." Consequently, on December 6, 1993, the Polish American Congress reinvigorated the Central and East European Coalition (CEEC), composed of fourteen ethnic organizations. On the same day, PAC President Edward J. Moskal directed an urgent plea to the organization's state and local units, as well as to CEEC member groups. He warned of Russian "neo-imperialistic policy," and exhorted them to express their "dismay and astonishment" that PFP might allow Moscow once again to engulf Poland.[15]   The urgency arose from Clinton's impending speech at NATO headquarters scheduled for early 1994.

An ensuing torrent of phone calls prompted White House operators to ask Jan Nowak for his help in curbing the deluge of communications. "Our switchboard is completely tied up by calls from your people," they told him.[16]   The president also got the message, and invited PAC and CEEC leaders to meet at a "Round Table" with him and his foreign-policy team in Milwaukee in early January. Indeed Clinton liked to speak to domestic groups before jetting to Europe to discuss NATO issues. The night before the session, his mother died, requiring Vice President Gore to act as stand-in. CEEC activists found little new in the vice president's remarks, for he mainly reiterated Central Europe's importance to U.S. security. On the eve of Gore's talk, however, Dan Fried arranged a private dinner between Deputy National Security Adviser Berger and approximately twenty coalition leaders from the Polish, Hungarian, Czech, and Slovak communities. Organizers expected that heavy snow and extreme cold would limit the gathering to about forty-five minutes. The ethnic participants hit it off so well with their guest that the discussion stretched to three hours. "You could even tell by his body language that he understood our concerns," noted one participant.[17] The unpretentious Berger, a product of a small town in upstate New York, came across not as a Washington bigshot, but as a regular guy. He seemed particularly down-to-earth when, bereft of a cellular phone, he asked to borrow a quarter to respond to a beeper message in the middle of the meeting. Above all, the participants implored the administration to publish explicit criteria for NATO membership and, if it would not, to tell them why.[18] "Going into the dinner, Berger worried and grumbled; afterwards he said it was one of the best meetings he had had," Fried recalls.[19] The White House reacted to presentiments voiced in Milwaukee by sending Albright, Shalikashvili, and Gati to Warsaw,

Prague, and Budapest to inform the host governments of PFP II; specifically, Washington's intentions for PFP affiliation to open a pathway to a seat on the NATO council, not an alternative to membership as the Pentagon envisioned.

Its initial hostility to PFP aside, Poland became the first Central European country after Romania to join the program. It hoped that an impressive performance by its armed forces would convert naysayers into believers with respect to its ability to strengthen the alliance.

Stage 2: January 1994 to late Fall 1994

Clinton made his speech to the NATO summit on January 10, 1994. From Brussels he flew to Prague, where he made his now famous "not if, but when and how" statement. After returning home, the president turned his attention to domestic and non-NATO foreign-policy issues. Although generally favorable toward alliance enlargement, his administration showed no deep commitment to such an initiative and pursued an essentially reactive policy with respect to European security.

Some CEEC activists took heart from Clinton's post-Brussels remarks in Prague. But Colonel Casimir Lenard, an extremely prominent national director of the Polish American Congress, still expressed skepticism owing to the vagueness of Clinton's comments.[20]

Walesa sought to invigorate Poland's pro-expansion efforts in the United States by naming Jerzy Kozminski, then first deputy minister of foreign affairs, as ambassador to Washington. Kozminski's strengths lay in his renowned intelligence, his systematic approach to problem solving, his contagious enthusiasm, his capacity for hard work, and his apolitical background. The latter trait enabled him to function in an effective and nonthreatening manner with Polish politicians across the ideological spectrum. Unlike the envoys in some Central European embassies in Washington, Kozminski represented Poland, not a particular political party or coalition. No stranger to challenges, the forty-one-year-old Tarnow native, a graduate of Warsaw's Central School of Commerce, had served as undersecretary of state and the closest associate of Deputy Prime Minister Leszek Balcerowicz, architect of his nation's daring recovery plan. Upon arriving in June 1994, Kozminski set about at once to map a successful strategy for NATO enlargement. He befriended key GOP activists like Bruce Jackson, who wound up conceiving the U.S. Committee to Expand NATO. Kozminski also identified potential allies in U.S. firms with economic interests in Poland;[21] he nurtured ties

Ethnic Lobbies

The Polish American Congress shares traits with two of the most powerful ethnic lobbies in Washington, namely the American Israel Political Action Committee (AIPAC) and the Cuban American National Foundation (CANF). The three groups each boast substantial memberships, and their supporters tend to reside in large states rich with electoral votes. They maintain a significant lobbying presence in Washington, and they work closely with U.S. media publishing in their native languages. Their appeals have included opposition to communism, support for democracy, and reminders of historic victimization. Finally, their leaders know how to play hardball. For example, the PAC jointly with the CEEC sought to block the Clinton administration's appointment of Stephen Sestanovich as special coordinator for the New Independent States. Why? Sestanovich—a former NSC staff member and vice president for Russian and Eurasian Affairs at the Carnegie Endowment at the time of his nomination— had voiced concerns about NATO expansion.

Nevertheless, while demonstrating skill in coalition-building over NATO expansion, the PAC exhibits weaknesses vis-à-vis its Israeli American and Cuban American counterparts. While neither is a lobbying organization, AIPAC—and to a lesser extent CANF—enjoy support from political action committees that provide general financial support to candidates attentive to their agendas. In contrast, the Polish American Congress has chosen neither to form its own political action committee nor to encourage the formation of such committees within the Polish American community. AIPAC and CANF also demonstrate substantially more organizational cohesion, boast larger Washington offices, and benefit from a greater number of younger activists, especially in the case of Cuban Americans. A majority of Polish Americans emigrated to the United States early in the century or, at the latest, near the outbreak of World War II. Although eager to redress the betrayal at Yalta, many of these elderly or late-middle-aged citizens have greater interest in health-care and Social-Security reform than issues relating to Poland's internal policies or its relationship to NATO. Moreover, although emphasizing that it is an American group, AIPAC can communicate readily with the Israeli government, a strategy denied the PAC during forty years of foreign occupation of Poland.

with think tanks and opinion leaders; and he launched an increasingly active courtship of decisionmakers in the executive and legislative branches, often inviting them to the embassy to savor Darkowski's *pièces de résistance*. Kozminski also renewed his acquaintanceship with Strobe Talbott, whom he had hosted in Warsaw while holding the post comparable to Talbott's in the Polish Foreign Ministry. In addition, he revived ties with David Lipton, a senior treasury department official who had advised Poland on reforms along with Harvard economist Jeffrey Sachs's team.

Besides the growing list of well-placed contacts, the highly respected Polish embassy benefitted from a first-rate team that included several young diplomats in the embassy's political section: Deputy Chief of Mission Andrzej Jaroszynski, 47; First Secretary Mariusz Handzlik, 30; First Secretary and Political Counselor Boguslaw Winid, 36; Michael Wyganowski, 37; and later, Dariusz Wisniewski, 32.

Wyganowski called the drive toward expansion "a long, long process, making it impossible to cite a single pivotal event." Like his boss, he realized the importance of seizing the moral high ground. Thus, in public pronouncements and in exchanges with officials, the embassy reiterated that "expansion would contribute to democracy, promote [European] stability . . . [and] that it was moral, normal, natural, and of great benefit to all parties." By mid-1993, he believed NATO enlargement constituted a "realistic possibility," citing Clinton's Holocaust Museum meeting with Havel and Walesa as an important occurrence."[22]

Still, the embassy left nothing to chance. The dynamic Kozminski continually kept in touch with two distinguished Polish Americans, Jan Nowak and Zbigniew Brzezinski. Hitler's assault on Poland had prevented Nowak from completing his doctoral studies at the University of Poznan. During the conflict, he traveled between Poland and London as an emissary for the Polish Underground. He documented his cloak-and-dagger feats in *Courier from Warsaw*.[23]   Following the war, he worked at the British Broadcasting Corporation before assuming the directorship of Polish services at Munich-based Radio Free Europe. There, he supervised, wrote, and delivered broadcasts to the Polish people. In 1977, Nowak, then 64, left Europe for the United States and soon became a national director of the Polish American Congress. His encyclopedic knowledge of Central Europe attracted the attention of official Washington, allowing Nowak to advise Republican and Democratic administrations in both official and unofficial capacities. For example, he consulted at the National Security Council from 1979 to 1992. President Clinton recognized his contributions by awarding him the Presidential Medal of Freedom in

Table 5: Comparison of Three Ethnic Lobbying Groups

	Polish American Congress (PAC)	American Israel Public Affairs Committee (AIPAC)	Cuban American National Foundation (CANF)
Date of founding	1944	1954 (evolved out of American Zionist Council)	July 6, 1981
Purpose	National umbrella group promoting the interests of 20 million Americans of Polish descent and origin	Promote a special relationship between the U.S. and Israel	Reestablish freedom and democracy in Cuba
Membership	1 million*	35,000	50,000
Number of staff members	5		
Annual budget		$15,000,000	
Offices	Chicago and Washington	Washington, Los Angeles, San Francisco, Houston, Chicago, Atlanta, Jerusalem, Seattle**, Columbus**, Missoula**, and Trenton**	Washington and Miami (chapters in Chicago, Dallas, Jacksonville, Los Angeles, New Jersey, New York, New Orleans, Orlando, San Juan, Puerto Rico; as well as in Caracas, Hong Kong, Madrid, Mexico City, Moscow, Santo Domingo, and Valencia, Spain.
Campus affiliates	None		
Board of Directors	170-member Council of National Directors embraces all prominent Polish-American organizations	42 members	64 members

Table 5: Comparison of Three Ethnic Lobbying Groups (Contd.)

	Polish American Congress (PAC)	American Israel Public Affairs Committee (AIPAC)	Cuban American National Foundation (CANF)
Executive Committee	Eleven members	412 members, including an honorary member from every organization represented in the New York-based Conference of Presidents of Major American Jewish Organizations such as the American Jewish Committee, the American Jewish Congress, B'nai B'rith, and the Union of Hebrew Congregations	8 members
Amount contributed by Political Action Committee	No political action committee	No political action committee	No political action committee
Publications	*Polish American Congress News* (3 to 4 times per year)	*Near East Report* (bimonthly)	*Actualidad Cubana* (monthly)

*PAC bases this figure on the number of individuals estimated to belong to the organization's 31 state Divisions and 20 city and county Chapters (Colonel Casimir Lenard, National Director, telephone interview by author, PAC, December 17, 1998).
**Satellite office.
***CANF also has 71 trustees, who have contributed $5,000 or more to the organization compared with a minimum contribution of $10,000 by directors.

Source: Bruce C. Wolper, ed., *Lobbying Congress: How the System Works* (Washington, D.C.: Congressional Quarterly, 1990); web sites of the three organizations; Pamela J. Komorowski, Administrative Assistant to the President, PAC; Guy Brenner, Research Analyst, AIPAC; and Carrie Simmons, Assistant to the Director, CANF.

1996. The Polish government likewise honored Nowak with its highest award, the Order of the White Eagle, bestowed on only seventy-two people.

During the NATO debate, Nowak met frequently with top policymakers, for whom he sometimes functioned as a sounding board. Lake invited Nowak to a session with the administration's top international-affairs team in late 1993, after a "post-communist" had regained the presidency of Poland. In light of this event, the national security adviser asked Nowak whether the United States should continue to explore NATO membership for his homeland. The elderly gentleman emphatically answered "yes," because of the imperative to build bridges to former enemies. He saw immediate relief on the faces of his government hosts. Doubtless, they feared that a negative response would have signified the Polish American community's opposition to Washington's forging close ties with the government of Alexander Kwasniewski.[24] Even with the postcommunists in power, Nowak incessantly lectured, wrote, and lobbied on behalf of expanding the Atlantic alliance. He also worked with the Polish American Congress to keep the pressure on decisionmakers.

Nowak often found himself in meetings with his close friend Brzezinski, who had served as national security adviser in the Carter administration. Born in Warsaw in 1928, Brzezinski earned a Harvard doctorate, taught at Columbia University and elsewhere, and has written prolifically on both security questions and Central Europe. As a result, he received invitations to discuss his views on NATO's future with Lake, Christopher, Albright, Lugar, and dozens of other Washington foreign-policy elites. As referred to in Chapter 3, Brzezinski's astute, well-reasoned attack on the Partnership for Peace represented one of his many contributions to the enlargement debate. Many Poles admired his staunch anticommunism, commitment to integrating their country into Europe's bosom, and his international prestige.[25] In fact, Brzezinski's fame on both sides of the Atlantic prompted brief speculation in Warsaw that the country's moderate and conservative parties might unite behind him in the 1995 presidential campaign. This suggestion "disturbed" Brzezinski.[26] While an avid supporter of Poland, he takes enormous pride in his American citizenship. Like Nowak, Brzezinski received the Presidential Medal of Freedom (1981) from the U.S. government and the Order of the White Eagle (1994) from Poland. Brzezinski, Nowak, and Kozminski formed a triangle that kept in close contact with most constituencies committed to enlarging NATO.

Stage 3: Fall 1994 to September 1995

In the fall of 1994, Senator Brown and Representative Gilman continued crafting legislation to open the Atlantic alliance to Central European states. Meanwhile, as the November 1994 elections approached, House Republicans issued their "Contract With America," which included a call for NATO expansion. Michael Franc, director of congressional relations for the Heritage Foundation, helped organize groups to work on specific elements of the contract. He asked Larry Di Rita, then-deputy director of foreign policy and defense studies at Heritage, to chair a think tank team that concentrated on the NATO provision. His colleagues included Heritage Vice President Kim R. Holmes, an expert on European security; Ariel Cohen, Heritage's senior policy analyst in Russian and European studies; and Doug Seay, a former diplomat who had served in Romania.[27]

For its part, the Clinton administration shifted from a reactive to a proactive strategy on NATO with the appointment of Holbrooke as assistant secretary of state. At approximately the same time, Dan Fried's rise to the post of NSC's senior director for European Affairs brought another friend of Poland into an extremely influential position. Fried enjoyed good ties with Kozminski, whom he had met when assigned to the U.S. embassy in Warsaw in the early 1990s. The two men's professional acquaintance blossomed into a warm, personal friendship in Washington, where Fried became the envoy's closest contact in the White House. They regularly lunched together on roast pepper and cheese sandwiches at the Vox Populi restaurant, dined at each other's homes in the capital's Chevy Chase area, and talked daily in person or by telephone. Kozminski reiterated the view of many that "Fried was a key player" in adding the Central European countries to NATO.[28]

Warsaw's change in its approach toward NATO smoothed Kozminski's relationship with pro-expansionists in the United States. When Walesa and others began espousing Poland's entry in the alliance, their justification centered on the threat posed by a resurgent Russia. By 1994-95, Foreign Minister Olechowski, then-Foreign Affairs Committee Chairman Geremek, and Kozminski subtly shifted the rationale for membership to advancing European security as a whole. By accepting parallel tracks—NATO enlargement and NATO-Russian rapprochement—Poland's policy dovetailed with U.S. goals.

As discussions of expansion became more focused, the Polish embassy increasingly coordinated its activities with its Czech Republic and

Hungarian counterparts. Neither America's highly divided Czech community nor the Hungarian population boasted organizations that commanded the membership, leadership, and reach of the Polish American Congress. In forming the Hungarian American Coalition, Frank Koszorus, Jr., a prominent Washington attorney, and other talented leaders used the PAC as a model. Although receiving high marks for his persuasiveness on Capitol Hill, Hungary's ambassador developed only limited contacts with Hungarian Americans. They deeply resented his association with the government whose prime minister had helped suppress freedom fighters in the 1956 Budapest uprising.

For their part, leaders of the Polish American Congress, still skeptical of the administration's intentions, embarked upon a two-pronged strategy. On one hand, the PAC drummed up support for pro-NATO legislation introduced by Senators Brown, Dole, Lieberman, Simon, Roth, and Mikulski, and by Representative Gilman. On the other hand, PAC members bombarded the administration with bristling communications about both the merits of enlarging the Atlantic alliance and the dangers posed by the Kremlin. A letter from PAC President Moskal to Lake typified these exchanges. On March 15, 1995, Moskal asserted that Washington's efforts to placate Moscow's leaders over the past year and a half have failed. Instead of making Russians more reasonable, Russia has become "increasingly confrontational and aggressive. Russia has taken numerous actions around the world that are against the interests of the U.S. and its allies."[29]

Stage 4: September 1995 to Clinton's "Detroit Speech," October 22, 1996

An unresolved Balkan situation also helped to promote NATO enlargement. First, the strife demonstrated that the alliance still served a valuable purpose. Second, persistent problems in and around Bosnia revealed that the Europeans still needed sustained American involvement to resolve crises on the Continent. Third, as discussed below, Bosnia provided an opportunity for Central European governments to cooperate with members of the Atlantic alliance. Fourth, in the course of its own response to the Balkan conflict, the French government came to realize the value of involving several Central European states in the pact. Finally, Bosnia indicated that NATO could work in tandem with Russia, giving credence to the double-track policy advocated by Brzezinski, the NSC troika, and the Polish government.

Until September 1995, Defense Secretary Perry, like most Pentagon officials, had shown no enthusiasm for enlarging NATO. In that month, however, he traveled to Europe, making visits to Warsaw, Prague, Budapest, and other regional capitals. Observers insist that this experience convinced Perry of the existence of two Central Europes: one—embracing Poland, Hungary, and the Czech Republic—appeared economically, politically, and culturally linked to the West; the other reportedly left a far less favorable impression in terms of political, economic, and institutional reforms.

In September 1995, Perry reemphasized NATO's mission to protect and promote economic and political pluralism in member states. Policies along such lines undertaken by Poland, Hungary, and the Czech Republic enhanced Perry's support for expansion. Even before the secretary formally suggested these criteria, Poland's leaders anticipated such guidelines and used them as policy-making benchmarks. As outlined below, Hungary and the Czech Republic also implemented initiatives congruent with these tenets.

Perry Principles[30]

Economic Reforms

Poland

More relentlessly than other Central European governments, Polish leaders moved to open their nation's once-statist, heavily centralized economy, which suffered from hyper-inflation, a huge foreign debt, ubiquitous shortages of essential goods, a nonconvertible currency, and the absence of a real pricing system. Although the cerebral Finance Minister Balcerowicz had studied economic reforms undertaken in postwar West Germany, in Pinochet's Chile, and by the Asian Tigers, no model existed for converting an economy from communism to capitalism. Nonetheless, the intrepid professor-turned-practitioner applied high-voltage shock therapy by abandoning subsidies for foodstuffs, coal, gasoline, electricity, and transportation. Increasingly, he let the market determine prices of key goods. To promote disciplined management across the board, the plan also required that the government privatize hundreds of state-owned companies. To institute a stable, globally tradeable currency, Balcerowicz slashed the budget deficit and instituted a tax system. To save the country from bankruptcy, he had to do the near impossible: In the words of Walesa, Balcerowicz "made eggs from an omelette." In addition, Poland later cofounded the Central European Free Trade Association (CEFTA), crafted to reduce commercial barriers among Poland, Hungary, the Czech Republic, and Slovakia. Parties to CEFTA agreed to begin liberalization of trade in raw materials and noncompetitive imports, followed by opening markets for agricultural products and most industrial goods. Signatories committed themselves to addressing sensitive, high-value-added items—cars, textiles, and steel— by 2001. In recognition of Poland's economic attainments, the EU extended an offer of "associate membership" to Warsaw in May 1994— with accession to the union expected early in the next century.

In November 1997, two Solidarity-offshoot parties took power, placing Jerzy Buzek in the prime minister's seat. Buzek has accelerated efforts to broaden health-care coverage, reform the pension system, decrease the size of the coal and steel sector, and privatize remaining state-owned industries. He has also speeded up Poland's preparations for NATO entry.

Czech Republic

Less grave conditions in the postcommunist period explain more modest economic changes in Czechoslovakia. After all, observers regarded the Prague regime as the "economic champion of the former Soviet bloc states."[31] After the January 1, 1993 "Velvet Divorce" that divided Czechoslovakia, Czech Prime Minister Václav Klaus instituted substantially milder reforms than those achieved in Poland. A series of problems—decreased outlays for agriculture, diminished spending on pensions, and financial and banking scandals—magnified popular distaste for the government's belt-tightening programs. In the spring of 1997, Klaus, who faced a declining GDP, mounting unemployment, and an annual 10.3 percent inflation rate, imposed austerity measures to redress imbalances and reignite growth. These reforms included slashing the budget, devaluing the currency, accelerating privatizations, and imposing stricter regulatory mechanisms. Still, devastating floods contributed to a 2.7 percent drop in economic activity. The public's negative reaction to this strong medicine accounted for President Havel's late-1997 encouragement of Klaus to step down in favor of an interim prime minister, independent economist Josef Tosovsky.

Hungary

Interestingly, Hungary's Marxist regime began reforming its command economy in the late 1980s, obviating the immediate need for the kind of abrupt liberalization implemented by the Polish government. A UN study showed that Hungary attracted more direct foreign investment than did any other former Soviet-bloc state, some $14 billion in the 1990-97 period. Nonetheless, budget and current-account deficits forced the Horn government to enact a sweeping stabilization plan in 1995. This unpopular action bore fruit in 1998 when gross domestic product grew 3.5 percent amid low unemployment and inflation. At the same time, the ruling Socialist-Liberal coalition continued to privatize large state-owned enterprises, even weathering official wrongdoing that linked private firms to prominent politicians. Impressive progress led the World Bank to approve a $225 million loan to restructure the country's archaic banking sector.

Commitment to Democracy

Poland

In mid-1990, martial-law-era leader General Jaruzelski announced he would step down as president, opening the way for Walesa's winning the election to succeed the communist chief that December. Walesa supporters and other Solidarity-related forces also captured a robust majority in the 460-seat Sejm, the lower house of Poland's parliament.

Austerity initiatives soon diminished Walesa's popularity, and the Polish electorate swung to the left in September 1993. The former Communist Party, renamed Social Democracy of the Republic of Poland Party (SDRP), formed the heart of the Alliance of the Democratic Left (SLD), which captured enough seats to forge a legislative coalition with the left-populist Polish Peasant Party (PSL). By November 1995, government power had again changed hands peacefully as SLD candidate Kwasniewski won a majority in a multiparty election, ousting Walesa from the presidency. Many voters blamed the former Solidarity chief for the economic and social hardships they suffered during Poland's economic opening after 1989. Others castigated Walesa's mercurial behavior; a few believed that he had failed to pay taxes on a $1 million contract for movie rights to his life story; and some younger citizens resented Walesa's opposition to abortion rights and other social positions influenced by the Roman Catholic Church. The defeated president's supporters unsuccessfully attempted to invalidate Kwasniewski's victory because he had lied about holding a university degree in economics. Evidence of Poland's political maturation lay in the consolidation of more than one hundred parties—which emerged in the postcommunist burst of pluralism—to five significant parties in 1999, four of which hold seats in the Sejm.

Democratic rule in Poland continued to consolidate, even outside of elections for public office. Poles voted 52.7 percent to 45.9 percent to approve a new constitution that continues the post-1989 parliamentary system with several modifications, one of the most important of which shifts from the president to the prime minister formal responsibility for national defense. The 1998 fundamental law also guarantees a minimum wage, free education, and universal health care. Thus, a social safety net complements the state's commitment to a market economy.

Czech Republic

In the Czech Republic, the reaction to sweeping economic reforms undermined Klaus's coalition, composed of his own Civic Democratic Party, the Christian Democrats which embrace the People's Party, and the Civic Democratic Alliance. In mid-1998 voters brought to power the Social Democrats, who named former communist Milos Zeman as prime minister. This election signified the smooth transition to a new, leftist government, following eight years of moderate-conservative rule.

Hungary

Hungarian Socialists joined the government in 1994, after the splintering of Prime Minister Antall's center-right coalition. Ex-communist Gyula Horn emerged as the head of a Socialist-Liberal amalgam, which—to the amazement of many observers—pursued reforms initiated by its predecessors. Indeed, Horn actively campaigned for Hungary's NATO membership, backed by two-thirds of voters in a mid-November 1997 referendum. As noted earlier, evidence of official corruption surfaced with respect to the privatization program. While these revelations did not stall the sale of state-owned firms, the electorate did hold the ruling coalition to account. The Alliance of Young Democrats (Fidesz), the Smallholders' Party, and the Hungarian Democratic Forum formed a new government after the May 1998 national contests. Accentuating the rightward drift of Hungarian politics, Istvan Czurka's conservative, nationalist Hungarian Justice and Life Party won parliamentary seats for the first time.

International Policies

Poland

In November 1992, Poland's National Defense Committee—including Walesa, Prime Minister Hanna Suchocka, and other cabinet officials—unveiled a new security doctrine based on the assumption that Poland had no natural enemies and no territorial claims on its neighbors.[32] Post-cold war Polish governments have signed peace and cooperation agreements with contiguous countries, which grew from three to seven in number after the Soviet Union's breakup. As evidenced by Walesa's welcome to Yeltsin in August 1993, Poland has made a special effort to allay Russia's concerns about NATO expansion. Anti-Russian rhetoric, quite prevalent after 1989, has sharply diminished. In 1993, Poland also began to champion economic assistance to Ukraine at the UN, the IMF, the World Bank, and other international organizations. In May 1997, President Kwasniewski signed a reconciliation pact with his Ukrainian counterpart Leonid Kuchma. This accord condemned the deportation of some 100,000 Ukrainians from south-eastern Poland in 1947 and the killings of thousands of Poles by Ukrainian extremists during World War II. In addition, Poland and Ukraine formed a joint peacekeeping battalion. As a result, policymakers in Kiev moved from "hesitant," to "ambivalent," to "positive" with respect to Poland's joining NATO.[33] Furthermore, Poland conciliated the Vilnius government by participating in a joint peacekeeping battalion with Lithuania.

Czech Republic

In preparation for NATO membership, Czech defense officials agreed with their Hungarian and Polish counterparts to coordinate military policies and procurements, beginning in 1995. But Czech-Slovak relations have deteriorated since the Czech Republic promised to turn over part of the gold confiscated from Slovak Jews in World War II to a Jewish foundation. President Havel's criticism of Slovak Prime Minister Vladamir Meciar's disdain for NATO enlargement sharpened bilateral tensions.

Hungary

Hungary has also mended fences with nearby countries. During a visit by President Yeltsin in November 1992, the Budapest government dropped demands that Russia compensate it for environmental damage done at Soviet bases between 1956 and 1991. Hungary's leadership promised to provide humanitarian aid "commensurate with its means" to Russian troops previously stationed in its country. Furthermore, Hungary agreed to purchase $800 million worth of military equipment and spare parts to partly offset Russia's trade deficit of $1.7 billion. In a speech to Hungary's National Assembly, Yeltsin voiced hope that the two countries could put their "mutual bitter past" behind them, and relaunch bilateral relations on a "fresh sheet." He also denounced the Soviet invasion of Hungary in 1956, and visited the grave of Imre Nagy, chief of Hungary's revolutionary government during the aborted uprising.[34]

Hungary has resolved most outstanding differences with its neighbors. The Antall regime concluded basic treaties on understanding, cooperation, and good-neighborliness with several of its neighbors: Ukraine (1991), the Soviet Union (1991), Croatia (1992), and Slovenia (1992). Although the Horn government signed treaties with Slovakia (1995) and Romania (1996), these accords were deficient with respect to the protection of Hungarian minorities.

In addition, Hungary, Italy, and Slovenia promised to form a joint military brigade and to hold regular maneuvers. At the same time, however, Hungarian-Slovakian relations deteriorated when Slovak Prime Minister Meciar suggested that the Hungarian minority could leave Slovakia at any time. Analysts project that Meciar's defeat in the September 1998 elections will reduce tensions in Central Europe.

Human Rights (an Indicator of Commitment to Democracy)

Poland

Poland's population includes far fewer minorities than either Hungary or the Czech Republic. Post-1989 governments have allocated four Sejm seats to the country's German population. President Walesa's principal advances in human rights involved Jews, long the target of attacks in Europe and the principal victim of the Nazi holocaust carried out on occupied Polish soil. In May 1991, the shipyard-worker-turned-politician flew to Israel. Speaking before the Knesset, he apologized for anti-Semitic acts that had taken place in Poland. In early 1994, Pope John Paul II sought to resolve a long-simmering dispute between the Polish Church and the Jewish community by calling on Carmelite nuns to abandon their convent at the Auschwitz-Birkenau concentration camp. In January

1995, Poland hosted a commemoration of the fiftieth anniversary of the camp's liberation. Delegates from more than twenty countries issued a joint resolution, calling the Holocaust "the biggest crime in history."

Kozminski took extreme care in dealing with the powder keg of Jewish issues, both in Poland and the United States. He understood the moral importance of these questions for the American Jewish community and worked with Nowak, Fried, and the government in Warsaw to achieve a sensitive resolution of the Auschwitz site imbroglio. In mid-1996, Kwasniewski vetoed a commercial development at Auschwitz-Birkenau, thereby preserving a place of Jewish martyrdom. In addition, with the president's blessing, Prime Minister Buzek's government has removed all crosses from the "field of ashes" at the Auschwitz II death camp, and joined the Roman Catholic Church in urging removal of provocative new crosses erected by an anti-Semitic fringe group near Auschwitz I. Buzek himself participated in the Israeli-sponsored "March of the Living" at Auschwitz and attended the rededication of the major synagogue at Wroclaw on the sixtieth anniversary of the Nazi Kristallnacht. Poland's deft handling of these symbolic, emotionally charged questions ensured the support of mainstream American Jews for NATO enlargement.

Czech Republic

Meanwhile, ethnic controversies continue to churn in the Czech Republic. In early 1997, an organization of expatriate Sudeten Germans (CSSD) decried the biased composition of a council established to study Czech-German relations. The council originated as the result of a January 1997 declaration of reconciliation between the two countries covering Nazi Germany's annexation of Czech territory in 1938-39 and the postwar expulsion of three million Sudeten Germans by the Prague government.[35] Partially in response to this dispute, Havel, after beginning his final term as president, committed himself to combating the increased "nationalism" and "xenophobia" in Czech society.[36]

Even as the Czech Republic has begun to make amends to its German population, the Roma—or Gypsy—minority continues to decry discrimination and repression. Officials in the city of Ostrava even discussed giving the Roma free air tickets to emigrate to the United Kingdom, Canada, and other countries. In 1997 the Czech government issued a special report promising to improve the Roma's conditions and establishing an "inter-ministerial commission for Roma community affairs"—efforts scorned by critics as "mere window-dressing."[37]

Hungary

After two years of preparatory work, parliament passed a law on the status of national and ethnic minorities. This legislation recognized the rights of all ethnic groups that have lived in the country for at least a century, and whose members are Hungarian citizens, to have their own language, culture, and traditions. These groups include Armenians, Bulgarians, Croats, Germans, Greeks, Poles, Roma, Romanians, Ruthenians, Serbs, Slovaks, Slovenes, and Ukrainians. Nevertheless, leaders of the 500,000 Romanies claimed that their people continued to suffer de facto discrimination in employment and housing, while falling victim to skinhead attacks and vigilante justice. Such complaints prompted parliament to add hate crimes, punishable by up to three years in prison, to its penal code.

In 1991, Hungary launched a program to compensate surviving Jewish victims of the Holocaust, and pledged to return property to the Roman Catholic Church that communists had confiscated after World War II.

Civilian Control of the Military and Ability to Contribute Militarily to NATO

Poland

Civil-military relations have sparked controversies in Poland. In April 1992, Walesa fired Jan Parys, Poland's first civilian defense minister, stating that Poland "had still not yet settled the relations between a civilian minister of defense and professional military matters."[38] Parys himself forced the retirement of his predecessor Kolodziejczyk. He warned that politicians like Walesa might use the army for "political intrigues," offering promotions to officers in return for their support, and put himself at the prime minister's disposal. In part, the problem stemmed from the constitution's vagueness about whether responsibility for security questions rested with the cabinet or the president.[39]

In February 1996, after protracted debate, the Sejm passed legislation clarifying civilian dominance over the military relations in defense matters. The tension over control of Poland's armed forces abated with the March 1997 removal of General Tadeusz Wlecki, chief of the country's general staff, who voiced his misgivings concerning civilian dominance of the military. General Henryk Szumski, his successor, has adopted a more progressive position on this key element of the Perry Principles.

Czech Republic

The Czech Republic has achieved the most success among aspiring NATO members in establishing civilian control of the military. The government named the president commander in chief of the armed forces, and in October 1990 a parliamentary commission appointed the first civilian defense minister. The following year, a new defense minister arrived to reorganize the ministry with an eye to strengthening civilian authority even further.

Hungary

Legislative and constitutional provisions empower the Parliament to exercise oversight functions over the Defense Ministry, which in turn controls the armed forces. The Constitution vests Parliament with authority over the military budget, structure, deployment, and senior leadership. The 1993 National Defense Law specifies that the chief of staff, commander of the armed forces, answers to the minister of defense, a member of Parliament.

Polish Lobbying

Fulfilling the Perry Principles did not distract Poland's Washington embassy from developing close relationships all over Capitol Hill. At the ambassador's direction, political officers Wyganowski and Winid categorized the Senators under five rubrics: (1) emphatically committed to ratification, (2) pro-enlargement without emphatic commitment, (3) uncommitted but leaning in favor, (4) uncommitted but leaning against, and (5) opposed. The political section then arranged meetings between Kozminski and individual senators—with emphasis on categories 2, 3, and 4, but ignoring neither emphatic friends nor perceived foes of expansion. Sometimes, the ambassador made courtesy calls alone, as did his associates from other aspiring members; after the mid-1997 Madrid Summit, Kozminski increasingly visited Capitol Hill with colleagues from Hungary and the Czech Republic. When legislators themselves had no time to meet, the diplomats arranged to speak with key foreign-affairs aides. By 1996 the embassy had targeted more than thirty key Congressional staff members, four of whom were deemed "critical": Ian Brzezinski, Senator Roth's legislative assistant for national security affairs; Steve Biegun, an American of Polish extraction who served on the senior professional staff of the Senate Foreign Relations Committee; Michael Haltzel, Senator Biden's top aide on the SFRC staff; and Mark Gage, an aide to House Inter-national Relations Committee Chairman Representative Benjamin Gilman.[40]

The fact that two senators and seven representatives boasted Polish ancestry did not hurt embassy access to Capitol Hill.[41] Crucially, Polish embassy staff regularly exchanged information with Rosner's NERO office.

The Polish embassy actively cooperated in arranging visits of the Visegrad countries' foreign ministers, each of whom traveled to the United States twice before the final Senate vote. For instance, the three ambassadors made certain that all three ministers met with the twenty-two-member Senate NATO Observer Group (SNOG), discussed in Chapter 6. In addition, they helped ensure that key senators attended dinners hosted by Jackson's U.S. Committee to Expand NATO for the visiting dignitaries.

During the four years before the crucial Senate vote, Poland had two presidents, four prime ministers, four foreign ministers, and five defense ministers. Kozminski turned what might seem like the vice of instability into the virtue of continuity: despite numerous changes in *dramatis personae*, each new member of the cast reiterated his full-throated commitment to the Perry Principles. Furthermore, the emergence of new players afforded the embassy an excuse for scheduling even more visits to congressional offices to introduce the new actors.[42]

The Polish American Congress assisted with the get-acquainted activities. For instance, on May 1, 1997, the PAC in cooperation with the embassy commemorated Polish Constitution Day by hosting a highly successful Capitol Hill breakfast for Premier Wlodzimierz Cimoszewicz. Kozminski, Senator Mikulski, and Representative Gilman served as honorary sponsors for the event, which attracted thirty senators and thirty-six House members as cosponsors.[43]

Stage 5: October 22, 1996 to the Madrid Summit, July 7, 1997

With President Clinton fully supporting NATO expansion, Poland's Washington embassy no longer concentrated on the executive branch. Instead, it stepped up efforts to build firmer support in Congress and among interest groups. Myra Lenard and her colleagues at the Polish American Congress joined in this endeavor. Specifically, the PAC sponsored a three-day fact-finding trip to Poland for eleven congressional staff members. The visitors, who joined Senator Richard Durbin (D-IL) in Warsaw, met with Polish cabinet members, legislative leaders, military specialists, and scholars at the Lech Walesa Institute, a think tank for policymakers and political activists.[44]

Even as it rolled the red carpet out for influential Americans, Warsaw kept a close eye on negotiations over the NATO-Russia Founding Act. Above all, Polish authorities wanted to avoid the inclusion of language that would consign Poland to second-class status within the alliance. Consequently Kwasniewski, his foreign minister, and Kozminski labored to avoid limitations on the stationing or movement of NATO troops, the construction of military infrastructure, or the introduction of nuclear arms in Poland. While the Poles achieved their goal in a technical sense, the United States and Russia had tacitly agreed that the Atlantic alliance would neither concentrate military units in Central Europe nor locate nuclear weapons in the region. The Polish government also scrutinized the conventional-force negotiations, lest provisions in the final accord constrain its freedom of action.

In the United States, Ambassador Kozminski appealed more and more to Poland's consulates to stir up grass-roots support for ratification. Upon reaching Washington in 1994, Kozminski had initiated annual meetings with Poland's three consuls-general in the United States, residing in Chicago, New York, and Los Angeles, as well as with the two honorary consuls, in Boston and San Juan, Puerto Rico. While the envoys discussed cultural exchanges, Polish-Jewish relations, Poles in America, and economic matters, NATO expansion devoured fifty percent of their agenda. The consuls-generals helped build support among local businesses, trade unions, civic associations, and fraternal organizations. Polish diplomats actually took the lead in obtaining endorsements from nineteen state legislatures. Later, they joined Rosner in soliciting support from governors, mayors, and city councils, an activity the embassy had begun before NERO's formation.[45]

During the 1996 electoral campaigns, the Poles carefully monitored candidates to determine their position on NATO's future. They were particularly impressed by the internationalist views of Senate aspirant Chuck Hagel, to whom the ambassador paid a congratulatory visit soon after his decisive victory. During their conversation, the men discovered that the Nebraska lawmaker's grandmother was born in Poznan, making him a Polish American.[46]

In July 1997 after the Madrid summit, President Clinton addressed 30,000 cheering Poles in Warsaw's Castle Square. Ex-communist President Kwasniewski startled the crowd when he turned to Walesa, whom he had defeated in 1995, and praised him for doing so much for their country. The Solidarity leader rose and bowed, prompting the assemblage to applaud both men for their civility.

Immediately after his speech, Clinton met with Solidarity veterans inside the Royal Castle, once the seat of parliament. Former Prime Minister Olszewski recalled that, as a boy, he had seen the castle in flames at the beginning of World War II. "I know," he said, "what insecurity can lead to. And I know that this Castle and this city will not burn again." Solidarity stalwart Maciej Jankowski pointed out that, as far back as anyone could remember, someone in his family had to fight—and sometimes die—for Poland. "But now, Mr. President," he said, "because of what you have done, I believe that my children will not have to die in war. We will have peace at long last." At this point, fellow Solidarity activist Marion Krzaklewski added, simply, "We know NATO membership means responsibilities. We are ready."[47]

Stage 6: Madrid Summit to Ratification, April 30, 1998

For the run-up to this vote, Ambassador Kozminski continued to work with Polish consulates and other nations' embassies to broaden and mobilize the network of supporters identified throughout the United States. He applauded efforts by the Polish American Congress—in concert with other ethnic interest groups—to keep letters, facsimiles, visits, and calls pouring onto Capitol Hill. Kozminski and his lieutenants spoke to audiences around the country, taking part in dozens of background media interviews. In addition to keeping NERO apprised, embassy personnel also maintained active ties with the U.S. Committee to Expand NATO and other allies. The ambassador himself became the diplomatic version of perpetual motion.

In late 1996, SFRC ranking member Biden had wondered publicly, "who cares about NATO expansion?" He soon found out when Richard J. Bartkowski, a Polish American politician in Wilmington, Delaware, went into action. Although the only Republican on the body, Bartkowski convinced his twelve fellow city council members to unanimously pass a pro-enlargement resolution, which Senator Roth promptly entered in the *Congressional Record*. At the same time, Delaware's Polish American community assiduously cultivated Biden, who tended to publicly articulate the potential pitfalls of enlargement. In September 1997, standing under a banner emblazoned with the words "POLAND-NATO-USA," Ambassador Kozminski proclaimed both of Delaware's senators "heroes" at a gathering of some five-hundred Polish Americans in Wilmington's venerable Hotel DuPont. Biden later joined Roth as a key leader in the ratification effort much to the delight of residents of Hedgeville and Browntown, Wilmington's predominantly Polish American neighborhoods.[48]

Meanwhile, Colonel Lenard, Koszorus, and Joseph Pritasil, a leader of the Czechoslovak Council of America, took part in a five-country European tour in October 1997. Sponsored by the departments of State and Defense, this trip afforded twenty leaders of military, veterans', ethnic-American, and religious organizations an opportunity to observe first-hand the preparations that Poland, Hungary, and the Czech Republic had made to join NATO.

Poland, Inc.'s multiple endeavors emboldened the embassy to estimate that the "yea" vote would fall between 78 and 84.

Conclusion

Chef Darkowski planned to lay on his most extravagant meal on May 1. That evening, approximately 530 people would swarm into Poland's English Renaissance-style embassy. Celebrating the legislative triumph here seemed particularly appropriate, inasmuch as ex-Senator John Brooks Henderson, a Unionist from Missouri, had constructed the building in 1910. Nine years later, he sold the majestic, four-storey structure to Prince Casimir Lubomirski, Poland's first envoy to the United States. The second-floor Salon would overflow with guests, some of whom would find themselves pinioned against a Steinway grand piano. World-renowned musician and statesman Ignacy Jan Paderewski had presented the instrument to the embassy in 1941. But Darkowski, Kozminski, the embassy staff, and other pro-expansionists had to endure a long day of debate, proposed amendments, and parliamentary maneuvers before the first celebratory course left the kitchen.

Whatever the outcome, the Poles could take pride in the contributions they had made to the European-security debate. They had exerted consistent, effective pressure on decisionmakers in NATO capitals; influenced the conversion of PFP I to PFP II; championed Brzezinski's "dual-track" approach toward Russia; encouraged a new European security architecture that, in addition to NATO expansion, included the OSCE, the CFE, and the Russia-NATO Founding Act; emerged as the prime advocate for the Ukraine; and stressed the importance of integrating Europe rather than the less appealing idea of eliminating a security vacuum in Central Europe.[49]   Chapter 6 analyzes the Senate's final action on the ratification protocols.

Notes

1. Rey, interview by author, August 5, 1998.
2. Kozminski, telephone interview by author, November 3, 1998.
3. Quoted in Vladimir Kusin, "Security Concerns in Central Europe, *Report on Eastern Europe*, March 8, 1991, p. 35; see Larrabee, *East European Security after the Cold War* (p. 55) on which I have relied heavily in this section.
4. Quoted in Michael Simmons, "Poles Want More Power for NATO," *The Guardian*, January 10, 1991.
5. Reportedly, Kohl assented only after Claiborne Pell, then-chairman of the Senate Foreign Relations Committee, threatened to introduce legislation whereby the United States would refuse to recognize a unified Germany (Nowak, interview, October 16, 1998).
6. "A Time of Dizzying Change," *Polityka*, August 8, 1992; translated in Foreign Broadcast Information Service (FBIS), EEU-92-152, August 6, 1992, pp. 24-29.
7. Rey, interview, August 5, 1998.
8. Anna Marszalek, "A Meeting by Polish and U.S. Intelligence," *Rzeczpospolitca*, October 28, 1997; in Foreign Broadcast Information Service, *Daily Report: East Europe*, FBIS-EEU-97-301, October 28, 1997, Internet edition.
9. Larrabee, *East European Security after the Cold War*, p. 60.
10. For the adumbration of these stages, I am indebted to Ambassador Kozminski, interview, October 19, 1998.
11. One former adviser to the U.S. government claimed that Olechowski's anger exploded in his pounding the desk of a senior State Department official. If so, such behavior would have been out of character for the urbane, witty, and gregarious public servant. For example, Secretary of State Lawrence Eagleburger told a leading Polish American that he enjoyed meetings with Olechowski, especially compared with sessions with other foreign ministers from the region for which he had to "take a half-dozen aspirin" in preparation (Nowak, telephone interview, November 14, 1998).
12. Polish American Congress, "Review of the Role of the Polish American Congress in Bringing Poland into NATO, Historical Background: 1939-1991," Internet.
13. Polish American Congress, "Review of the Role of the Polish American Congress," Internet.
14. Polish American Congress, "Review of the Role of the Polish American Congress," Internet.
15. Polish American Congress, "Review of the Role of the Polish American Congress," Internet.
16. Nowak, interview, October 16, 1998.

17. Nowak, telephone interview, November 16, 1998.

18. Nowak, interview, October 16, 1998.

19. Fried, electronic mail to author, December 15, 1998.

20. Colonel Casimir Lenard, Polish American Congress, Washington, D.C., interview by author, June 30, 1998.

21. For example, the embassy helped alert the Polish American Southeast Chamber of Commerce in Atlanta and other business associations with interests in Poland of the merits of enlarging the alliance.

22. Michael Wyganowski, first secretary, political section, Embassy of the Republic of Poland, telephone interview by author, June 29, 1998.

23. (Detroit: Wayne State University Press, 1982).

24. Nowak, interview, October 16, 1998.

25. Alexander J. Groth, "Poland," *Encyclopedia Americana 1995 Annual* (n.p.: Grolier, 1995), pp. 420-21.

26. Brzezinski, letter to author, December 4, 1998.

27. Larry Di Rita, legislative director for Senator Kay Bailey Hutchison, telephone interview by author, November 4, 1998.

28. Kozminski, telephone interview, November 3, 1998.

29. Polish American Congress, "Role of the Polish American Congress," Internet.

30. This section benefits greatly from Appendix 3 (pp. 439-44) and Adrian Karatnycky, Alexander Motyl, and Boris Shor, eds., "Excerpts from: 'Nations in Transit'" (pp. 445-87), in U.S. Senate, Committee on Foreign Relations, *The Debate on NATO Enlargement*.

31. Carol Skalnik Leff, "Could this Marriage Have been Saved? The Czechoslovak Divorce," *Current History* 95, no. 599 (March 1996): 133.

32. *Keesing's Record of World Events 1992* (Cambridge, UK: Longman, 1992), p. 39200.

33. Anonymous, interview, October 19, 1998.

34. *Keesing's Record of World Events 1992*, p. 39200.

35. *Keesing's Record of World Events 1997*, p. 41461.

36. *Keesing's Record of World Events 1997*, p. 42087.

37. Sharon L. Wolchik, "Czech Republic," *The Americana Annual 1998* (n.p.: Grolier, 1998), p. 209; "Slovacs v Czechs on Gypsies," *The Economist*, November 7-13, 1998, p. 52.

38. *Keesing's Record of World Events 1992*, p. 38880.

39. *Keesing's Record of World Events 1992*, pp. 38880-1.

40. Until Senator Hank Brown retired in 1996, his top foreign-policy aide, Carter Pilcher, was also a "key figure" (Kozminski, interview, October 19, 1998).

41. The senators are Barbara A. Mikulski (D-MD) and Frank H. Murkowski (R-AL); the representatives are Robert A. Borski (D-PA), David E. Bonior (D-MI), John D. Dingell (D-MI), Paul E. Kanjorski (D-PA), Marcy Kaptur

(D-OH), Gerald D. Kleczka (D-WI), and William O. Lipinski (D-IL). David R. Obey (D-WI) is married to a Polish American.

42. Kozminski, telephone interview, November 3, 1998.
43. Polish Constitution Day actually falls on May 3, a Saturday in 1997; however, few legislators turn out for weekend events.
44. Polish American Congress, "US Congressional Staffers Visit Poland," *News Release*, Washington, D.C., February 27, 1997.
45. Kozminski, interview, October 19, 1998.
46. Kozminski, interview, October 19, 1998.
47. This scene was recounted by Fried, electronic mail to author, December 15, 1998.
48. City Councilman Paul T. Bartkowski, twenty-nine-year-old son of former councilman Richard J. Bartkowski, telephone interview, November 4, 1998.
49. Kozminski emphasized the warmer reception that he and his colleagues received when urging European integration rather than addressing a security vacuum (interview, October 19, 1998).

Chapter 6

ℰᴂ

Senate Action

Introduction

The administration's support for the NATO Enlargement Participation Act of 1996, combined with President Clinton's pro-expansion speech in Detroit near the end of the 1996 campaign, signaled a growing consensus linking both ends of Pennsylvania Avenue with respect to inviting the Visegrad states into the alliance. Nevertheless, relatively few lawmakers focused on NATO's future in early 1997. The questions that swirled about the cost of expansion and the possibility of explosive developments abroad—like American troop fatalities in Bosnia—meant that enlargement advocates could take nothing for granted.

The Senate Staff: Hearings and Bill Drafting

A medley of factors—the myriad of bills, the complexity of issues, ever-longer sessions, and growing nonpolicy demands on legislators' time—has expanded the role professional staff members play on Capitol Hill. Preparations for the NATO vote exemplified this trend. Individuals on the SFRC's majority staff (Steve Biegun and Beth Wilson) and minority staff (Michael Haltzel) worked extremely well together.   They also cooperated closely with Ian Brzezinski, a security expert in Senator Roth's office, Fred Downey, a professional staff member for Senator Lieberman, and Ken Myers III of Senator Lugar's office. The intelligent, politically savvy, and typically young Senate personnel established effective bonds with Rosner and NERO's virtual office.

Among the early challenges they faced was recruiting witnesses for the eight hearings scheduled by the Senate Foreign Relations Committee. The staff's enthusiastic support for adding members to the Atlantic alliance tempted them to load the docket with likeminded speakers.   Although eager for pro-expansionist testimony, Rosner, Haltzel, and Biegun agreed on the desirability of also inviting the best-informed and most articulate opponents of expansion. This striving for balance manifested itself during the October 9, 1997 hearing when Senator Roth, Zbigniew Brzezinski, and former UN Ambassador Kirkpatrick spoke in favor of enlargement, while Ambassador Dean and Professor Mandelbaum excoriated the initiative.   Proponents outnumbered opponents three-to-one during the seven committee sessions held between October 7 and November 5, 1997. The predominance of pro-expansion participants sprang not from any stacking of the deck, but from the opponents' inability to present more experts in what increasingly loomed as a losing cause for their side. Nevertheless, the senators heard from nearly a dozen foes of enlargement. In addition, three other Senate committees conducted hearings on the NATO protocols.

David A. Harris, executive director of the New York-based American Jewish Committee (AJC), founded in 1906 in response to pogroms carried out by czarist officials, surprised some senators with his organization's resounding support for augmenting the alliance.   After all, Polish membership would add to the pact a country where anti-Semitism had long thrived, and perceived anti-Semitic statements by President Moskal sparked tensions even within his own Polish American Congress.   Yet Harris spoke passionately about Munich, Yalta, and the "West [having] watched from the sidelines as Soviet power squashed fledgling and promising democratic movements in Hungary in 1956, in Czechoslovakia in 1968, and in Poland in 1981."[1] Enlarging NATO, he averred, would mean "greater stability and security for Central Europe, a region that has already been the cockpit for two World Wars that brought such horror to the world."[2] In other words, stabilizing this region through NATO expansion would sharply diminish the likelihood of future pogroms, holocausts, and other crimes against humanity. As an AJC official stated,

"If NATO ends at Check-Point Charlie [in Berlin], then the alliance withers."[3]

Whether by design or chance, the AJC participated in a virtual minuet with Polish Jews, especially young professionals. Leaders of Poland's 3,500-member Jewish community would apprise Harris of their government's remarkable strides in combatting bigotry; the AJC would then praise such efforts in statements featured in the Polish press; and, the dissemination of these accolades spurred even greater efforts by Polish leaders to improve the climate for religious tolerance.[4] Ironically, one of the few Jewish organizations to oppose enlargement was the Jewish Institute for National Security Affairs, which specializes in defense matters.

Jan Nowak, who also offered moving testimony on the same day as Harris, later observed the large number of Jews in the administration who had championed expansion: Berger, Fried, Holbrooke, Rosner, Steinberg, Vershbow, and others. "Without the active, enthusiastic support of the Jewish community, there would have been no enlargement," he affirmed.[5]

The AJC's emphatic support made it easier for staff members to prepare ratification legislation that would enjoy broad appeal on Capitol Hill. Senator Biden's assistant Haltzel favored introducing a "clean" streamlined version of the protocols, then marshalling pro-expansionists to defeat threatening amendments. Only after the legislation hit the floor would he consider acceptable changes in the language to garner additional votes. Senator Helms's aide Biegun agreed on the need to fend off all amendments, lest even minor floor changes throw open the floodgates to harmful modifications in the legislation. But Biegun realized that initially accepting a handful of changes advocated by key senators would swell the ranks of opponents to floor amendments inasmuch as more legislators would become invested in securing final passage of a measure they had helped draft.

After assessing both ideas, NERO chief Rosner agreed with Biegun's approach, which Biden's staff graciously accepted. Thus, Rosner worked with Helms's and Biden's top lieutenants to stitch relatively minor, but symbolically important, provisions into the original text. Above all, Biegun sought to propitiate GOP conservatives by reiterating opposition to any Russian veto over the accession of new NATO members. To quell concerns about cost issues, the drafters inscribed a requirement for annual reports on expansion funding. In addition, to reassure senators who worried that a larger alliance would dilute NATO's central mission,

they stressed that NATO's military goal remained "collective defense."
Finally, Haltzel applauded the administration's proposal to eliminate
gratuitous Russia-bashing and insert a reference to "democratic Russia"
in hopes of winning over more Democrats, even liberals like Paul
Wellstone.[6] The additional language extended the length of the ratification
resolution to more than one thousand words, while the original legislation,
as well as measures to admit Germany, Greece, Turkey, and Spain, fell
under one hundred words.

Senate Foreign Relations Committee

The ideologically riven Senate Foreign Relations Committee that
took up NATO expansion in 1998 paled in comparison to its 1949
predecessor, which had molded and approved the Washington Treaty.
Nonetheless, committee consideration of the expansion protocols marked
an important step in the ratification process. It's a tribute to Biegun's
drafting strategy that the committee accepted no amendments except a
proposal by Senator Dianne Feinstein to require more reports on costs.
Most of the discussion among SFRC members centered on Ashcroft's
concerns (mentioned in the Introduction) about missions, strategic doctrine,
and NATO evolving into some kind of "globo-cop"—questions sure to
excite discussion at the April 1999 Washington summit and other future
NATO meetings.

SFRC's action on the enlargement legislation in no way overcame its
sharp fall in status, evident by examining international, national, and
institutional factors. International relations remains extremely important
for the United States. However, the cold war's end has radically changed
the challenges faced overseas. The demise of the Soviet Union has obviated
the need for grand popular, bipartisan ventures like the United Nations,
the Greek-Turkish relief program, the Marshall Plan, the Berlin airlift,
and NATO. More often than not foreign policy involves complex,
intractable problems that seldom yield clear-cut and popular outcomes.
These include pursuing Mideast peace, preventing Saddam Hussein-style
tyrants from deploying weapons of mass destruction, curbing North
Korea's appetite for nuclear arms, keeping civil strife from further
rupturing the Balkans, providing relief to disaster victims in Africa and
Central America, stemming the influx of boat people from Caribbean
islands, and crafting rescue packages for Indonesia, Russia, Brazil, and
other wobbly economies.

In such thorny areas, lawmakers seem inclined to defer to the executive branch, reserving the right to castigate policies that fail or yield incomplete results, or suggest partisan motivation or vulnerability. Majority Leader Lott's immediate, barbed criticism of President Clinton's December 1998 air attack on Iraq exemplifies this tendency. The new array of international issues works against the emergence of latter-day Arthur Vandenbergs and William Fulbrights, whose reputations as statesmen sprang from leadership in foreign policy.

On the national scene, the crumbling of the Berlin Wall has diminished the public's concern for foreign affairs vis-à-vis domestic matters. This change has produced three outcomes: First, voters resonate to candidates pledging to improve employment opportunities, health-care coverage, educational opportunities, transportation needs, and pension benefits. Second, Senate aspirants emphasize these bread-and-butter issues, and—if elected—seek posts on committees relevant to their constituents' interests. Third, the changing national agenda finds ever more parochial men and women arriving on Capitol Hill. Just a few years ago, candidates for national office extolled their study, travel, or work abroad; many of the current crop of politicians tend to downplay such experiences, if they have had them at all.

At the institutional level, the style, objectives, and performance of the chairman and ranking member strongly affect a committee's status. Although Lugar tried to raise the SFRC's profile during his tenure as chairman in 1985-86, his successors—Democrat Claiborne Pell of Rhode Island (1988-96) and Republican Helms (1981-85 and 1996-)—have contributed significantly to the panel's decreasing attractiveness.

A former foreign service officer, the cerebral, nonassertive Pell exuded lethargy, and—during his penultimate term—dissipated his energies in Hamlet-like vacillation over whether to seek reelection. In the SFRC chair, the patrician Pell found himself caught in the crossfire as Helms and other hard-right conservatives battled moderates and liberals. The casus belli frequently involved the effort of unabashed conservatives to attach anti-abortion amendments to bills unrelated to population control. Such proposals generate divisive, confrontational exchanges that can poison the committee-room atmosphere and detract from debates on major policies. The average rating by the American Conservative Union (ACU) for the entire committee has risen from 40 percent in 1982 to 54.7 percent in 1998. During the same period, the ACU score for SFRC Republicans increased from 59.4 percent to 98.1 percent. In addition, the 1996 retirements of Nancy Landon Kassebaum (R-KS) and Hank Brown deprived the foreign-relations panel of two moderates, widely respected for their commitment to international affairs. Although Helms's staff boasts more moderates since the reorganization of his office in 1992, his lieutenants still vigorously pursue their boss's zealous program. Helms, who gloried in propounding his ideological goals as ranking member, has hewn to a right-wing line in the chair. His personal credo encompasses God, country, law and order, and anticommunism. Observers have noted that in "foreign policy, these beliefs translate into a view of the world that is largely distrustful of international entanglements, unless they involve confronting Communist regimes that pose a direct threat to the United States."[7]

Regardless of partisan control, the Foreign Relations Committee has traditionally adopted an internationalist stance, working closely with the State Department, the United States Information Agency, the Agency for International Development (AID), the Arms Control and Disarmament Agency (ACDA), and other elements of the foreign-affairs bureaucracy. Rather than champion these agencies' causes, however, the parochial Helms—who has only left the United States to visit England—berates them as overstaffed, overfunded, and overextended. The son of a North Carolina police chief and an ardent proponent of states' rights, Helms barely masks his contempt for the diplomatic community which he regards as dominated by eastern elites.[8]

Putting his chairmanship in service of his politics, he drafted and won passage of legislation abolishing AID, USIA, and ACDA and folding their functions into the State Department. When Clinton balked at such a root-and-branch reform, Helms held up ratification of the 1996 Chemical Weapons Convention, which bans the use of poison gas and similar weapons, until the administration threw in the towel. Capitulation by the White House opened the way for passage of the Helms-Biden Foreign Affairs Reform and Restructuring Act (FARR), which the administration will implement in 1999. The measure does, however, create a new departmental bureau responsible for East European and Eurasian Affairs, defined as the "newly independent states of the former Soviet Union."[9] In addition, Helms has enthusiastically joined efforts to slash budgets of the State Department and sister agencies.

Helms has also blocked ambassadorial appointments to demonstrate his disdain for either the nominees themselves or particular foreign-policy ventures. The most publicized controversy erupted in 1997 when Clinton nominated former Massachusetts Governor William Weld, a moderate Republican, as envoy to Mexico. Helms—who disliked both Mexico's "ineffective, corrupt" antidrug policy and Weld's support for the medicinal use of marijuana—refused to meet with the nominee or hold more than a pro forma confirmation hearing, forcing Weld to withdraw his name from consideration in mid-September 1997.

Senator Lugar's backing of Weld only thickened the bad blood between the Indiana Senator and Helms. Helms purposely left Lugar's name off the list of conferees hammering out the final version of the Foreign Affairs Reform and Restructuring Act, despite the former committee chairman's recognized competence in international relations.

"I was unpleasantly surprised when the House-Senate conference started to meet on this very large and complex piece of legislation, and I got word that I was not to be part of it," Lugar said. "It's fair to say that Sen. Helms is trying to marginalize me in this debate, and I'm asserting he will not succeed."[10]

Helms's autocratic approach to issues, his ideological fervor, his no-holds-barred treatment of opponents, and the zeal of some of the committee's staff have diminished the desirability of serving on a panel no longer regarded as especially powerful or prestigious by its own members. As one senator said:

> Well, you know, it is fun to hobnob with foreign leaders and discuss world affairs, but it doesn't get me any place with my Senate colleagues. . . . Foreign Relations doesn't have much legislative jurisdiction that's important to other senators—it's nothing like Finance or Appropriations.[11]

Though not citing these reasons, in 1997 Senator Biden told Helms—with whom he entered the Senate in 1973—that on the North Carolinian's watch the committee's standing had reached a "25-year low."[12]

In all fairness, Ranking Member Biden bears some responsibility for the SFRC's declining fortunes. In the Pell era, for instance, the chairman and ranking member endowed their subcommittee counterparts with great leeway in spending subcommittee budgets and permitted them to hire their own staffs. In contrast, Biden micromanages subcommittee budgets available to Democrats, and even places his own choices in subcommittee staff positions once filled by ranking minority members.[13]

Moreover, the imperative to raise huge reelection war chests has spurred some lawmakers to opt for other "Super A" committees—finance, appropriations, or armed services—whose members attract more attention and funds from interest groups.[14] Nevertheless, some generous domestic groups carefully monitor the work of the SFRC. When Feinstein and Charles S. Robb (D-VA) left the committee in 1999, their replacements, Barbara Boxer (D-CA) and Robert G. Torrecelli (D-NJ), were poised to win substantial financial support from donors interested in Israel and Cuba, respectively.

Several factors demonstrate the committee's decline in influence. First, except for executive-sponsored treaties and the FARR, the Senate Foreign Relations Committee approved few if any major pieces of legislation in the 1994-98 period. In all fairness, the committee has never functioned as a "big producer" like, say, the finance and commerce committees. Still, it has failed to send to the floor a foreign-aid authorization bill since 1986. Inaction by the authorizing or functional committee shifts even greater power to the appropriations committee, which ultimately approves funding. Once a SFRC member himself, Senator Mitch McConnell (R-KY) shrewdly transferred to the appropriations committee in 1994. As chairman of the foreign operations subcommittee, he exerts far more influence on the U.S. foreign-policy apparatus than when he served on the often-stalemated Foreign Relations Committee.[15]

Second, the rancor and deadlock afflicting the SFRC has led the Senate leadership to refer an increasing number of important bills to other committees.

Third, even when the Senate parliamentarian might have allowed the committee to exercise joint authority over matters affecting international affairs such as NAFTA's implementing legislation, the SFRC's chairman did not seek such a role, leaving the Finance Committee to scrutinize the initiative. Similarly, the Judiciary Committee has dominated bills on narcotics control, even though drugs and drug-trafficking play an ever-more salient role in U.S. relations with other countries.[16]

Fourth, in recent years more members have transferred off the committee, an ever-larger contingent of first-term senators occupy committee seats, and fewer chairmen and ranking members of other committees choose to serve on what senators once regarded as a premier assignment on Capitol Hill. As early as the mid-1960s, Senator George Smathers (D-FL) quit the committee, saying, in essence, that sitting on the SFRC wasn't such a big deal. Table 7 illuminates the committee's changing composition.

Table 6: Evolution of the Senate Foreign Relations Committee, 1948-1998

Year (Number of Congress)	Number of Republican Members	Number of Democrat Members	Number of Chairmen of Other Committees	Number of Ranking Members of Other Committees	Number of First-term Members	Number of Members Who Transferred Off
1998 (105)	10	8	1	1	10	2
1996 (104)	10	8	2	3	9	6
1994 (103)	9	11	2	4	8	6
1992 (102)	8	11	5	1	4	1
1990 (101)	9	10	3	3	6	1
1988 (100)	9	11	3	4	7	1
1984 (98)	9	8	2	3	6	2
1982 (97)	9	8	2	2	9	0
1986 (99)	9	8	2	4	5	0
1980 (96)	6	9	2	2	6	0
1978 (95)	6	9-10*	4	3	5	3
1976 (94)	7	10	4	6	2	1
1974 (93)	7	10	6	4	0	1
1972 (92)	7	9	4	4	1	1
1970 (91)	6	9	2	5	0	0
1968 (90)	7	12	1	6	0	1
1966 (89)	6	13	2	5	1	1
1964 (88)	5	12	2	5	1	0
1962 (87)	6	11	2	6	3	0
1960 (86)	6	11	3	5	2	0
1958 (85)	7	8	4	5	9	0
1956 (84)	7	7	4	4	1	0
1954 (83)	7	8	4	3	2	0
1952 (82)	6	7	3	3	1	0
1950 (81)	5	8	4	1	4	0
1948 (80)	7	6	4	5	2	1

*The committee was expanded to sixteen members

Source: Michael Barone and Grant Ujifusa, *Almanac of American Politics* (Washington, D.C.: National Journal, 1991, 1993, 1995, and 1997); and Garrison Nelson, *Committees in the U.S. Congress* (Washington, D.C.: Congressional Quarterly, 1994).

Finally, formation of special task forces indicates another way the leadership can circumvent or attenuate the influence of standing committees. The majority leader has established such ad hoc bodies to consider arms control, legislation on economic sanctions, and the expansion of NATO.

Senate NATO Observer Group (SNOG)

The idea to establish such a group for NATO—one that would formalize contacts between the executive and legislative branches—surfaced from several sources. Paula Dobriansky, Senator Dole's foreign-policy adviser during the presidential campaign, discussed the concept with legislative staff members in the fall of 1996.[17]   Upon accepting the NERO assignment, Rosner recommended in his memorandum to top State Department and NSC officials the "creation of a Senate leadership group to meet with the administration regularly and go to Madrid."[18] Randy Scheunemann, the majority leader's principal foreign-policy adviser devised the plan that Lott ultimately broached in an op-ed contribution to the *Washington Post*.

In his essay, the majority leader admonished the president to forgo ambiguity and specify the candidates for admission to NATO; to assure the Baltic states and others not included in the first round that they might enter the alliance in the future; to deal firmly with Moscow, and avoid placing "the Russian cart before the NATO horse"; and to involve the U.S. Senate in the enlargement process at once.[19]   His staff members spread the word that Lott would welcome participants in the group on a first-come, first-served basis.

He asked Roth, chairman of the Senate Finance Committee and president of the North Atlantic Assembly,[20] to chair the Senate NATO Observer Group, commonly referred to as the SNOG. Minority Leader Thomas A. Daschle (D-SD) invited Roth's colleague Biden to serve as cochair.

Tensions usually fray relations between senators from the same state, especially if they fly different party banners. As a rule, they compete for media attention, campaign funds, judicial appointments, committee assignments, bragging rights for delivering federal funding, and recognition as potential national candidates. If both are Democrats or Republicans, they may also vie for control of the state party apparatus.

Lott and fellow Mississippi Republican Thad Cochran epitomize this rivalry. Not so in the "First State" where the low-key Roth matches yin to the flamboyant Biden's yang.[21]

All told, the SNOG numbered fourteen Republicans and fourteen Democrats, including the majority and minority leaders and the chairmen and ranking members of the committees on foreign relations, armed services, and appropriations. Lott chose not to invite Lugar to become a member, reportedly because of the strained relations between Lugar and Helms. As discussed earlier, the Indianan's challenge to Bob Dole for the GOP presidential nomination in 1996 and his support for the moderate Cochran over the bellicose Lott for majority leader have also diminished his standing among GOP colleagues, some of whom find him "slightly arrogant" and "stand-offish." In any case, Lugar did not request appointment to the group.

Senate leaders contemplated modeling the SNOG after the Arms Control Observer Group (ACOG) that facilitated contacts between Capitol Hill and the White House with respect to the SALT and START agreements. Lott, who proposed the NATO group, had served on ACOG when a member of the House. Still, the latest observer group would exhibit several major differences. Chaired by Lugar, ACOG operated with a budget of $500,000, which helped to pay for its own staff. Roth insisted that SNOG could accomplish its tasks without special funding, drawing on the existing expertise in Senate offices and committees. Ian Brzezinski and Bob Nickel from Roth's staff played leading roles in coordinating the group's activities. Before concluding its work, SNOG had held seventeen members-only, off-the-record meetings, including sessions with the president, the secretaries of state and defense, NATO Secretary General Javier Solana, and the foreign and defense ministers of Poland, Hungary, and the Czech Republic.[22]

The SNOG, which opened its doors in May 1997, got off to a rocky start with the State Department. The administration had negotiated the NATO-Russia Founding Act, but refused to divulge the final text to the twenty-eight senators, even though drafts had reached all alliance capitals and the Kremlin. In reaction, "Senate Republicans complained angrily that the administration was too slow to produce information. Republicans blamed Strobe Talbott . . . but Rosner also got clobbered at a meeting with GOP aides."[23]

The well-connected Ian Brzezinski mooted the issue by obtaining a copy of the document for Roth from non-U.S. government sources, and

Rosner strongly urged the administration to practice better cooperation, lest this episode incite distrust between the two branches of government. In a memorandum to Secretary Albright, Rosner emphasized that it is "in the interest of getting NATO enlargement ratified to reach some accommodation with the Observer Group on information sharing." He added, however, that "we must avoid setting an adverse precedent, and we must bear in mind that the Senate will likely want 'a second bite of the apple'—more information—during the advise and consent process."[24]

The White House quickly patched up its relations with the lawmakers by inviting Senators Roth, Biden, and Gordon Smith (R-OR) to fly with Clinton aboard Air Force One to Paris for the signing of the NATO-Russia Founding Act. At the invitation of the French government, the ceremony took place in the ornate garden ballroom of Elysée Palace. With the gold-tipped cane that Yeltsin had given Clinton following his recent knee surgery resting beside the lectern, the American and Russian presidents placed their signatures on the accord, after which Clinton exulted, "For all of us, this is a great day."[25]

After the dustup over information-sharing, NERO arranged for an exclusive two-hour meeting between Clinton and SNOG members in the White House residence on June 11. (Even veteran lawmakers find such parleys with the chief executive a heady experience.) The gathering started on a light note, when—after Roth and Biden playfully bragged that the group's leadership was an "all-Delaware" affair—Clinton responded by saying that those, like himself, who originated from states further west had always been glad that the initial thirteen states had maintained an "open door" policy. In a more serious vein, the president told his guests—relaxed on couches and in armchairs—that he was considering recommending the admission to NATO of Poland, Hungary, and the Czech Republic at the upcoming Madrid summit.

This announcement could have excited an uproar, because that day Biden and ten other senators had urged membership for Slovenia, which, despite impressive reforms, would have added little to NATO's military capabilities. Before anyone could second-guess Clinton, President pro tempore Strom Thurmond piped up to support the Visegrad three, using his seniority to move the informal session toward consensus.[26] Although he announced no decision that evening, the president assured his guests that Sandy Berger would be in touch with them soon. The only sour note sounded when, after the lawmakers had left, someone released the names of the three preferred Central European states without informing NERO and before Washington could consult with alliance allies. In the words of one administration insider who asked that his name not be used, "the NSC really fucked NERO."27

What sparked this vulgarity? NERO and the State Department had promised NATO partners they would wait until the July summit in Madrid to name the new members. The premature disclosure particularly offended the French, who had lobbied openly for Romania's affiliation, and the Italians, who shared Biden's enthusiasm for its neighbor, Slovenia. Representatives of three U.S. allies said the American "diktat" stunned them. One observer remarked that "Yeltsin, Chirac and other Europeans seem[ed] to fear that the Clintonites will attempt to turn Madrid into an event that combines holding a beauty contest for potential members and a crowning of the American president as king of NATO."28

After SNOG's session at the White House, twenty-five senators—mostly members of the observer group—took up the president's offer to respond to any lingering questions about enlargement. Specifically, they included fifteen queries in a letter dispatched to Clinton on June 25, 1997. These questions, which ranged from probing to puerile, included: "What is the military threat that NATO expansion is designed to counter? How does expansion increase the security of Europe and the American people? Are we creating a new dividing line that will breed instability and friction in Europe? What guidelines will NATO establish to resolve these [border, ethnic, nationalist, and religious] types of disputes or other problems that may well arise among the new member nations? What would be the impact of extending coverage of the U.S. nuclear umbrella to them?"29

Apparently, John Warner and Kay Bailey Hutchison had spearheaded the collection of signatures on the letter. Hutchison even employed her southern charm to persuade the courtly Helms to sign on—an act that dismayed some SFRC staff members. The letter, which greatly worried the administration, marked the "low point of the enlargement effort" for NERO. If the twenty-five signatories were to cast "nay" votes, only nine more dissenters could have sunk the protocols.30

The likelihood of SNOG's leading the anti-expansion charge abated in July 1997, when four representatives of the group—Roth, Biden, Mikulski, and Gordon Smith—attended the Madrid summit where the alliance formally invited applications from the three Visegrad states. The administration astutely arranged for Roth to deliver a speech to the North Atlantic Council, NATO's leading decision-making forum, with heads of state occupying their countries' seats. This was the first time a legislator from any country had addressed the body. The presence of four members of the House of Representatives in the U.S. contingent further underlined the importance that official Washington placed on full congressional involvement in the ratification process.[31]   In a lighter vein, the Americans quickly removed the "SNOG" sign from their delegation's meeting room after a U.K. official gleefully advised that the British employed the word to describe a messy, furtive form of kissing.[32]

Establishing the observer group proved less crucial to ultimate ratification in 1998 than gaining allies with which to combat hostile amendments, while broadening NATO's congressional constituency for future legislation. The administration learned the concerns of a number of legislators. Rosner, Munter, and other U.S. representatives became better acquainted with senators and their key aides, enhancing their credibility with lawmakers. The twenty-eight members also gained access to a plethora of data about the alliance and its operations, obviating the complaint—which occurred with the Chemical Weapons Convention—that "we don't have enough information on which to base a vote."[33]   As a result, the overwhelming majority of SNOG participants lined up in favor of the protocols, while helping to defeat several of the most threatening amendments.

Senate Debate

In launching the Senate debate on April 27, Helms stressed that Poland, Hungary, and the Czech Republic would strengthen NATO's ability to defend Europe and ensure the security of alliance members. Moreover, he emphasized that prospective members stood ready to "strike out of area" against any regime that employed chemicals, biological weapons, or other nonconventional arms against NATO members: "While many of our current NATO allies stuck their heads in the sand and wiggled their fannies [in an early 1998 confrontation with Saddam Hussein], Poland and Hungary and the Czech Republic . . . immediately and without hesitation said, 'We will send troops in alongside the American forces if a military response is necessary in Iraq.'"[34]

Helms concluded his remarks by stressing a theme carried in Biden's prevote speech—namely, that the United States had a moral obligation to the Central Europeans. By supporting ratification, he told his colleagues, they would "right the historical wrongs of Yalta," site of the February

1945 conference among Roosevelt, Churchill, and Stalin at which Poland lost Eastern lands to the Soviets. As discussed earlier, this strategic bargain sparked bitter opposition in Poland and in the United States, particularly in the Polish American community.[35]

Indiana's Lugar offered yet another argument for enlargement. The prospect for membership, he asserted, "has given the countries of Central and Eastern Europe the incentive to accelerate reforms, to settle disputes with neighbors, and to increase regional cooperation."[36] As a result, not only would the alliance emerge stronger militarily with the three new countries, but membership would enable them to complete their democratic transitions and deepen their commitment to the free market.

As for the belief of some analysts that the Visegrad states should join the European Union before seeking NATO affiliation, Lugar underlined the EU's "cumbersome and slow" decision-making procedures and the union's tendency to produce policy outcomes "expressing the lowest common denominator." Such traits, he added, "are antithetical to the demands of a military alliance which places a premium on timely, decisive action . . . ."[37]

Drawing on his experience in foreign affairs, Lugar went on to articulate a fundamental argument for NATO expansion; that is, keeping the United States fully engaged in the Euro-Atlantic community. In contrast, "subordinating NATO to the EU . . . would make the Alliance, not a cornerstone of European security, but an appendage. The role of the U.S., Canada, and Turkey, none of whom are members of the EU, would be significantly diminished in the enlargement process."[38] Briefly stated: in the aftermath of the cold war, the United States must lead as the world's only superpower or retreat into isolationism and relinquish its status as a global leader.

Yet, the very issue of the U.S. role in the Atlantic community persuaded Virginia's Warner, a former navy secretary and vigorous NATO supporter, to turn thumbs-down on the addition of Poland, Hungary, and the Czech Republic. Their membership, he feared, would dilute NATO's mission, converting an effective military alliance into an organization pursuing vague social and economic objectives. As discussed in the Introduction, his amendment to impose a three-year freeze on the admission of new members to the alliance came within ten votes of succeeding.

Equally troublesome to Warner was Secretary Albright's alleged assertion that the alliance could respond to threats posed by countries in Africa or the Mideast. In embracing indefinite new missions, he warned, we run the risk of creating a 911 organization: "Call if there is a problem—dial a cop, dial-a-soldier." After all, the Caspian Sea area, like Bosnia, is rife with border disputes and ethnic and religious hatreds that date back centuries. Thus, "we cannot allow this organization to become a response unit to any crisis in that part of the world."[39]

Representing a state where balancing the budget constitutes a sacred rite, Warner also raised the question of the cost of expansion. Over the course of eighteen months, figures had varied from $150 million to $3.5 billion. Turning to Helms, he asked, "What is his view as to the costs and what are the basic facts on which he relies in bringing forth this treaty at this time to the Senate?"

Caught off guard, the gravel-throated North Carolinian answered:

Mr. President [of the Senate], my response to my friend from Virginia has to be in many parts. I just told my helpmate here that we did a drivel here and a drivel there, all formal and official estimates. Before we go any further, I want to get the Senator's question on paper, and then we give the citations for the various figures . . . . Why don't we get together and get the specific question about the specific figures, and we will give the Senator the responses on which we based our judgment.

Rather than press his fellow southerner, the gentlemanly Warner called Helms's reply "most reasonable" and promised to submit the requested letter. Helms pledged to answer fully. "I am not inclined ever to give anybody a blank check for their American taxpayers' money," he added.[40]

Daniel Patrick Moynihan next joined the fray. While reiterating concerns articulated by Warner, the New York Democrat expressed fear that expanding NATO might be the one action that could unify, galvanize, and radicalize Russia, strengthening the hand of extremists at the expense of moderates. If convinced that a "ring of steel" is descending around them, such firebrands—aware of the weakness of their conventional forces—might think about the unthinkable: the "first use" of nuclear weapons. "Don't you understand our situation. Back to the hair trigger of the 1950s."[41]

Washington had failed to cast off its cold-war mentality, he averred. Otherwise, the Senate would not be debating the addition of Poland, Hungary, and the Czech Republic to NATO—with Croatia, Slovenia, Romania, Bulgaria, and the three Baltic states standing in the wings for eventual entry.

He concluded with this dire warning:

NATO could defend the Baltics by only one means, nuclear attacks. . .
Nuclear attack and nuclear response. We are right back to where we
were in the 1950's, or we will be as we continue this. We have
already signaled we are going to move into the Baltic States. I cannot
imagine the thinking process that has led us to this point. I can only
note that the persons who conceived this extraordinarily successful
strategy in the 1940s look up today and say: Have you all gone mad?
Do you realize what you are doing?[42]

Moynihan also inserted into the record an article quoting the four-
line "moral of the work" emblazoned across the first page of Winston
Churchill's *History of World War II*: "In War—Resolution; In Defeat—
Defiance; In Victory—Magnanimity; In Peace—Goodwill." He stressed
that the victors' ostracism of Germany after World War I led inexorably
to World War II; in contrast, the incorporation of Germany into the
bosom of Europe after World War II fostered peace, prosperity, and
democracy in the West. In his view, extending NATO four hundred
miles closer to Russia resembles the error of 1919, not the prudence of
1945.

Finally, the professorial Moynihan admitted the cultural affinities of
Central Europeans with their western neighbors. But, he asked, "[w]hich
has made a larger contribution to European culture: Hungary or the land
of Tolstoy, Dostoevsky, Pushkin, Prokofiev, Kandinsky, and
Shostakovich?" "Bringing Russia firmly into the West is a goal worthy
of the United States—and its Senate," he concluded.

Wellstone, one of two members of the Foreign Relations Committee
to oppose enlargement, fleshed out the Russia-first case. He noted that
his father fled czarist Russia one step ahead of the pogroms. Later,
members of his family perished at the hands of the Bolsheviks. But the
Soviet Union disintegrated, and he insisted that the West must now be
sensitive to "democratic forces" who fear a backlash against democracy
if NATO expands to their doorstep.

Wellstone quoted Dr. Georgy A. Arbatov of Moscow's Institute of
USA and Canadian Studies that "NATO expansion will plant a permanent
seed of mistrust between the United States and Russia. It will worsen
everything from nuclear arms control to policies in Iraq and Iran. It will
push Moscow into alliance with China and rogue regimes." The Minnesota
liberal also called attention to a front-page article in that day's *New York*

Times, which disclosed the substantial fund that military contractors had expended on behalf of NATO enlargement.[43]

The Final Vote

Proponents first tried to obtain a vote on NATO enlargement during the week of March 16. Although Lott allowed the measure to advance, he kept alternating it with an education bill sponsored by conservative Paul Coverdell (R-GA). In fact, the majority leader appeared to be holding the NATO legislation hostage to the Coverdell initiative, which the White House vehemently opposed. Supporters of expansion and the press in general expressed outrage at Lott's failure to accord the treaty amendment full-time attention. This reaction led the Mississippian, just minutes after the president's White House event on NATO, to halt floor debate on the measure, postponing consideration until late April—a move that made Lott appear inexperienced in handling an issue of major gravity. CANE rejoiced at the delay, hoping it could be extended, while Ashcroft used the additional weeks to work energetically on his floor amendment, and NERO officials worried that the head of steam they had developed— a flood of endorsements, a February visit of three foreign ministers, a March 20 White House ceremony—would dissipate.

"I am convinced that if the senators had voted in late March, we would have been in the mid- to high-80s," Rosner said in retrospect.[44]

In any case, at 11 p.m. on Thursday, April 30, Senator Chuck Hagel (R-NE) gaveled the chamber to order.[45] After some twenty hours of debate, beginning on Tuesday, the Senate finally prepared itself to decide upon the admission of three new members to NATO. Majority Leader Lott, a strong advocate of enlargement, asked that the vote on this "historic" treaty be conducted with decorum—with the one hundred senators in their desks, rising when called to cast a "yea" or "nay."

Robert Byrd, the Senate's foremost expert on parliamentary procedure and its most flamboyant orator, rose to agree with Lott. Although known better during his thirty-eight years on Capitol Hill for shifting operations of agencies as diverse as the FBI and the Fish and Wildlife Service to his home state of West Virginia, the silver-haired legislator has written a history of the Senate and mastered its procedures. He said that a formal vote—rather than allowing a "stock market" frenzy in the well of the chamber—would make a "better impression on visitors" and bring "greater pride to the institution."

Senator Helms, the legislation's nominal floor manager, forewent closing remarks, asking unanimous consent to present them in written form. Senator Biden, who had directed the ratification effort, briefly lauded NATO for "keeping Soviet imperialism at bay" and providing "a security umbrella" under which Western European democracies could "recover socially and economically and thrive." Each previous addition of members, he insisted, had strengthened the alliance. Thus, admitting to the western security framework "three highly qualified countries which had chafed under the communist yoke for four decades . . . would mean righting a historical injustice forced upon Poland, the Czech Republic, and Hungary by Josef Stalin." Expansion would be good for the United States, good for Europe, and good for Russia by "stabilizing the historical crucible of violence in eastern central Europe . . . [and] beginning another 50 years of peace."

Finally, Virginia's Warner, aware that he and other opponents of enlargement were on the verge of suffering defeat, reiterated his misgivings about bringing three candidate-states into NATO, but in a statesmanlike gesture added that, if two-thirds of the Senate opted for expansion, he as the next chairman of the Senate Armed Services Committee would do everything in his power "to make it work," while maintaining a "vigil" about future members.

During the roll call, most senators rose quietly to voice a "yea" or "nay." Some, like New York's Al D'Amato (R) and Arizona's John McCain (R) popped up like jacks-in-the-box to cast their votes. Ninety-five-year-old Thurmond, who parachuted into Normandy on D-Day and had already entered middle age when the 1949 Washington Treaty establishing NATO took effect, stood erect as he shouted "yea" from his front-row desk. Max Cleland (D-GA), whose Vietnam-incurred injuries force him to use a wheelchair, raised his hand to signal an affirmative vote.

The absence of some senators from the chamber required a second roll call. When the last lawmaker had made his preference known, the Senate clerk read aloud the "ayes" and "nays" before presenting her tally to the presiding officer. After quickly perusing the document, Senator Hagel gravely intoned that "on this vote, the ayes are 80, the nays are 19 [and] two-thirds of the senators are present and having voted in the affirmative the resolution of ratification is agreed to."[46]

The announcement of the vote sparked spontaneous cheers and applause from the Diplomatic Gallery, which overflowed with observers from countries affected by the outcome. Jerzy Kozminski, Gyorgy Banlaki, and Alexandr Vondra, respectively ambassadors from Poland, Hungary, and the Czech Republic, limited themselves to broad smiles and exchanges of handshakes. Younger diplomats and interest-group activists—many of whom had been in the Capitol since noon—could not stifle their emotions. Officious, stern-faced assistant sergeants-at-arms nipped the celebration in the bud as they unceremoniously admonished the would-be revelers to "be quiet or leave!"

The Senate action would, in the words of President Clinton, send a clear message that "American support for NATO is firm, our leadership for security on both sides of the Atlantic is strong, and there is a solid, bipartisan foundation for an active US role in the world." He went on to say that the "vote stands in the tradition of Harry Truman, George Marshall and Arthur Vandenberg and other giants who kept America engaged in the world after World War II and were present at NATO's creation."[47]

Vote Analysis

A review of the final vote finds that forty-five of fifty-five Republicans (81.8 percent) supported the protocols compared with thirty-six of forty-five Democrats (80 percent). Only Patrick Leahy (D-VT) and Warner broke ranks with the twenty-eight-member SNOG to vote against the treaty. All nine female senators backed NATO expansion, a tribute—in part, at least—to assiduous proselytizing by Mikulski and Albright. Of the fourteen senators from states with the heaviest concentrations of defense plants and military installations, only Warner sided with the anti-expansionists. In "Ethniclandia," composed of ten northeastern and midwest states, eighteen of twenty senators opted for adding the three countries to NATO.[48] Ten of eleven senators in leadership posts favored enlargement—with the only exception being Senator Larry Craig (R-ID), who chairs the Republican Policy Committee. Thirty-nine of the body's forty-eight military veterans voted in the affirmative (81.3 percent), as did thirty of the thirty-six members of the armed services and foreign relations committees (83.3 percent). Proponents of the protocols averaged 57.6 years of age compared with 61.9 years for opponents and 58.8 for the entire Senate.

More than half of the senators had voted one or more times for hortatory resolutions, funding measures, or the NEFA of 1996. Although petty inconsistency may be the hobgoblin of small minds, taking apparently

Table 7: Ratification of Accession Protocols for Poland, Hungary, and the Czech Republic to Enter NATO

Country	Ratification	Action
Belgium	July 16, 1998	Approved by House of Representatives (Senate Approved on July 9)
Canada	February 4, 1998	Instrument of ratification deposited (Foreign Minister ratified on February 2)
Denmark	February 17, 1998	Instrument of ratification deposited (Parliament approved on February 3)
France	February 4, 1998	Instrument of ratification deposited (Senate approved on May 20; National Assembly on June 10)
Germany	April 24, 1998	Instrument of ratification deposited (Bundestag approved on March 26; Bundesrat on March 7)
Greece	May 14, 1998	Approved by Parliament
Iceland	June 4, 1998	Approved by Parliament
Italy	June 23, 1998	Approved by House of Representatives (Senate approved on May 13)
Luxembourg	May 27, 1998	Approved by Parliament
Netherlands	December 4, 1998	Approved by Parliament
Norway	March 17, 1998	Instrument of ratification deposited (Parliament approved on March 3)
Portugal	December 3, 1998	Approved by Parliament
Spain	June 23, 1998	Approved by Senate (Congress of Deputies approved on May 21)
Turkey	December 3, 1998	Approved by National Assembly
United Kingdom	August 18, 1998	Instrument of ratification deposited (House of Commons approved on July 17; House of Lords on July 31)
United States	April 30, 1998	Approved by Senate

Source: NATO, "Status of Ratification of Accession Protocols," *NATO Fact Sheet*, August 26, 1998, Internet.

contradictory stands on the same issue can supply potent ammunition to a lawmaker's challenger in the next election. Thus, a kind of "incremental" or "creeping" ratification of the alliance had begun several years before the protocols actually arrived on the Senate floor.[49] This legislative incrementalism gave the appearance of U.S. backing for NATO enlargement well before the final vote, conveying the impression in some quarters that negative action on April 30 would be tantamount to Washington's reneging on a commitment. As one highly regarded analyst wrote, "enlarging NATO was an unnecessary initiative but one that should nonetheless be seen through at this point given all that has been said and done."[50]

Lessons from the NATO Expansion Process

The end of the cold war has sharply diminished anticommunism as a lodestar—employed by Democrats and Republicans alike—to orient initiatives abroad. "I sincerely believe that this is the most important time to be a player in foreign policy since 1948. Absolutely everything is up for grabs," stated the loquacious Biden, adding that "[i]ssues such as NATO enlargement, the U.S. presence in Bosnia, trade agreements and arms control really boil down to a debate about what America's role in the world is going to be."[51]

What insights about this "America's role in the world" emerge from the drive to gain admission of Poland, Hungary, and Czechoslovakia to NATO?

First, nominal former enemies may emerge as America's best allies in this new era. Poland, for example, gained such overwhelming support on Capitol Hill neither because of the efforts of key executive- and legislative-branch officials nor because of backing from the Polish American Congress. Rather, the Warsaw government—through its reforms at home and its performance in Iraq, Bosnia, and the Partnership for Peace—convinced most of the U.S. foreign-policy community that the country would become an effective ally and a net security provider to the trans-Atlantic alliance.

Second, the decision of Albright, Asmus, and others to establish a single office on NATO expansion accentuates the importance of limiting the number of executive interlocutors with Congress, lest the White House message appear inchoate if voiced by numerous agency heads. In this regard, the NATO experience offered a sharp contrast to the drive to win approval of NAFTA.

Third, the NERO lobbying élan demonstrated that an old-style, grass-roots campaign can generate coast-to-coast endorsements for an issue that only tangentially affects Main Street America, especially if the cloistered foreign-affairs establishment fails to court rank-and-file citizens.

Fourth, Rosner and his governmental and nongovernmental colleagues showed the possibility of hammering together new public coalitions in support of private démarches in the current international environment. By stressing symbols and goals that unified rather than divided—"democracy," "Yalta betrayal," "integration of the West"—pro-expansionists rallied to their cause Big Business and Big Labor, Biden-style liberals and Helms-style conservatives, and Jewish and Polish groups.

Fifth, NERO's, USCEN's, PAC's, and the Polish embassy's unrelenting courtship of lawmakers on a bipartisan basis ensured that the issue never became embroiled in party politics. After the administration overcame its hesitation to share information about the NATO-Russia act with congressional offices, the White House not only kept legislators fully abreast of expansion-related developments, but also involved them thoroughly in the process. In addition, while the Senate has had a proprietary view of NATO since ratifying the Washington Treaty, Rosner et al. reinforced this tendency, particularly after the SNOG's formation.

Sixth, the expand-NATO coalition revealed the importance of fostering a sense of inevitability in the process of policy deliberation. Moving early—even in a haphazard way at first—to obtain endorsements from diverse groups across the country tended to put opponents on the defensive and infuse them with a "we-can't-win" attitude. This pessimism limited the time, energy, and resources contributed by enlargement foes. The success of this strategy manifested itself when no senator seized upon defeat of the NATO protocols as a personal crusade, when relatively few witnesses appeared to oppose enlargement, and when the final vote occurred.

Seventh, the NATO episode indicates that—even in an era of pragmatism—ideas still count in the formation of foreign policy. The Asmus-Kugler-Larrabee *Foreign Affairs* article (and their subsequent publications) made a compelling case for projecting the alliance eastward; it also set forth core provisions that attracted the attention of key players in the Senate, in the administration, in the German Foreign Ministry, in think tanks, in the media, and in interest groups. The RAND boys provided a framework in which the NSC troika could fashion an action plan, which the administration skillfully implemented.

Finally, enlargement proponents must take care, lest the exceptional coalition they forged in 1998 persuade the Senate to throw open NATO's portals to future states that satisfy the Perry Principles but prove incapable of advancing the members' vital interests. In other words, further expansion must adhere to an explicit geostrategic rationale that enhances the security of alliance allies.[52]

Postscript

After the historic vote with its sweeping consequences, Mary Daly, the outstanding foreign service officer who had foregone spending *Carnevale* in Venice to join the NERO team in early 1998, felt bone tired. Yet her enthusiasm remained undiminished even after other merrymakers had left the Capitol, and she and Rosner had to close up by themselves. "This meant that we had to schlep all our files, briefing books, and Jeremy's computer back to the State Department by taxi—only to find that we had no money and could barely scrape up the $5.00 fare between us," she reported. This chore did not detract from her sense of accomplishment one jot. "As someone who had experienced the cold war during my entire life, I relished the opportunity to have played a small role in advancing a secure, unified Europe." The next night Daly could relax at the Polish embassy party, where she felt an incredible bond with the scores of other people who had worked for NATO enlargement. It was like attending a wonderful wedding," she noted.[53]

Rosner missed the party because he and Asmus were aboard a 747 bound for an international-security conference in Istanbul. Once ensconced in his seat and after takeoff, he closed his eyes and let his mind drift across the events of the past several years and the large number of people who had contributed to NATO enlargement. "I came away from the experience," he remembered, "feeling that this is a very plastic moment for American leadership and the politics of American foreign affairs, when international initiatives often lack sharp definition and context, public and congressional attention is intermittent, and political coalitions highly fluid. All this means that there is a broad range of possible outcomes on many issues and the efforts of individuals can make a decisive difference."[54]

Notes

1. Quoted in *The Debate on NATO Enlargement*, pp. 310-11.
2. Quoted in *The Debate on NATO Enlargement*, p. 310.
3. Barry Jacobs, assistant director for International Affairs, American Jewish Committee, telephone interview by author, January 15, 1999.
4. Fried, interview, December 28, 1998.
5. Nowak, telephone interview, November 14, 1998.
6. Michael Haltzel, professional staff member, Committee on Foreign Relations, interview by author, Washington, D.C., November 6, 1998.
7. James Kitfield, "Jousting with Jesse," *National Journal*, September 27, 1997, p. 1888.
8. Kitfield, "Jousting with Jesse," p. 1888.
9. Congress included the reorganization scheme in its giant catchall spending bill for fiscal year 1999. See, Thomas W. Lippman, "USIA and ACDA Workers All to Retain Employment," *Washington Post*, January 5, 1999, p. A-9.
10. Quoted in Kitfield, "Jousting with Jesse," p. 1887.
11. Quoted in Christopher J. Deering and Steven S. Smith, *Committees in Congress*, 3rd ed. (Washington, D.C.: CQ Press, 1997), p. 81.
12. Quoted in Kitfield, "Jousting with Jesse," p. 1887.
13. The ranking minority members are Paul S. Sarbanes (D-MD), International Economic Policy, Export & Trade Promotion; Christopher J. Dodd (D-CT), Western Hemisphere & Peace Corps Affairs; John F. Kerry (D-MA), East Asian & Pacific Affairs; Charles Robb (D-VA), Near East & South Asian Affairs; Dianne Feinstein, International Operations; and Russell D. Feingold (D-WI), African Affairs. In 1999, Robb transferred from SFRC to the Finance Committee.
14. There is no Senate rule against it, but the parties' leadership typically allow members to sit on only one "Super-A" committee. Waivers can be obtained, however. Virginia's Robb, who held seats on both armed services and foreign relations, now is the only Democrat assigned to armed services and finance. Senate reformers have discussed the possibility of demoting the SFRC from the "Super-A" list. In terms of fundraising, political action committees contributed, on average, $911,435 to each senator in 1996, while the mean contribution to an SFRC member totaled $793,526, substantially less than the comparable figure for members of the finance ($1,055.116), commerce ($1,002,538), and appropriations ($914,500) committees. See Michael Barone and Grant Ujifusa, *The Almanac of American Politics 1998* (Washington, D.C.: National Journal, 1997).
15. An analogous situation exists in the House, where colleagues regard Benjamin A. Gilman (R-NY), the seventy-six-year-old chairman of the ideologically splintered International Relations Committee (IRC), as a

lackluster and unimaginative leader. Capitol Hill observers report that his staff once prepared a speech using a version of WordPerfect software that required using tiny "o"s rather than bullets to highlight key points. Supposedly, Gilman read his comments, which appeared briefly in the *Congressional Record*, that found him beginning a half-dozen sentences with "O"s. Just as in the Senate, the IRC's inertia enhances the power of the House Appropriations Committee and its thirteen subcommittee chairmen, known as the "college of cardinals." Congressional insiders recall that Sonny Callahan (R-AL), chairman of the Foreign Operations Subcommittee that controls the State Department's budget, used to live on a rickety houseboat on Washington's waterfront. When Callahan invited Warren Christopher, a multimillionaire lawyer with impeccable social tastes, to a gathering on his houseboat, the secretary of state is said to have asked his legislative affairs liaison, "Do I really have to go?" She answered emphatically, "Yes, you do."

16. Of course, the Finance Committee enjoys prime responsibility for tax, tariff, and trade issues, while the Judiciary Committee plays the same role with respect to narcotics.

17. Ian Brzezinski, legislative assistant for national security affairs, Office of Senator William V. Roth, Jr., interview by author, Washington, D.C., August 31, 1998.

18. Rosner, Memorandum to Secretary Albright, Deputy Secretary Talbott, APNSA Berger, DAPNSA Steinberg on "Initial thoughts on NATO enlargement ratification strategy," February 26, 1997, xeroxed.

19. Trent Lott, "The Senate's Role in NATO Enlargement," *Washington Post*, March 21, 1997, p. A-27.

20. Not a part of NATO's decision-making structure, this assembly is constituted by legislators from the sixteen NATO nations.

21. For insights into tensions between senators, I am indebted to my William & Mary colleague, Professor John J. McGlennon.

22. Schedule conflicts meant that attendance ranged from four or five to more than twenty senators at these sessions.

23. Milbank, "SNOG Job," p. 15.

24. Rosner et al., "Sharing Information and Documents with the Senate NATO Observer Group," unclassified *Action Memorandum*, May 23, 1997, p. 1.

25. Craig R. Whitney, "Russia and NATO Sign Cooperation Pact," May 28, 1997, Internet edition.

26. Milbank, "SNOG Job," p. 15.

27. NSC officials disavow responsibility for the leak, suggesting that one or more senators may have talked with the press after leaving the White House.

28. Jim Hoagland, "'Diktat' from Washington," *Washington Post*, June 25, 1997, p. A-19.

29. The letter appears in Council for a Livable World Education Fund, *Briefing Book on NATO Enlargement*, pp. 55-58.
30. Rosner, memorandum to author, December 21, 1998.
31. Representing the House counterpart to the SNOG were Gilman, Rules Committee Chairman Gerald B. H. Solomon (R-NY), Samuel Gejdenson (D-CT), and Norman Sisisky (D-VA).
32. Milbank, "SNOG Job," p. 15.
33. Ian Brzezinski, interview, August 31, 1998.
34. Helms quoted in floor speech in a debate on "Protocols to the North Atlantic Treaty of 1949 on the Accession of Poland, Hungary, and the Czech Republic" (April 27, 1994), *Congressional Record*, Internet edition.
35. Helms, floor speech on "Protocols."
36. Lugar, floor speech on "Protocols."
37. Lugar, floor speech on "Protocols."
38. Lugar, floor speech on "Protocols."
39. Warner, floor speech on "Protocols." The "globo-cop" notion sprang from faulty press reports of Albright's speech to the New Atlantic Initiative on February 11, 1998. At the end of her presentation on NATO, she said that enlargement showed that the trans-Atlantic partnership continued to be an important force in a broad range of ways: from liberalizing trade to promoting peace from Africa to the Pacific. A reporter erroneously construed her words—framed in the context of trade—to imply her advocacy of NATO ventures around the world.
40. Helms, floor speech on "Protocols."
41. Moynihan, floor speech on "Protocols."
42. Moynihan, floor speech on "Protocols."
43. Wellstone, floor speech on "Protocols."
44. Rosner, memorandum to author, January 11, 1999.
45. These descriptions of the final vote derive from a video of the session provided by Sophia Miskiewicz, legislative and public affairs director, the Polish American Congress.
46. As mentioned in the Introduction, only Senator Kyl, an Arizona Republican, missed the vote because he had left the chamber to catch a flight.
47. The White House, Office of the Press Secretary, "On Senate Approval of NATO Enlargement: Statement by the President," April 30, 1998, Internet.
48. Minnesota's Wellstone and New York's Moynihan cast the "nay" votes from this artificial zone, which embraces Massachusetts, Rhode Island, New York, New Jersey, Maryland, Ohio, Illinois, Minnesota, Indiana, and Wisconsin.
49. Former senators Brown (telephone interview, September 21, 1998) and Nunn (telephone interview, December 14, 1998) agree with the idea of incremental ratification.
50. Haass, "Fatal Distraction: Bill Clinton's Foreign Policy," p. 119.

51. Kitfield, "Jousting with Jesse," pp. 1886-87.
52. Hans Binnendijk and Richard L. Kugler, "NATO after the First Tranche: A Strategic Rationale for Enlargement," *Strategic Forum*, Institute for National Strategic Studies, National Defense University, no. 149, October 1998.
53. Daly, interview, October 2, 1998.
54. Rosner, memorandum to author, January 11, 1999.

Chronology

The Senate's vote on the accession of Poland, Hungary, and the Czech Republic marked the culmination of a four-year effort by the Clinton Administration. Significant events in the development and pursuit of that goal include:

1989
: Democratic governments begin to assume power in Central Europe; fall of the Berlin Wall. President George Bush, Congress, support democratic transformation.

1990-91
: Germany reunites with U.S. support. Baltic states declare and maintain independence.

1991
: Boris Yeltsin foils communist putsch in Moscow; USSR dissolved and independent Russia, Ukraine, and other states emerge.

1993
: At Vancouver summit with Yeltsin, President William Clinton greatly increases assistance for Russia; begins to forge partnership.

1/10-11/94
: President Clinton and the other NATO leaders, at a summit in Brussels, signal their willingness to enlarge the alliance, declaring that "the membership of the alliance remains open to other European countries."

1/12/94
: President Clinton, in Prague, declares that "the question is no longer whether NATO will take on new members but when and how."

7/7/94
: President Clinton addresses the Polish Sejm (parliament), affirms his intent to pursue NATO's expansion, and calls on the organization to begin concrete, careful steps toward bringing in new members.

late 1994
: House Republicans include NATO enlargement as part of their "Contract with America."

12/94   NATO launches comprehensive study of enlargement; approved by NATO ministers the following December, it establishes principles for membership, including democratic governance, civilian control of the military, and peaceful relations with neighbors.

10/22/96   President Clinton reaffirms his support for NATO's growth during a major foreign-policy address in Detroit.

3/20-21/97   President Clinton and Russian President Yeltsin meet for a summit in Helsinki, and conclude major agreements concerning arms control and economic cooperation.

4/22/97   Majority Leader Trent Lott and Minority Leader Tom Daschle announce the creation of the Senate NATO Observer Group (SNOG), composed of 28 senators from both parties, charged with working with the administration to examine NATO enlargement. The administration immediately welcomes the creation of the group, and conducts over a dozen briefings for the group over the next nine months.

5/27/97   President Clinton and the other NATO leaders join Yeltsin in signing the "Founding Act on Mutual Relations, Cooperation and Security Between the North Atlantic Treaty Organization and the Russian Federation."

5/31/97   President Clinton devotes his commencement address at the U.S. Military Academy at West Point to the case for NATO's enlargement.

6/12/97   President Clinton announces that he has decided the United States will favor invitations to NATO membership for three countries, Poland, Hungary, and the Czech Republic.

7/3/97   Joined by leaders of major veterans groups at the White House, President Clinton stresses his support for NATO enlargement and lays out his goals for the upcoming Madrid summit.

7/8-9/97   President Clinton and the other NATO leaders gather for a NATO summit in Madrid, and extend invitations to Poland, Hungary, and the Czech Republic to begin accession talks with the alliance. The summit also declares that NATO will keep an "open door" to membership for other qualified European democracies. The president is joined by eight members of Congress from both chambers and both parties, whom he invites to participate as part of his delegation.

7/97   Following the Madrid summit, President Clinton, Secretary of State Madeleine Albright, and Secretary of Defense William Cohen visit nearly a dozen European capitals to explain the decisions at Madrid, including the open-door policy. The president is welcomed by over 100,000 cheering Romanians in Bucharest; he and his national security team receive expressions of support from leaders throughout the region.

9-11/97   NATO staff and military authorities hold four rounds of accession talks with Poland, and five each with Hungary and the Czech Republic.

10/7/97   The Senate Foreign Relations Committee begins a series of five hearings devoted to NATO's growth. These will be among twelve hearings by four Senate committees between 4/97 and 3/98.

11/10/97   Senators Helms and Biden write a joint letter to their colleagues declaring that, on the basis of the Senate Foreign Relations Committee hearings, they believe NATO enlargement is "squarely in the American national interest."

12/97   Defense and foreign ministers accept studies conducted by NATO military authorities and staff on the military requirements and costs of enlargement.

12/16/97   Secretary of State Albright and her NATO counterparts sign the three protocols of accession for Poland, Hungary, and the Czech Republic, which make them full NATO members, subject to ratification by all current and incoming NATO member states.

2/11/98   President Clinton transmits the protocols of accession to the Senate, accompanied by a detailed report by Secretary Albright.

2/24/98   Secretary Albright, Secretary Cohen, and Chairman of the Joint Chiefs of Staff General Henry H. Shelton appear for the final hearing on NATO enlargement before the Senate Foreign Relations Committee.

3/3/98   The Senate Foreign Relations Committee votes 16-2 in favor of NATO enlargement.

3/14/98   The president writes to Senators Lott and Daschle, declaring that "the enlargement of NATO directly will benefit America's security."

4/30/98   Senate votes 80-19 in favor of ratification.

4/99   NATO celebrates fiftieth anniversary and admits Poland, Hungary, and the Czech Republic to membership.

Glossary of Organizations

ACCHAN	Allied Commander in Chief Channel
ACDA	Arms Control and Disarmament Agency
ACOG	Arms Control Observer Group
ACU	American Conservative Union
ADA	Americans for Democratic Action
AEI	American Enterprise Institute
AFL-CIO	American Federation of Labor - Congress of Industrial Organizations
AID	Agency for International Development
AJC	American Jewish Congress
BLSP	Business Leaders for Sensible Priorities
CANE	Coalition Against NATO Expansion
CEEC	Central and East European Coalition
CEFTA	Central European Free Trade Association
CFE	Conventional Forces in Europe
CFR	Council on Foreign Relations
CLW	Council for a Livable World
CSCE	Conference on Security and Cooperation in Europe
CSIS	Center for Strategic & International Studies
CSSD	organization of expatriate Sudeten Germans (Czech Republic)
CTR	Cooperative Threat Reduction Program (Nunn-Lugar bill)
CWC	Chemical Weapons Convention
EDC	European Defense Community
ESDI	European Security and Defense Identity
ESSG	European Strategic Steering Group
EU	European Union
EUCOM	European Command
FARR	Foreign Affairs Reform and Restructuring Act
Fidesz	Alliance of Young Democrats (Hungary)
GATT	General Agreement on Tariffs and Trade
"H"	State Department's Bureau of Legislative Affairs
HAC	Hungarian American Coalition
IFOR	Implementation Force (NATO)
IISS	International Institute for Strategic Studies
IMF	International Monetary Fund
INF	Intermediate-Range Nuclear Forces in Europe Treaty

IRC	International Relations Committee, U.S. House of Representatives
IWG	Inter-Agency Working Group
JCS	Joint Chiefs of Staff
NAC	North Atlantic Council
NACC	North Atlantic Cooperation Council
NAFTA	North American Free Trade Agreement
NAI	New Atlantic Initiative
NATO	North Atlantic Treaty Organization
NEFA	NATO Enlargement Facilitation Act of 1996
NERO	NATO Expansion Ratification Office
NIC	National Intelligence Council
NSC	National Security Council
NSC-68	National Security Council Memorandum
NWG	NATO Working Group
OEEC	Organization for European Economic Cooperation
OSCE	Organization for Security and Cooperation in Europe
PAC	Polish American Congress
PFP	Partnership for Peace
PJC	Permanent Joint Council (created by the Russian Founding Act)
PRC	People's Republic of China
PSL	Polish Peasant Party
SAC	Strategic Air Command
SACEUR	Supreme Allied Commander Europe
SACLANT	Supreme Allied Commander Atlantic
SAIS	School of Advanced International Studies, The Johns Hopkins University
SDRP	Social Democracy of the Republic of Poland Party
SFOR	Stabilization Force (NATO)
SFRC	Senate Foreign Relations Committee
SHAPE	Supreme Headquarters Allied Powers Europe
SLD	Alliance of the Democratic Left (Poland)
SNOG	Senate NATO Observer Group
S/P	State Department's Policy Planning Staff
START I	Strategic Arms Reduction Treaty
START II	Strategic Arms Reduction Treaty (second phase)
UN	United Nations
UOP	State Protection Office (Poland)

USCEN	United States Committee to Expand NATO
USIA	United States Information Agency
Versailles Treaty	(treaty concluding World War I)
Visegrad States	Czech Republic, Hungary, and Poland
Washington Treaty	(treaty establishing NATO in 1949)
WEU	Western European Union
WTO	World Trade Organization

Bibliography

Books and Monographs

Acheson, Dean. *Present at the Creation: My Years in the State Department.* New York: W. W. Norton & Co., 1969.

Adenauer, Konrad. *Memoirs, 1945-64.* Chicago: Henry Regnery Co., 1965.

Archer, Clive. *Organizing Europe: The Institutions of Integration.* 2nd ed. London: Edward Arnold, 1994.

Bailey, Thomas A. *A Diplomatic History of the American People.* 7th ed. New York: Appleton-Century-Crofts, 1964.

Barone, Michael, and Grant Ujifusa. *The Almanac of American Politics.* Washington, D.C.: National Journal, 1991, 1993, 1995, and 1997.

Berghahn, V. R. *Modern Germany: Society, Economy and Politics in the Twentieth Century.* Cambridge: Cambridge University Press, 1982.

Bush, George, and Brent Scowcroft. *A World Transformed.* New York: Alfred A. Knopf, 1998.

Christopher, Warren. *In the Stream of History: Shaping Foreign Policy for a New Era.* Stanford: Stanford University Press, 1998.

Clemens, Clay, ed. *NATO and the Quest for Post-Cold War Security.* New York: St. Martin's Press, 1997.

Council For a Livable World Education Fund. *Briefing Book on NATO Enlargement.* Washington, D.C.: Council for a Livable World Education Fund, 1998.

David, Jules. *America and the World of Our Time: United States Diplomacy in the Twentieth Century.* New York: Random House, 1964.

Deering, Christopher J., and Steven S. Smith. *Committees in Congress.* 3rd ed. Washington, D.C.: Congressional Quarterly, 1997.

Desse, David A. *The New Politics of American Foreign Policy.* New York: St. Martin's Press, 1994.

Dodd, Lawrence C., with Bruce I. Oppenheimer, eds. *Congress Reconsidered.* Washington D.C.: Congressional Quarterly, 1997.

Duncan, Phil, ed. *Politics in America 1994.* Washington, D.C.: Congressional Quarterly, Inc., 1993.

Dupuy, R. Ernest, and Trevor Dupuy. *Encyclopedia of Military History from 3500 B.C. to the Present.* New York: Harper & Row, 1986.

Fleming, Denna F. *The United States and the League of Nations, 1918-1920.* New York: Putnam, 1932.

Forschler, Mary, ed. *Federal Yellow Book.* Leadership Directories, 1990-98.

Gaddis, John Lewis. *The United States and the End of the Cold War: Implications, Reconsiderations, Provocations.* New York: Oxford University Press, 1992.

Gati, Charles. *Hungary and the Soviet Bloc*. Durham: Duke University Press, 1986.

Gordon, Philip H., ed. *NATO's Transformation: The Changing Shape of the Atlantic Alliance*. Lanham: Rowman and Littlefield Publishers, 1997.

Gore, Al. *Earth in the Balance: Ecology and the Human Spirit*. Boston/New York: Houghton Mifflin Company, 1992.

Heller, Francis H., with John R. Gillingham, eds. *NATO: The Founding of the Atlantic Alliance and the Integration of Europe*. New York: St. Martin's Press, 1992.

Hill, Dilys M., and Phil Williams. *The Bush Presidency: Triumphs and Adversities*. New York: St. Martin's Press, 1994.

Holbrooke, Richard C. *To End a War*. New York: Random House, 1998.

Holt, W. Stull. *Treaties Defeated by the Senate*. Baltimore: Johns Hopkins University Press, 1933.

Johnson, Loch K. *The Making of International Agreements: Congress Confronts the Executive*. New York: New York University Press, 1984.

Kalb, Marvin. *The Nixon Memo: Political Respectability, Russia, and the Press*. Chicago: University of Chicago Press, 1994.

Kaplan, Lawrence S. *NATO and the United States: The Enduring Alliance*. Boston: Twayne Publishers, 1988.

Keegan, John. *Six Armies in Normandy: From D-Day to the Liberation of Paris*. New York: Viking, 1982.

Kugler, Richard L., with Mariana V. Kozintseva. *Enlarging NATO: The Russian Factor*. Santa Monica: RAND Corporation, 1996.

Larrabee, F. Stephen. *East European Security After the Cold War*. Santa Monica: RAND Corporation, 1993.

Lieber, Robert J., ed. *Eagle Adrift: American Foreign Policy at the End of the Century*. New York: Longman, 1997.

Mandelbaum, Michael. *The Dawn of Peace in Europe*. New York: The Twentieth Century Fund Press, 1996.

——. *NATO Expansion: A Bridge to the Nineteenth Century*. Washington, D.C.: Center for Political and Strategic Studies, 1997.

McCullough, David. *Truman*. New York: Simon and Schuster, 1992.

Morris, Dick. *Behind the Oval Office: Winning the Presidency in the Nineties*. New York: Random House, 1997.

Nathan, James A., with James K. Oliver. *Foreign Policy Making and the American Political System*. Baltimore: Johns Hopkins University Press, 1994.

Nelson, Garrison. *Committees in the U.S. Congress*. Washington, D.C.: Congressional Quarterly, 1994.

O'Neill, Tip, with William Novak. *Man of the House: The Life and Political Memoirs of Speaker Tip O'Neill*. New York: Random House, 1987.

Powell, Colin L., with Joseph E. Persico. *My American Journey*. New York: Random House, 1995.

Roberts, Brad, ed. *U.S. Foreign Policy after the Cold War*. Cambridge: MIT Press, 1992.

Rosner, Jeremy. *The New Tug-of-War: Congress, the Executive Branch, and National Security*. Washington, D.C.: Carnegie Endowment for International Peace, 1995.

Rozek, Edward J. *Allied War Diplomacy*. New York: Wiley & Sons, 1958.

Russell, Ruth B. *A History of the United Nations Charter*. Washington, D.C.: Brookings Institution, 1958.

Sherwen, Nicholas, ed. *NATO's Anxious Birth: The Prophetic Vision of the 1940s*. New York: St. Martin's Press, 1985.

Smith, Joseph, ed. *The Origins of NATO*. Exeter: BPCC Wheatons Ltd., 1990.

Snow, Donald M., with Eugene Brown. *Puzzle Palaces and Foggy Bottom: U.S. Foreign and Defense Policy-Making in the 1990s*. New York: St. Martin's Press, 1994.

Trubowitz, Peter. *Defining the National Interest: Conflict and Change in American Foreign Policy*. Chicago: University of Chicago Press, 1998.

Truman, Harry S. *Years of Trial and Hope 1946-1952*. Garden City: Doubleday and Company, 1956.

Vandenberg, Arthur H., ed. *The Private Papers of Senator Vandenberg*. Boston: Houghton Mifflin Company, 1951.

Woodward, Bob. *The Agenda: Inside the Clinton White House*. New York: Simon and Schuster, 1994.

Articles and Chapters in Books

American Enterprise Institute. "NAI Releases Statement in Support of NATO Enlargement." Internet. ‹http://www.aei.org/›

Arms, Thomas S. "RAND Corporation." In *Encyclopedia of the Cold War*, p. 476. New York: Facts on File, 1994.

Asmus, Ronald D., Richard L. Kugler, and F. Stephen Larrabee. "Building a New NATO." *Foreign Affairs* 72, no. 4 (September/October 1993): 28-40.

——. "NATO Expansion: The Next Steps." *Survival* 37, no. 1 (spring 1995): 7-33.

——. "Strategic Alliance." *New York Times*, August 27, 1993, p. A-29.

——. "What Will NATO Enlargement Cost?" *Survival* 38, no. 3 (autumn 1996): 5-26.

Asmus, Ronald D., and F. Stephen Larrabee. "NATO and the Have-Nots: Reassurance after Enlargement." *Foreign Affairs* 75, no. 6 (November/December 1996): 13-20.

Auerbach, Stuart. "Bush, Clinton Differ on Government's Role." *Washington Post*, October 8, 1992, pp. 23, 30.

Binnendijk, Hans. "NATO Can't Be Vague About Commitment to Eastern Europe." *International Herald Tribune*, Paris, November 8, 1991, p. 6.

Binnendijk, Hans, and Richard L. Kugler. "NATO after the First Tranche: A Strategic Rationale for Enlargement." *Strategic Forum*, Institute for National Strategic Studies, National Defense University, no. 149, October 1998.

Brzezinski, Zbigniew. "The Premature Partnership." *Foreign Affairs* 73 (March/ April 1994): 67-82.

Clark, Bruce. "How the East Was Won." *Financial Times*, July 5 and 6, 1997, p. 1.

Clifford, Clark M. "A Landmark of the Truman Presidency." In André de Staercke et al. *NATO's Anxious Birth: The Prophetic Vision of the 1940s*, pp. 1-10. New York: St. Martin's Press, 1985.

Council for a Livable World Education Fund. "An Open Letter to President Clinton." *Briefing Book on NATO Enlargement*, pp. 59-62. Washington, D.C.: Council for a Livable World Education Fund, April 1998.

——. "Founding Declaration of the Coalition against NATO Expansion." *Briefing Book on NATO Enlargement*, pp. 69-72. Washington, D.C.: Council for a Livable World Education Fund, April 1998.

Crow, Suzanne. "Russian Stand on Poland's NATO Membership Biased." *RFE/ RL Research Report* 2, no. 41, October 15, 1993, pp. 21-22.

Daley, David. "Pitchman for the Politically Correct." *National Journal* 40 (October 3, 1992): 2266.

Democratic Party Headquarters. "1996 Democratic National Platform," as adopted by the Democratic National Convention on August 27, 1996, p. 23. Internet. ‹http://ourworld.compuserve.com/hompages/democraticparty›

"Democratic Platform." *1992 Congressional Quarterly Almanac*.

Dobbs, Michael. "Wider Alliance Would Increase U.S. Commitments." *Washington Post*, July 5, 1995, pp. A-1, A-16.

Drozdiak, William. "NATO Ponders Future, Effectiveness." *Washington Post*, May 30, 1998, p. A-16.

"Ego and Error on Gay Issues." *New York Times*, January 29, 1993, p. 26.

Eisenhower, Susan. "Russian Perspectives on the Expansion of NATO." In *NATO and the Quest for Post-Cold War Security*, ed. Clay Clemens. New York: St. Martin's Press, 1997.

Ellingwood, Susan. "Unplanned: Bureaucratic Decay at State; U.S. State Department Policy Planning Office." *The New Republic*, October 6, 1997, p. 6.

Flanagan, Stephen J. "NATO and Central and Eastern Europe: From Liaison to Security Partnership." *Washington Quarterly* 15, no. 2 (spring 1992): 141-51.

Fournier, Ron. "Russian Opposition to NATO Expansion Another Problem for Clinton." Associated Press, December 6, 1994. Internet edition.

Foreign Broadcast Information Service (FBIS), EEU-92-152. "A Time of Dizzying Change." *Polityka*, August 8, 1992.

Friedman, Thomas. "Now a Word from X." *New York Times*, May 2, 1998, p. 15.

Goldgeier, James M. "NATO Expansion: The Anatomy of a Decision." *Washington Quarterly* 21, no. 4 (winter 1998): 85-102.

Gordon, Michael R. "U.S. Opposes Move to Rapidly Expand NATO Membership." *New York Times*, January 2, 1994, pp. A-1, A-7.

Groth, Alexander J. "Poland." *Encyclopedia Americana 1995 Annual,* pp. 420-21. N.p.: Grolier, 1995.

Haass, Richard N. "Fatal Distraction: Bill Clinton's Foreign Policy." *Foreign Policy,* no. 108 (fall 1997): 112-23.

Hargreaves, Ian. "The Commanding Heights: A European View." *IntellectualCapital.com*, July 16, 1998. Internet. ‹http://www.IntellectualCapital.com›

Harries, Owen. "The Collapse of the West." *Foreign Affairs* 72, no. 4 (September/October 1993): 42-53.

——. "'The West' is only a Flag of Convenience." *New York Times*, August 28, 1993, p. 19.

Harris, John F. "Clinton Vows Wider NATO in 3 Years." *Washington Post,* October 23, 1996, p. A-1.

——. "NATO and the Campaign." *Washington Post* (editorial), October 23, 1996, p. A-22.

Hoagland, Jim. "'Diktat' from Washington." *Washington Post*, June 25, 1997, p. A-19.

Kempe, Frederick. "NATO: Out of Area or Out of Business." *Wall Street Journal Europe*, August 11, 1993, pp. A-6, A-8.

Kennan, George F. "The Sources of Soviet Conduct." *Foreign Affairs* 25, no. 4 (July 1947): 566-82.

Kissinger, Henry. "It's an Alliance, Not a Relic." *Washington Post*, August 16, 1994, p. A-19.

——. "NOT This Partnership." *Washington Post*, November 14, 1993, p. 17.

——. "Reflections on Containment." *Foreign Affairs* 73, no. 3 (May/June 1994): 113-30.

Kitfield, James. "Jousting with Jesse." *National Journal*, September 27, 1997, pp. 1886-89.

Korbonski, Andrej. "The Warsaw Pact." *International Conciliation,* no. 573 (May 1969): 5-73.

Kugler, Richard L. "Costs of NATO Enlargement: Moderate and Affordable." *Strategic Forum*, Institute for National Strategic Studies, National Defense University, no. 128, October 1997.

Kusin, Vladimir. "Security Concerns in Central Europe." *Report on Eastern Europe*, March 8, 1991, p. 35.

Lardner, George, Jr. "Lugar Can Cross Allies, Charm Foes and Outdo Roger Staubach." *Washington Post*, April 27, 1982, p. A-2.

Larrabee, F. Stephen. "East Central Europe: Problems, Prospects and Policy Dilemmas." In *NATO and the Quest for Post-Cold War Security*, ed. Clay Clemens, 87-108. New York: St. Martin's Press, 1997.

Lawrence, W. H. "12 Nations Sign Atlantic Treaty; Stress Aim to Uphold the U.N.; Truman Sees Aggression 'Shield.'" *New York Times*, April 5, 1949, pp. 1, 3.

Leff, Carol Skalnik. "Could this Marriage Have been Saved? The Czechoslovak Divorce." *Current History* 95, no. 599 (March 1996): 129-34.

Lippman, Thomas W. "Perry May be Named to Try to Salvage Pact with N. Korea." *Washington Post*, October 4, 1998, p. A-27.

——. "Senators Lukewarm on NATO Expansion: Even Backers Say Administration Has Not Fully Explained Need." *Washington Post*, October 8, 1997, p. A-24.

——. "WSIA and ACDA Workers All to Retain Employment." *Washington Post*, January 5, 1999, p. A-9.

Lott, Trent. "The Senate's Role in NATO Enlargement." *Washington Post*, March 21, 1997, p. A-27.

Lugar, Richard. "Viewpoint." *Aviation Week & Space Technology*, August 30, 1993, p. 66.

Mandelbaum, Michael. "Foreign Policy as Social Work." *Foreign Affairs* 75, no. 1 (January/February 1996): 16-32.

——. "Open the Ranks to Eastern Europe." *Washington Post*, September 6, p. A-23.

Marszalek, Anna. "A Meeting by Polish and U.S. Intelligence." *Rzeczpospolitca*, October 28, 1997; in Foreign Broadcast Information Service, *Daily Report: East Europe*, FBIS-EEU-97-301, October 28, 1997. Internet edition.

McGrory, Mary. "For Whom the Phone Tolls." *Washington Post*, January 31, 1993, p. C-1.

Mesler, Bill. "NATO's New Arms Bazaar." *The Nation*, July 21, 1997, pp. 3-6.

——. "NATO's Stealth Costs." *The Nation*, July 21, 1997, pp. 21-23.

Milbank, Dana. "SNOG Job." *The New Republic*, May 25, 1998, pp. 14-15.

"Nominee Clinton Describes Vision of 'New Covenant.'" *1992 Congressional Quarterly Almanac*, vol. 48, pp. 55-A-56-A. Washington, D.C.: Congressional Quarterly, 1993.

Omestad, Thomas. "Why Bush Lost." *Foreign Policy*, no. 88 (winter 1992-93): 70-81 .

"Other Defense Issues Considered in 1996." *1996 Congressional Quarterly Almanac*, vol. 51, pp. 8-16. Washington, D.C.: Congressional Quarterly, 1997.

Polish American Congress. "Review of the Role of the Polish American Congress in Bringing Poland into NATO, Historical Background: 1939-1991." Internet.

Rosner, Jeremy D. "The Know-Nothings Know Something." *Foreign Policy*, no. 101 (winter 1995-96): 116-29.

——. "NATO's Enlargement's American Hurdle: The Perils of Misjudging Our Political Will." *Foreign Affairs* 75, no. 4 (July/August 1996): 9-16.

Rühe, Volker. "Shaping Euro-Atlantic Policies: A Grand Strategy for a New Era." *Survival* 35, no. 2 (summer 1993): 129-37.

Schmitt, Eric. "NATO Opponents Vocal, Diverse and Active." *New York Times*, April 21, 1998. Internet edition.

Seelye, Katharine Q. "Arms Contractors Spend to Promote an Expanded NATO." *New York Times*, March 30, 1998, p. A-6.

Sieff, Martin. "Yeltsin Fears 'Cold Peace' in Europe; at Odds with U.S. on NATO, Bosnia." *Washington Times*, December 6, 1994, p. A-1.

Simmons, Michael. "Poles Want More Power for NATO." *The Guardian*, January 10, 1991.

"Slovaks v Czechs on Gypsies." *The Economist*, November 7-13, 1998, p. 52.

Sultzberger, C. L. "Senate, 82 to 13, Votes Atlantic Pact Binding 12 Nations to Resist Attack; Truman to Move Soon for Arms Aid." *New York Times*, July 22, 1949, p. 2.

Talbott, Strobe. "Why NATO Should Grow." *New York Review of Books*, August 10, 1995, pp. 27-30.

Trussell, C. P. "Senator for Speed." *New York Times*, July 29, 1945, p. 1.

"Vandenberg Resolution." In *Encyclopedia of the Cold War*, pp. 564-65. New York: Facts on File, 1994.

White, William S. "Pledge to Europe: Three Efforts to Soften Text by Restrictions Decisively Beaten." *New York Times*, July 22, 1949, p. 1.

Whitney, Craig R. "Russia and NATO Sign Cooperation Pact." *New York Times*, May 28, 1997. Internet edition.

Wolchik, Sharon Lee. "Czech Republic." *The Americana Annual 1998*, p. 209. N.p.: Grolier, 1998.

Wolfowitz, Paul D. "Clinton's First Year." *Foreign Affairs* 73, no. 1 (January/February 1994): 28-43.

Government Documents

Baker, James A., III, former U.S. secretary of state, and Hans-Dietrich Gencher, former German foreign minister. "US-German Joint Statement on Transatlantic Community." *US Department of State Dispatch*, October 7, 1991, p. 736.

Bureau of Public Affairs, U.S. Department of State. *The Enlargement of NATO: Why Adding Poland, Hungary, and the Czech Republic to NATO Strengthens American National Security*. Washington, D.C.: U.S. Department of State, 1998.

Marszalek, Anna. "A Meeting by Polish and U.S. Intelligence." *Rzecz-pospolitca,* October 28, 1997. In Foreign Broadcast Information Service, *Daily Report: East Europe,* FBIS-EEU-97-301, October 28, 1997. Internet edition.

"National Security Council Memorandum-68." In *The Cold War 1945-91,* vol. 3, ed. Benjamin Frankel, pp. 213-14. Detroit/Washington: Gale Research, Inc., 1992.

NATO. *Declaration of the Heads of State and Government.* Ministerial Meeting of the North Atlantic Council/North Atlantic Cooperation Council, NATO Headquarters, Brussels, 10-11 January 1994, Press Communiqué M-1 (94) 3, Internet, p. 4. ‹http://www.nato.int/›

——. *Founding Act on Mutual Relations, Cooperation and Security between NATO and the Russia Federation.* Internet. ‹http://www.nato.int/›

——. "The Partnership between NATO and Russia." *NATO Basic Fact Sheet* No. 20, July 1997. Internet. ‹http://www.nato.int/›

——. "Rome Declaration on Peace and Cooperation." Press Communiqué S-1 (91) 86, November 8, 1991. Internet. ‹http://www.nato.int/›

——. "Status of Ratification of Accession Protocols." *NATO Fact Sheet,* August 26, 1998. Internet. ‹http://www.nato.int/›

NERO. *NATO Enlargement News Alert.*

"Protocols to the North Atlantic Treaty of 1949 on Accession of Poland, Hungary, and the Czech Republic." April 27, 1998. *Congressional Record.* Internet edition.

Rosner, Jeremy. Memorandom on "Initial Thoughts on NATO Enlargement Ratification Strategy." February 26, 1997; "Weekly Update on NATO Enlargement Ratification," dated October 10, 1997.

Rosner, Jeremy, and Cameron Munter, "Mission Statement: NATO Enlargement Ratification Office (NERO)," photocopy, March 5, 1998.

Rosner, Jeremy, et al. "Sharing Information and Documents with the Senate NATO Observer Group." Unclassified *Action Memorandum,* May 23, 1997.

Sloan, Stanley R., with assistance of J. Michelle Forrest. *NATO's Evolving Role and Missions.* CRS Report for Congress, Congressional Research Service, The Library of Congress, 97-708F (updated March 13, 1998), Washington, D.C.

U.S. Department of State, Office of the assistant secretary/spokesman. "Intervention by Secretary of State James A. Baker, III at the North Atlantic Council, June 6, 1991." Press Release, Copenhagen, June 7, 1991.

U.S. Government. *Public Papers of the President, William J. Clinton.* "The President's News Conference with Visegrad Leaders in Prague," VI, pp. 39-43. Washington, D.C.: Office of the Federal Register, National Archives and Records Administration, 1994.

U.S. Senate, Committee on Foreign Relations. *The Debate on NATO Enlargement: Hearings before the Committee on Foreign Relations, United*

States Senate, 105th Congress, October 7, 9, 22, 28, 30 and November 5, 1997. Washington, D.C.: U.S. Government Printing Office, 1998.

U.S. Senate. *The Charter of the United Nations*, Hearing before the Senate Committee on Foreign Relations, 79 Cong. 1 sess. (1945), p. 405.

The White House. "President Transmits Accession Protocols to Senate." *NATO Enlargement News Alert*, no. 15, February 11, 1998, p. 1.

Magazines and Newspapers

Facts on File, 1949-99.
Keesing's Record of World Events, 1990-99.
New York Times, 1945-99.
Newsday, 1992.
Wall Street Journal (Europe), August 11, 1993, p. A-8.
Washington Post, 1990-99.

Interviews by Author

Acheson, David, president, U.S. North Atlantic Council. Telephone interview by author. January 6, 1999.

Albert, Thomas, director, Office of Ethnic Outreach, Democratic National Committee. Telephone interview by author. June 13, 1998.

Ansley, Judith, national security director, Office of Senator John Warner. Interview by author. June 29, 1998.

Asmus, Ronald D., deputy assistant secretary of state for European and Canadian affairs, U.S. Department of State. Interview by author. Washington, D.C., October 1, 1998.

Bartkowski, Paul T., city councilman, Wilmington, Delaware. Telephone interview by author. November 4, 1998.

Biennendijk, Hans, director, Institute for National Security Studies, National Defense University. Interview by author. Washington, D.C., November 6, 1998.

Brown, Hank, former U.S. Senator. Telephone interview by author. September 21, 1998.

Brzezinski, Ian, legislative assistant for national security affairs, Office of Senator William V. Roth, Jr. Interview by author. Washington, D.C., August 31, 1998. Telephone interview by author. December 29, 1998.

Buchanan, Elizabeth, publicist, Fenton Communications. Interview by author. Washington, D.C., September 30, 1998.

Carpenter, Ted Galen, vice president, CATO Institute. Interview by author. Washington, D.C., July 13, 1998.

Cleary, Colin, desk officer for Hungary, U.S. Department of State. Interview by author. Washington, D.C., August 31, 1998.

Cleveland, Peter, professional staff member, U.S. Senate Select Committee on Intelligence. Interview by author. Washington, D.C., December 14, 1998.

Cohen, Scott, former staff director, Senate Foreign Relations Committee, and former senior foreign affairs adviser to Senator Charles Percy. Telephone interview by author. December 7, 1998.

Daly, Mary, Foreign Service officer. Interview by author. Washington, D.C., September 28, 1998. Telephone interviews by author. October 2, 1998 and January 5, 1999.

Dean, Ambassador Jonathan, consultant to Union of Concerned Scientists. Interview by author. Washington, D.C., June 23, 1998.

Di Rita, Larry, legislative director for Senator Kay Bailey Hutchison. Telephone interview by author. November 4, 1998. Interview by author. Washington, D.C., November 6, 1998.

Downie, Fred, professional staff member, Office of Senator Joseph Lieberman. Telephone interview by author. November 9, 1998.

Eagleburger, Lawrence S., former secretary of state. Telephone interview by author. December 11, 1998.

Fenton, David, president of Fenton Communications. Interview by author. Washington, D.C., September 30, 1998.

Ferdman, Gary, executive-director and political consultant, Business Leaders for Sensible Priorities. Telephone interview by author. October 5, 1998.

Fingerhut, Victor, associate professor of political science, Mary Washington College. Telephone interview by author. August 5, 1998.

Finley, Julie, District of Columbia Republican state chairman. Telephone interviews by author. December 17, 1998, January 6, 1999, and January 11, 1999.

Fisher, Cathleen S., senior associate, Henry L. Stimson Center. Interview by author. Washington, D.C., June 23, 1998.

Flanagan, Stephen J., special assistant to the president and senior director for Central and Eastern European Affairs, National Security Council. Interview by author. Washington, D.C., October 21, 1998.

Fried, Daniel, U.S. ambassador to Poland. Interview by author. Washington, D.C., December 28, 1998.

Gati, Charles, former adviser to the Policy Planning Staff, U.S. Department of State. Interview by author. Washington, D.C., November 6, 1998.

Gedmin, Jeffrey, director, New Atlantic Initiative. Telephone interview by author. October 10, 1998.

Gensler, Martin D., legislative assistant to Senator Paul Wellstone. Interview by author. Washington, D.C., June 23, 1998.

Gompert, David C., former director for European and Soviet Affairs, National Security Council. Telephone interview by author. January 4, 1999.

Haltzel, Michael, professional staff member, Committee on Foreign Relations. Interview by author. Washington, D.C., November 6, 1998.

Hunter, Robert, former U.S. ambassador to the North Atlantic Treaty Organization. Interview by author. Washington, D.C., October 21, 1998.

Isaacs, John, president, Council for a Liveable World. Telephone interview by author. July 7, 1998.

Jackson, Bruce, founder and cochairman, U.S. Committee to Expand NATO. Telephone interviews by author. December 21, 1998 and January 11, 1999.

Jacobs, Barry, assistant director for International Affairs, American Jewish Congress. Telephone interview by author. January 14, 1999.

Koss, Andrew, United States Information Agency. Telephone interview by author. September 23, 1998.

Koszorus, Frank, Jr., executive director, Hungarian American Coalition. Telephone interview by author. Washington, D.C., July 14, 1998.

Kozminski, Jerzy, ambassador of the Republic of Poland. Interview by author. Washington, D.C., October 2, 1998 and October 19, 1998. Telephone interviews by author. November 3, 1998 and January 26, 1999.

Kugler, Richard L., National Defense University. Interview by author. Washington, D.C., August 18, 1998. Telephone interview by author. October 10, 1998.

Lake, Anthony W., former national security adviser. Interview by author. Georgetown University, Washington, D.C., August 24, 1998.

Larrabee, F. Stephen, senior analyst, RAND Corporation. Interview by author. Washington, D.C., September 25, 1998.

Lenard, Colonel Casimir, national director, Polish American Congress. Interview by author. Washington, D.C., June 30, 1998.

Mandlebaum, Michael, Christian A. Herter Professor of American Foreign Policy, The Paul H. Nitze School of Advanced International Studies, The Johns Hopkins University. Telephone interview by author. December 23, 1998.

Millar, Alistair, program director and director of Washington, D.C. office, Fourth Freedom Forum. Telephone interview by author. December 7, 1998.

Miskiewicz, Sophia, legislative and political affairs director, Polish American Congress. Telephone interview by author. Washington, D.C., June 30, 1998.

Munter, Cameron, foreign service officer. Interview by author. Washington D.C., July 21, 1998. Telephone interview by author. September 1, 1998.

Murphy, Michael, NATO desk officer, U.S. Department of State. Interview by author. Washington, D.C., July 1, 1998.

Nowak, Jan, national director, Polish American Congress. Interview by author. Annandale, VA, October 16, 1998. Telephone interviews by author. November 14, November 16, 1998, and January 10, 1999.

Nunn, Sam, former senator. Telephone interview by author. December 14, 1998.

Rey, Nicholas, former U.S. ambassador to Poland. Interview by author. Washington, D.C., August 5, 1998.

Robb, Charles, U.S. senator. Interview by author. Washington, D.C., December 14, 1998.

Rosner, Jeremy. Interview by author. Washington, D.C., August 5, 1998. Telephone interviews by author. July 31, 1998, August 21, 1998, September 30, 1998, October 12, 1998, and January 5, 1999.

Rozek, Edward J., professor emeritus of political science, University of Colorado. Telephone interview by author. November 28, 1998.

Schake, Kori, Institute for National Security Studies, National Defense University. Interview by author. Washington, D.C., November 23, 1998.

Schnetzer, Amanda, research assistant, New Atlantic Initiative. Telephone interview by author. October 9, 1998.

Sedláček, Michal, counselor, embassy of the Czech Republic. Interview by author. Washington, D.C., July 13, 1998.

Serfaty, Simon, director, European Studies, Center for Strategic International Affairs. Telephone interview by author. October 1, 1998.

Thompson, Gayden E., director, Program on NATO and European Security, The Atlantic Council of the United States. Interview by author. Washington, D.C., July 1, 1998. Telephone interview by author, January 12, 1999.

Valasek, Tomas, research analyst, Center for Defense Information. Interview by author. Washington, D.C., July 21, 1998.

Wasley, Jon Liam, desk officer for Hungary, U.S. Department of State. Interview by author. Washington, D.C., August 31, 1998.

Waters, Laughlin E., senior federal judge. Telephone interview by author. December 28, 1998.

Wisniewski, Dariusz, first secretary, political section, Embassy of the Republic of Poland. Interview by author. Washington, D.C., July 13, 1998.

Wojtasiewicz, James, desk officer for Poland, U.S. Department of State. Interview by author. Washington, D.C., August 18, 1998.

Wormuth, Christine, assistant to the Special Adviser for Public and Legislative Affairs. Interview by author. Arlington, VA, August 24, 1998.

Wyganowski, Michael, first secretary, political section, Embassy of the Republic of Poland. Telephone interview by author. June 29, 1998.

Yazdgerdi, Tom, desk officer for the Czech Republic, U.S. Department of State. Interview by author. Washington, D.C., August 18, 1998.

Zakaria, Fareed, managing editor, *Foreign Affairs*. Telephone interview by author. November 2, 1998.

Letters, News Releases, Facsimiles, Electronic Mail, and Memoranda

"Address by President Lech Walesa of Poland on the Occasion of His Visit to NATO July 3, 1991." Press Release, Republic of Poland, Brussels.

Asmus, Ronald D. Electronic mail to author, October 21, 1998, October 23, 1998, and January 5, 1999.

Brzezinski, Zbigniew, former national security adviser. Letter to author, December 4, 1998.

Carter, James E., Jr., former president of the United States. Electronic mail communicated through his biographer, Steven H. Hochman, to author, November 16, 1998.

Clemens, Clay. Memorandum to author, November 5, 1998.

Davis, Lynn E., former undersecretary of state for international security. Electronic mail to author, November 30, 1998.

Freden, Brad, foreign service officer, U.S. embassy, the Czech Republic. Electronic mail to author, January 21, 1999.

Fried, Daniel. Electronic mail to author, December 15, 1998.

Gati, Charles. Written communication to author, November 30, 1998. Electronic mail to author, January 10, 1999.

Koszorus, Frank, Jr. Facsimiles to author, December 9 and 18, 1998.

Kugler, Richard. Facsimile to author, September 11, 1998.

Larrabee, F. Stephen. Electronic mail to author, October 25, 1998.

Millar, Alistair. Electronic mail to author, December 9, 1998.

Perry, William J., former secretary of defense. Letter to author, November 30, 1998.

Pew Research Center. "Public Indifference about NATO Expansion." News Release, Washington, D.C., January 24, 1997.

Polish American Congress. "US Congressional Staffers Visit Poland." *News Release*, Washington, D.C., February 27, 1997.

Powell, Colin L., former chairman of the Joint Chiefs of Staff. Letter to author, January 4, 1999.

Rey, Nicholas. Facsimile to author, October 30, 1998.

Rosner, Jeremy. Letter to author, December 21, 1998; electronic mail to author, January 6, 1999.

Schnetzer, Amanda. Electronic mail to author, October 14, 1998.

Serfaty, Simon, director of European Studies, Center for Strategic & International Studies. Washington, D.C. Letter to author, October 5, 1998.

Swiers, Peter Bird, retired diplomat and former vice president and director of the Harriman Chair for East-West Studies, The Atlantic Council of the United States. Facsimiles to author, January 14 and January 15, 1999.

Talbott, Strobe, deputy secretary of state. Facsmile to author, January 8, 1999.

Vershbow, Alexander "Sandy," U.S. ambassador to NATO. Electronic mail to author, December 10, 1998 and January 4, 1999.

Walker, Jenonne, former senior director for European Affairs, National Security Council. Facsimile to author, January 8, 1999.

Waters, Laughlin E. Facsimile to author, January 12, 1999.

Wormuth, Christine. Facsimiles to author, November 5 and 6, 1998; and electronic mail to author, January 12, 1999.

Zakaria, Fareed, managing editor, *Foreign Affairs*. Facsimile to author, November 18, 1998.

Zoellick, Robert B., former undersecretary of state for economic and agricultural affairs. Letter to author, December 19, 1998.

Speeches

Acheson, David. "Realities in the Trans-Atlantic Relationship." The 1998 Ernest Bevin Memorial Lecture, January 24, 1998. Published as an "Occasional Paper" by The Atlantic Council of the United States, February 1998.

Clinton, Bill. "Reforming the United Nations." Academic Universe, Lexis-Nexis, September 27, 1993. Internet. ‹http://phoenix.lib.ohio-state.edu/lexis-nexis/›

——. Speech to the Foreign Policy Association, "Major Foreign Policy Speech," LEXIS-NEXIS, Academic Universe, April 1, 1992.

——. Speech to the World Affairs Council of Los Angeles, August 13, 1992.

——. "Stump Speech: Clinton at University of Wisconsin," broadcast on National Public Radio, Academic Universe, LEXIS-NEXIS, October 13, 1992.

Lake, Anthony W. "From Containment to Enlargement." *Vital Speeches of the Day* 60 (October 15, 1993): 13-19.

Lugar, Richard G. "NATO's 'Near Abroad': New Membership, New Missions." Speech to the Atlantic Council of the United States, December 9, 1993.

"Remarks by President Bill Clinton at Fisher Theater, Detroit, Michigan." *Federal News Service,* Lexis-Nexis, October 22, 1996.

"Remarks by President Clinton to the Polish Parliament, July 7." *U.S. Newswire, Inc.*, Lexis-Nexis, July 8, 1998.

"Remarks in Cleveland, Ohio, at the White House Conference on Trade and Investment in Central and Eastern Europe, January 13, 1995." *Administration of William J. Clinton, 1995*, pp. 41-46.

"Testimony February 8, 1994 *Strobe Talbott* Nominee Deputy Secretary of State Senate Foreign Relations State Department Nomination." Academic Universe, LEXIS-NEXIS, February 8, 1994.

Index

Photos

October 11, 1944 - President Franklin D. Roosevelt meets the leaders of the Polish American Congress. The map shows the prewar boundaries, which Roosevelt and Stalin had secretly altered at their meeting in Teheran in November 1943. Among those shown are U.S. Congressman John Dingell of Michigan and Thadeus Adesko (first and second from the left), Frank Dziob (sixth from the left), PRCUA President John Olejniczak (seventh from the left); and from the right PNA/PAC President Charles Rozmarek, Polish Women's Alliance President Honorata Wolowska and Polish Falcon's Alliance President Teofil Starzynski.

January 4, 1994 - Meeting of 20 ethnic leaders with representatives of the Administration. In Milwaukee, Wisconsin, leaders of Central European ethnic groups discussed
the need for NATO expansion to include Poland, Hungary and the Czech republic.
Photo shows Mr. Edward J. Moskal, President of the Polish American Congress and
Mr. Sandy Berger and Mr. Daniel Fried of the National Security Council.

1994 – Polish American Congress President Edward J. Moskal introducing Poland's
President Lech Walesa at the 50th anniversary of the PAC in Buffalo, New York.

April, 1997 – Polish American Congress National Directors Meeting, Niagara Falls, NY – (left to right) Les Kuczynski, Polish American Congress National Executive Director, Jeremy Rosner, Special Advisor to the President and Secretary of State for NATO Enlargement Ratification, Witold Lukaszewski, PAC National Director and Mr. Zbigniew A. Kruszewski, PAC National Vice President.

Meeting at the Polish Embassy in **July 1998** – His Excellency Jerzy Buzek, Poland's Prime Minister, and Col. Casimir I. Lenard (Ret) PAC National Director. His Excellency Jerzy Kozminski, Ambassador of the Republic of Poland in the background.

Discussion concerning Poland's membership in NATO with sponsors of NATO expansion legislation. (right to left) Jan Olechowski, Poland's Foreign Minister, in discussion with Senators Paul Simon of Illinois, and Hank Brown of Colorado, and His Excellency Jerzy Kozminski, Ambassador of the Republic of Poland.

Representatives of the Polish American Congress leading the Congressional Staffers trip: Mr. Les Kuczynski, National Executive Director and Sophia Miskiewicz, Director of Legislative and Public Affairs, with Polish officers at military base.

Representatives of the Polish American Congress leading the Congressional Staffers trip: Mr. Les Kuczynski, National Executive Director and Sophia Miskiewicz, Director of Legislative and Public Affairs, with Polish officers at military base.

May 21, 1998 – President Clinton signing the *Resolution of Ratification of the Protocols to the North Atlantic Treaty of 1949 on the Accession of Poland, Hungary, and the Czech Republic as agreed to by the U.S. Senate, Washington, DC, April 30, 1998.* Witnessing the signing were: the Vice President, Secretary Albright, Secretary Cohen, Senators Roth, Biden, Levin, Lieberman, Lugar, Mikulski and Smith, also General Ralston, Sandy Berger, Jeremy Rosner, the Ambassadors of Poland, Hungary and the Czech Republic, other members of the diplomatic corps, and many representatives of ethnic, veteran and religious organizations.

NERO virtual office with Secretary Albright

May, 1998 – Jeremy Rosner and Ronald Asmus with Polish Foreign Minister Geremek

May, 1998 – Jeremy Rosner and Ronald Asmus with Polish Defense Minister Janusz Onyszkiewicz

May, 1998 – Jeremy Rosner and U.S. Ambassador to Hungary Peter Tufo with President Arpad Goncz

February 11, 1998 – President Bill Clinton signs the Instrument of Transmittal for the Protocols of Accession as General Henry Shelton, National Security Advisor Samuel Berger, Senator William Roth, Vice President Al Gore, Secretary Madeline Albright, Senator Joseph Biden and Deputy Secretary John Hamre look on.